PUBLISH A
PHOTO BOOK

Other books by the author:

Publish Your Genealogy: A Step-by-Step Guide for Preserving Your Research for the Next Generation

Publish Your Family History: A Step-by-Step Guide to Writing the Stories of Your Ancestors

Publish a Local History: A Step-by-Step Guide from Finding the Right Project to Finished Book

Publish a Memoir: A Step-by-Step Guide to Saving Your Memories for Future Generations

Publish a Biography: A Step-by-Step Guide to Capturing the Life and Times of an Ancestor or a Generation

Publish a Photo Book: A Step-by-Step Guide for Transforming Your Genealogical Research into a Stunning Family Heirloom

Publish a Source Index: A Step-by-Step Guide to Creating a Genealogically Useful Index, Abstract or Transcription

Publish Your Specialty: A Step-by-Step Guide for Imparting Your Research Expertise to Others

Set Yourself Up to Self-Publish: A Genealogist's Guide

PUBLISH A PICTURE BOOK

A Step-by-Step Guide for Transforming Your Genealogical Research into a Stunning Family Heirloom

by DINA C. CARSON

IRON GATE PUBLISHING
Niwot, CO

Publish a Photo Book:
A Step-by-Step Guide for Transforming Your Genealogical Research into a Stunning Family Heirloom

by Dina C. Carson

Published by:

Iron Gate Publishing
P.O. Box 999
Niwot, CO 80544

Copyright © 2015 by Dina C. Carson, Iron Gate Publishing
Printed in the United States of America
      ISBN   1-879579-67-7   ISBN 13 978-1-879579-67-5
      LCCN   2014914857

Publisher's Cataloging-in-Publication Data

Carson, Dina C, 1961 -

    Publish a Picture Book: A Step-by-Step Guide for Transforming Your Genealogical Research into a Stunning Family Heirloom
by Dina C Carson.

        p.   cm.
    Includes index.
    ISBN 9978-1-879579-67-5 (softbound) $24.95

    1. Reference—Writing.
2. Language Arts & Disciplines—Publishing.
3. Self-Publishing—United States   I. Title.

CT5. C239 2014   [Z285.5 C239 2014—Self-Publishing]
070.593

To Dad,

My most beloved photographer.

Who learned the craft as a U.S. Marine.

Who gave me my first Brownie camera and taught me to record my experiences in photographs.

Who gave me a patient, loving smile every time I needed one.

Acknowledgments

My kindest, most deeply held thanks to:

Dad—who supported my efforts in genealogy and who loved hearing about every delicious find I have made.

Mom—who had enough patience to read every word in this series of books and made each book better.

Charly Miller—whose Harry Potter Places travel guides have charmed me through and through, and who has supported every last thing I have done to make these books possible.

Buzzy Jackson—who wrote the stories of her ancestors in an enviable way, and was kind enough to lend her expertise to launch this project.

Silvia Pettem—whose remarkable local histories encourage me and so many others to poke about Boulder and write about our discoveries.

Dr. Thomas W. Jones—whose kind words and brilliant edits inspired me to share what I know about publishing.

Pat Roberts and Mona Lambrecht—who inspired an entire workshop on writing, research and publishing that lead directly to this series of books.

Sandi Pearce—my grammar goddess, who keeps me from tumbling headlong over my own words.

Gena Philibert-Ortega—for the most amazing week of social history studies. I have never had so much fun in a class.

Dr. John Philip Colletta—for providing the inspiration to take the next step to finish these books.

My friends at the Boulder Genealogical Society, the Jewish Genealogical Society of Colorado, the Boulder Heritage Roundtable, and the Colorado Council of Genealogical Societies—who have encouraged me to write, to lecture, and through steadfast community spirit have kept me going.

Strangers in the Box

"Come, look with me inside this drawer,
In this box I've often seen,
At the pictures, black and white,
Faces proud, still and serene.

I wish I knew the people,
These strangers in the box,
Their names and all their memories,
Are lost among my socks.

I wonder what their lives were like,
How did they spend their days?
What about their special times?
I'll never know their ways.

If only someone had taken time,
To tell, who, what, where and when,
These faces of my heritage,
Would come to life again.

Could this become the fate,
Of the pictures we take today?
The faces and the memories,
Someday to be passed away?

Take time to save your stories,
Seize the opportunity when it knocks,
Or someday you and yours,
Could be strangers in the box."

—Pamela A. Harazim

Updates

Websites come and go or change their structures. If you find a broken link or a website that has moved or changed its name, please help me update the book for the next generation of readers. Send an email to: alert@irongate.com.

Contents

SECTION 5: MARKETING

Preface

Because I am a photographer, I have an abundance of experience with shooting photographs and using image editing software to crop, correct and label my own images. And, because I am also a publisher, I have experience with the process of taking digital images and preparing them to look their best in print or on a screen. The requirements for print vs. digital images are different, so much of what you will find in this book will help you to prepare your images for your intended use and design page layouts to showcase your images in the best way.

My biggest challenge while writing this book was to give those of you who want to create a quick and simple photo book in time for the next holiday, and those of you who have historical photographs to preserve that also deserve some further research and explanation, what you both need.

For those of you who are only interested in writing short captions for your photographs and combining them into a book, there are instructions for preparing the images to look their best, at the correct resolution for screen and print. You can skip the sections on additional research and writing. Even though your books will not contain much text, you will not want to skip the section on explaining your images and editing. Every image (or group of images) deserves a caption or explanation and every book deserves a good edit to catch errors.

For those of you who will explain the meaning behind the images, have images with historical significance, or would like to tell a broader story along with the images, the bulk of this book is for you. There is ample advice for additional research that will benefit the explanation of the images, and for creating layouts leaving the focus on the images along with text that is easy to read.

It is also hard to know whether to refer to the book's intended recipients as readers or viewers. For the most part, I have chosen to use the term readers because even those books that have only short captions alongside each image will be read.

No matter what your intended project, you do not have to have any experience with publishing to take your images and mold them into a beautiful book.

Just keep reading.

Introduction

This book is a guide for anyone interested in creating a stunning family heirloom using images—to memorialize loved ones, to pass on memories and family lore, or to document your lineage.

This book is a conversation between you and me—one family historian to another. I have been where you are. I have accumulated a pile of images and scratched my head over how to put them together in a way my family members would appreciate. I have made sense of it, and so can you.

So, what if:

You have a box of old photographs but no research to explain the significance of the images?

You have research but no stories that tie the images to your family?

You have facts you would like to include but no pictures?

For the beginner, this book contains the elements needed to start with a box of inherited photographs and end with a finished book. For the intermediate, there are ideas for organizing your images, adding social and historical context, and captioning each image to explain or add interest. For the advanced, it is a polishing cloth for your writing, your research, and how to display your images to make your book the best it can be.

This book has technical explanations. If you are technologically challenged, there are suggestions for hiring help in critical areas.

This book contains some drudgery. Fixing damaged or faded photographs and writing succinct but informative captions to accompany them is hard work, and some of the rules for publishing are no fun to implement, but are endured by publishers everywhere for the sake of the reader.

This book is not death by grammar. There are suggestions for catching and correcting the little bugaboos we all use because our first inclination is to write as we speak. Even the most prolific professionals do not write perfect books on the first try. They, however, have the benefit of professional editing. Most of us do not. Trust me when I say that I can turn my editor, my grammar goddess, into a grammar grouch in one short phrase. The painful process of editing is not a punishment, it is performed so that the words on the page for posterity convey your meaning.

This book is lengthy. If you would rather jump right in and start with what interests you most, go right ahead. For the rest of you, I have organized the book in the steps that publishing projects follow.

Section One is full of ideas for additional publishing projects, describes how to pick a doable project, explains how traditional and self-publishing works, and examines the tools to facilitate the jobs of organizing, researching, writing, typesetting and layout.

Section Two is about preparation—identifying who you are creating the book for, conducting a review of the images you already have, adding research and images to make any accompanying stories come to life, what happens when you stare at a blank page one and have no idea what to do next, and how to draft an outline to jump start the process.

Section Three is all about the writing—explaining each image either with a caption or a longer narrative, saving time by implementing a style sheet, creating the first draft, and editing.

Section Four tackles the ins and outs of print publishing. The photo books that look the best use layouts that are easy on the eyes. This section will give you the instructions you need to make your book look its best.

Section Five will show you how to spread the word far and wide that your book is finished and available.

By the end of this book, you can expect to choose a doable project, to perform the kind of research that will help you gather a group of images that together tell a story, to caption or write about the images in a way that explains to future readers the people, places or events depicted, to successfully publish a book, and to let the world know it is available.

Throughout the book you will find references to:

Baby Steps. Baby Steps are essential. My objective, always, is to encourage you to do what you feel comfortable doing and to enjoy the process. It is not to make your book project a burden. If the only steps you take are the Baby Steps, no problem. Baby Steps also may identify more complicated tasks that you can skip if you are feeling overwhelmed, and still create a book your family will enjoy.

Next Steps. Next Steps build upon the Baby Steps and require more effort but will make the book look and read better. Many of these steps are about time—time to make another trip to the archives, time to learn the advanced features of your software, or time to re-write a caption or two. Even though I like to get projects off my desk, setting aside my expectations for finishing the project may be in the best interest of the book and my sanity. You may find the same is true.

Giant Leaps. Giant Leaps build upon Baby Steps and Next Steps and require significantly more effort, but are steps that professional writers, editors or publishers would take to make the book the best it can be. In fact, you *can* take the Giant Leaps. You can create a stunning family heirloom and package it in a way that even the snootiest, uptown publishing house cannot tell is self-published.

Enough with the soliloquy—on with the show.

Section 1

The goal in this section is to give you enough of an understanding about how publishing works to make you comfortable with the decision to self-publish.

Baby Steps

Take a look at the stages of all publishing projects—planning, writing, production and marketing. Consider a myriad of ideas before honing in on your own publishing project.

Next Steps

Learn how traditional book publishing works, and discover how everything a traditional publisher could do for you, you can do quite easily for yourself.

Giant Leaps

Examine the tools you will need to make your way from bright idea to a book in your hands.

Chapter 1

Who Needs This Book?

You need this book if:

- You want to pass the images of your family on to the next generation, and you do not know where to begin.
- You are just beginning to learn how to fix and correct images, and you want to focus your efforts on what to include in your first book.
- You want to issue a private publication that only you or your immediate family members will see, so that you can show images of and write about living people without worrying about privacy issues.
- You want to share what only you have access to, such as one-of-a-kind photographs or letters, the family bible or heirlooms.
- You are an experienced in photography or with photo restoration, and you want to cut your publishing teeth on images that are already restored, well researched or easy to describe in captions.

Keep reading. If you have images that are interesting enough to restore, research or include in a book, you will be able to create a stunning heirloom your family will greatly appreciate.

Why Publish a Photo Book?

With a little bit of knowledge, you can take old, faded photographs and make them come back to life. You can organize and present modern photographs alongside historic photographs, to tell a before and after story. Or, you could research the stories behind the images, and make a book available to family, friends or other researchers. Modern publishing technology makes it possible. In fact, publishing is one way to assure the legacy of your unique images.

Not only will your family members appreciate knowing more about their heritage through the images you have or will collect, the hours you spend repairing or researching the images deserves to become an everlasting record of your family's history.

Chapter 2

Publishing Projects

Every publishing project, whether it is a family-heirloom photo book or the next blockbuster novel, goes through four stages—planning, writing, production, and marketing.

Planning

The first step in any publishing project is the planning stage, where you decide what type of book to create—how much to include or how little. If you think you must include every image you have in a single volume, you do not.

In fact, I want discourage the data dump—purging your computer of every available image into one enormous manuscript. It may feel good to see how much you have. But once you start adding the captions and the historical or social context to numerous images, the project may become overwhelming.

In the next few chapters, I am going to help you pick a doable project and suggest material to make the book more interesting. Then, you will finish gathering what you will need to begin choosing photographs and writing about them.

Writing

The writing stage is perhaps the most feared part of the publishing process. All writers face that first blank page. All writers have doubts. "What if I can't think of anything to say? What if I don't like what I've written? What if no one else likes what I've written?"

Anxiety about writing is normal. Thankfully, the writing stage is not all writing. For a photo book, there may be less writing than a family history, but what captions a photograph may have to boil the information down succinctly, which is not always easy. This may also be a writing and research stage. Research, for many of us, is a much more comfortable, more familiar place. Feel free to retreat into the comfort zone every now and again to gather material to strengthen the stories behind the images. Be wary, however, of letting a small detour back into the research become an excuse to avoid writing. Eventually, you will want to finish the book.

Once the manuscript is complete, you must edit. Not even the most accomplished writer can produce a perfect manuscript in the first draft. Editing always means fixing typos and catching errors. Editing often means rewriting. Editing will make your manuscript better, more enjoyable for the reader.

Production

During the production stage, you will design the look and style of the book, and follow a set of rules to make the book easy on the eyes.

Production decisions include page layout, image placement, typesetting, cover design and final files. Fear not. There are ample tools to help you lay out the pages and make the images look their best.

During the production phase, you will decide whether to produce the book solely in print, whether an electronic or an online format may be better, or perhaps some combination of all three.

Marketing

Marketing is not necessarily about generating sales. It is a means of letting people who have an interest in your book know that it is available.

You may choose to give the book away to family as gifts or conduct a private sale, so only close family members can obtain a copy. You may want to sell the book to avoid financing the entire production yourself. Or, you may have a book with broader appeal that would warrant a sales campaign.

Marketing a photo book is a long-term process because unique books such as these do not go out of style and should not go out of print. If you find new information, you can issue a second edition or publish a new book. The most important part of marketing is letting family members know that your book is available.

❧❧

None of these stages has nice, neat beginnings and endings. Occasionally, you may need to return to the planning to gather more information to make the writing easier. You may discover errors or missing elements while you are typesetting that require research or may initiate a re-write. Later, you may discover some piece of blockbuster information that will inspire a second edition.

No photo book will roll off the press complete or perfect. Times ticks on. Families change. New information comes to light. Expect it and publish anyway.

Chapter 3

Pick a Project to Publish

The most important consideration for your publishing project is that you can complete it. Part of the fun of family history is that it is never done. There will always be a new discovery, another baby born or another group of photographs taken. The challenge for you, right now, is to pick the images (or a part of your research) that you are willing to focus on—to the exclusion of other interesting finds—and narrow the scope enough so that gathering, organizing, repairing and readying the images does not become overwhelming.

In Chapter 7: Review Your Photographs, you are going to take a critical look at the images you have already, and decide whether what you have fits the project you have in mind, whether they will with a little more research and a few more images, or whether an entirely different project may be best, for now. In the meantime, let us explore a few ideas in more detail.

Each of the books in this series was written with the genealogist or family historian in mind. You, however, may have a project idea is unrelated to any type of genealogical research. That is fine. Each of the book projects below has a corresponding guide book with information specific to each book type.

A Photo Book

There are some family stories best told by focusing on the photographs or illustrations with snippets of text (captions) to accompany the images. There are other projects where a collection of photographs is the focus for an entire book, but the book is mostly a narrative explaining the significance of the photos. What project you choose depends upon the types of images you have, what images you may add to your collection (if needed) and how much additional text will accompany each image.

PUBLISH A PHOTO BOOK

The following are ideas for family photo books or pictorial histories:

Familiar Genealogical Formats. There are some genealogical formats you may be very familiar with, that you could turn into beautiful images. Later in the formatting section, I will give you ideas for turning family group sheets, pedigree charts, bow-tie charts, or descendant charts into page formats. Using a format that is familiar from genealogical research is one way to display your research and your pictures together.

Heirloom Catalog. Share family heirlooms in pictures by showcasing them in a book. This is one way to preserve the historical items that belong to your family. Even if the items themselves have been scattered across the globe, you can use photographs of the items to tell your family's story.

Holiday Traditions. Maybe you have Christmas or other holiday cards or letters saved over the years that could accompany yearly pictures. Or, perhaps you have photos of other holidays celebrations that would make a good transition-through-time photo journal.

School Pictures. Starting in the 1950s, most school children had individual photographs taken each year as well as a class picture. Collecting the school pictures is one way to show what the family was doing every year across a decade or a generation.

A Biopic. That term usually refers to a biographical movie, but who says you cannot create a biography in pictures? Perhaps you could create a biopic tribute to your parents or grandparents?

A Chronology. You could tell your family's story across time by arranging your images in order of the events that occurred. Adding a bit of social history will get readers remembering what it was like during the hip '60s.

An Era. You could choose a small slice of time to showcase such as the WWII years along with what each member of the family was doing at the time.

Themes. Does your family have something in common? Eye or hair color? Freckles or jawline? Hobbies? Can you find a picture of different members of the family with their bikes, while skiing or fishing? Perhaps you have a collection of wedding photographs across many generations.

Travel Diary. If you have made the trip of a lifetime, or a trip to research your family's origins, show your family what the old country looked like through your modern-day experiences and photographs. You could also provide tips for other family members who wish to make the trip themselves.

Preservation. If you have a photo album or scrapbook made by one of your family members, preserve it by creating a more modern edition while adding stories gleaned from interviews or research.

Letters Home. Perhaps you have letters from a soldier written to those at home during a war, or from a student who traveled abroad. Combine the letters with photographs of the places and people mentioned in the letters. Add historical photographs, if appropriate, and write about what else was taking place at the time the letters were written.

Talents. Was your grandmother a knitter, or did she embroider or tat? Do you have examples of her work to show in a pictorial history? Perhaps your family's talent was acting or painting, scroll work or whittling, jewelry or quilting? I have a friend whose grandmother was a painter. Gathering examples of her paintings over her more than 80 year career would be a fabulous tribute and a treasure for her descendants.

A Family History

What is the difference between a genealogy and a family history?

In technical terms, a *genealogy* begins with an ancestor and moves forward in time through his or her descendants. A *pedigree*, on the other hand, starts with a descendant and moves backward in time through the ancestors.

For our purposes, consider a genealogy a way to pass on your well-documented *research* (with or without a lot of narrative). A family history, on the other hand, is less a numbered lineage, but rather the *stories* of your family.

The following are ideas for planning a family history:

Start to Finish. Pick the ancestor you wish to use as the first generation. Follow the family through the number of generations you have chosen to include describing the events that affect most families—the births, schooling, marriages, professions, and deaths. Enrich the stories with enough social history so that the reader understands what it was like to live in that time and place.

Photographs or Memorabilia. If you have inherited a box of photographs or memorabilia, plan your project around the people and events you find in that collection.

Letters or a Diary. Write about the people or person who wrote the letters or diary, weaving the actual text into the stories, or using the events described as the timeline for the book.

A Tragedy. Write about a defining event that affected the family, such as a natural disaster, becoming a prisoner of war, losing a fortune, or surviving the Great Depression or the Holocaust.

A Triumph. Triumphs are also defining events, such as suddenly becoming wealthy or famous, being elected to an important public office, and so on.

An Ancestor and the People Known to Him or Her. A book of this type could include parents, siblings, grandparents, children and grandchildren, cousins, aunts and uncles—essentially five generations—the two before and the two following your main character.

A Single Generation. If you would rather focus on an individual or a couple (e.g. your parents or grandparents) than a multi-generational family line, consult, *Publish a Biography: A Step-by-Step Guide to Capturing the Life and Times of an Ancestor or a Generation.* The difference is mostly in the level of detail required.

If you have done the research and are ready to write the stories of your family, you will find a detailed chapter on storytelling in *Publish Your Family History: A Step-by-Step Guide to Writing the Stories of Your Ancestors.*

A Genealogy

By my definition (above), a genealogy is a little less about writing and a little more about passing along your research to other researchers. Publishing your research is a valuable effort, in an of itself. If you have plenty of research to choose from, but are not quite ready to write the stories, publishing a genealogy will give you experience with the publishing process.

The following are ideas for planning a genealogy:

Every Descendant of a Single Ancestor. That may be your grandparents or the first immigrant. The more generations you go back, the more challenging it will be to ensure that the lines are complete.

Direct Descendants of a Single Ancestor. Include the siblings in each generation, but the detailed information only for your direct line.

Female Lines. Your mother and her mother, and her mother, and so on, as far back as you have researched.

A Surname Line. Beginning with the first ancestor of a given surname (a female), following her surname (male) line backward. Another section could include the wives of the male ancestors as collateral lines.

A Direct Line to a Specific Ancestor. Beginning with yourself, you could trace back across different surnames to a specific ancestor, such as an American President or a Salem witch (the kind of research to join a lineage society).

A Surname Study. Focus on a surname in a particular region (e.g. The Bakers of Campbell County, KY), within a national database (e.g. Revolutionary War soldiers or patriots), or across a complete record set (e.g. federal census records).

If you have done the research, but are not quite ready to write the narrative, you will find additional details about numbering systems and formal genealogical writing in *Publish Your Genealogy: A Step-by-Step Guide for Preserving Your Research for the Next Generation.*

A Local History

There are endless possibilities for writing local histories. All families have elements of local history in their stories, right? They attended local schools, worked in local businesses, joined community organizations, participated in local government, and lived in neighborhoods or rural communities.

The following are ideas for elements of local history to enhance your family history. Any of these ideas could become a local history unto itself:

Professions. Farming, mining, ranching, medicine, crafts, craftsmanship, banking, manufacturing, logging, science, technology, information, inventions, merchants, wholesalers, working conditions, etc.

Institutions. Schools, courts, military units, libraries, government agencies, fire departments, law and order, etc.

Associations. Sports teams, Masons, Odd Fellows, Boy Scouts, Girl Scouts, 4H, philanthropic, social, fraternal, activist, etc.

Religious Groups. Churches, synagogues, mosques, religious movements, religious colonies, etc.

Transportation. Freighters, wagon roads, railroads, stage companies, stations or airports, riverboats, barges, trails or roads, aerospace, aeronautics, etc.

People. Famous or notorious, leaders, office holders, women, children, what became of (e.g. a school class), the poor, ethnic groups, religious groups, etc.

Events. Natural disasters, on this day, during this year, anniversaries, economic depression, loss or gain of a major employer, politics, etc.

Architecture. Neighborhoods, downtown, building styles, building techniques, public buildings, historic homes, etc.

Transitions. Town into city, fort into town, farm into metropolis, etc.

Customs. Marriages, burials, holidays, celebrations, 4th of July, parades, rallies, expectations, manners, roles for men and women, expectations of children, economic class, etc.

Entertainment. Music, art, dance, theater, movies, plays, books, museums, carnivals, festivals, leisure, etc.

If you are considering writing a local history, consult, *Publish a Local History: A Step-by-Step Guide from Finding the Right Project to Finished Book*.

A Biography

A biography is different from a family history in that it focuses on an individual or a couple rather than trying to follow a family across generations. A biography requires a greater level of detail about people including where they lived, the era they lived in, what kind of schooling they had, associations they joined, and how they worked.

The following are ideas for family biographies:

Parent(s) or Grandparent(s). This book could be a tribute to a couple or an individual. These are people you may have the most information about, because they are people you know or knew well which means you can draw from memories as well as research.

Famous Ancestor. Whether famous or notorious, did your ancestor participate in a well-known historical event? Was he or she a professional athlete, or famous entertainer? Did he or she establish a town, or start a business?

Interesting Profession. Perhaps you had an ancestor who was a hatter, a furniture maker, or a smelter. Maybe your ancestor was an inventor who changed the lives of many people? Researching how an ancestor worked may be interesting to other people whose ancestors held similar jobs.

If you are interested in writing a biography, consult: *Publish a Biography: A Step-by-Step Guide to Capturing the Life and Times of an Ancestor or a Generation*.

A Memoir

While it may seem a strange exercise for family historians to do research on yourself or your generation, telling your story should not be. A generation from now, your children or grandchildren will be interested in how you lived.

The following are ideas for writing a memoir:

An Aspect of Your Life. Pick a part of your lifespan to write about—childhood, teenage years, college experiences, married life.

Professional Life. Perhaps it is your education, preparing for a profession, or your work life that you would most like to write about.

Military Life. Even if you did not choose the military as a profession, tell the stories of your experience in the service—during peacetime or at war.

Remembrances. If you have greeting cards or letters that help tell your story, consider weaving those into a memoir.

Journal or Diary. If you have kept a journal or diary, expand upon what you were thinking at the time you wrote the original entries.

Travel. If you have traveled extensively, create a lasting journal of the places you have gone, the experiences you had, the people you met along the way, and the things you saw.

If you are interested in writing a memoir, consult: *Publish a Memoir: A Step-by-Step Guide to Saving Your Memories for Future Generations.*

A How-To or Instructional Guide

If you have conducted extensive research in any one aspect of genealogy or local history, share your expertise with others. Everyone can benefit when you help others avoid the pitfalls of conducting family or local history research.

The following are ideas for how-to books:

Tips and Tricks. Give snippets of advice for people who are new to an area of research. This is especially useful for new members of groups such as re-enactors, so they can catch up with the more experienced members quickly.

Process. Describe how to do something from start to finish. This is where your knowledge of an earlier time may help readers understand what their ancestors did and how they did it. How were houses constructed in the 17th Century? How did hunters keep enough food on the table at a western fort? How did Paul Revere make copper-bottomed pans?

Lessons Learned. Reveal the techniques that *did not* work in your research so others can avoid making the same mistakes.

Record Type. You may have experience in land records or military records, for example, and can help others use those records effectively.

Research Facility. Do you have shortcuts to help make the best use of your time at a major repository? Or, perhaps you can shine a light on a repository that few researchers know about.

Recording or Preserving Records. Do you have photography tips for taking the best travel or cemetery pictures to use in a family history book, or advice for best practices to preserve the family bible?

Location. You may have conducted extensive research in a particular location (city, county, state or country) and could create a guide to what is available there.

If you are interested in writing a how-to book, consult: *Publish Your Specialty: A Step-by-Step Guide for Imparting Your Research Expertise to Others*.

A Source Index

Recently, I heard a speaker state that only two percent of all the material that could be digitized has been digitized. So, good records extractions will be necessary for a long time to come. If nothing else, creating an index that makes a record set easier to use is a valuable gift to other genealogists or researchers.

There is no limit to the places where records are kept. To name a few: government (e.g. schools, agencies, cities, counties, etc.); company (e.g. mortuary, ditch companies, banks, merchants, etc.); associations (e.g. religious groups, Masons, Odd Fellows, service clubs, philanthropic clubs, community groups, sports teams, etc.); publications (e.g. journals, newspapers, etc.), transportation (e.g. trains, freighters, ships, planes, etc.), or cemeteries (e.g. headstone transcriptions, lot purchasers, burial certificates, etc.).

The following are ideas for records extractions:

An Index. If you are in the records, you may as well do a thorough job and collect every name, every subject, and every location. In addition to record sets, many 19th century local histories could use an index.

An Annotated Index. If you want to take an index one step further, you could add useful information such as the role each individual played (e.g. juror, judge or witness) and the date each event occurred.

An Abstract. Without going as far as a full transcription, you could abstract the basic points of court cases, probate files, or meeting minutes.

A Transcription. While your first duty is to do no harm to the archive that holds the records, you can write a transcription in a way that encourages readers to visit the archive to obtain copies of the original records, so that the collection does not become less valuable as a result of your transcription.

An Annotated Transcription. You may be familiar enough with the records, or the people whose names appear in the records, that you could add information (an annotation) to make the transcription more useful.

Preservation Plus Extraction. Some records are so fragile that they are difficult to use without damaging them. In this case, photograph the records to display them in the book in their original form, along with an index, an abstraction, or a complete transcription.

A Comprehensive Index. Consider indexing each source within a single collection (e.g. California gold rush participants in the Bancroft Collection), or across many collections to create a comprehensive index (e.g. Boulder Pioneers in the Colorado State Archives).

If you are interested in publishing a source index, consult: *Publish a Source Index: A Step-by-Step Guide to Creating a Genealogically-Useful Index, Abstract or Transcription.*

Hybrid Projects

You may have a project in mind that does not fit neatly into any one category. Your book does not have to fit a mold. Be creative with some hybrid ideas.

The following are a few of the many possibilities for a hybrid family history:

Biography/Cookbook. While you write a biography, include a few recipes or family traditions sprinkled through the text.

Cookbook/Biography. Organize this one as a cookbook, but include some biographical information about the people who contributed the recipes, or how your family used the recipes according to tradition.

Biography/Professional Manual. You may have enough information about an ancestor's work or business to write a professional guide along with biographical information.

Photographic Timeline. Show how each family member fits into the photographic tree, or how they fit into the timeline of history.

Memoir/History. Use recollections from a memoir, letters or a diary, alongside the real-world history taking place.

Travel Guide/Family History. Let your family members follow your footsteps as you traveled to the homeland, along with information about the people who lived in the places you describe. Include travel guide information to help the reader make the trip, as well.

Perpetual Calendar. Include birth and death dates, anniversaries, graduations, immigration, travel—anything that puts family members on the calendar.

On This Day. Place historical events from your family history research or local history into a day-by-day collection.

Genealogical Gifts

While books are the most appreciated gifts according to reunion-goers, there are many other ways to give away your genealogical research as gifts.

The following are a few of the many possibilities for genealogical gifts:

Charts. You can create phenomenal family tree charts using software that makes it easy to upload your tree—fan charts, half-circles, full circles, or bow-tie charts. You can add photographs or background images, and information in as much detail as you desire.

Scrapbooks. There are books, clubs and stores devoted to creating amazing scrapbooks. If you can picture it as a pedigree, you can scrapbook it in a way that shows family relationships.

Photographs on Products. You can put a photograph on nearly anything—cakes, wall hangings, button covers, place mats, cups, mugs, and much more.

Cookbooks. Many companies specialize in producing cookbooks since so many groups use them as fundraisers. Use your next holiday or reunion to gather up the family's favorite recipes.

Card Decks. There are companies that specialize in playing card decks that you can create using photographs of your family. Sports cards are another idea along the same line.

Quilts. Quilting was one way to re-use scrap material and create a warm blanket before there was central heating. Quilting patterns can reveal something about your ancestors' ethnic heritage or the area where they lived. Other textiles such as tartans have similar meanings to family groups.

❧❧

Now that you have a great many ideas for turning your images and genealogical research into a photo book, read about the publishing process to determine the easiest way to finish your book and make it available to interested readers.

Chapter 4

How Publishing Works

Publishing has two essential parts—production and distribution. Before you determine whether to publish your book in print, electronically, or online, think about how your audience will want to read the book, and how you are going to deliver it to them.

It is hard to go wrong choosing print. The upside is that nearly everyone can read a printed book. The downside is that printed books must be produced and distributed (shipped) which cost money. Thankfully, print-on-demand technology has made it possible to print and ship books one at a time. Gone are the days when you had to order hundreds of books to keep the cost of each book down.

Publishing in an electronic format is tempting because there is almost no cost of production or distribution. Books can be sent to the reader electronically. The downside to electronic formats is that not everyone wants to read a book on a computer screen, dedicated eReader or tablet.

Publishing online is also tempting because most people have access to the Internet. Anyone with a web browser can read the book. The downside is that Internet companies come and go, so if your book is sitting on the server of a company that folds, the book disappears with it.

What is the best option? You do not have to make a decision about this yet. You may choose to publish in more than one format.

Before we move on to production, let us look at each publishing option in a little more detail.

Print Publishing

Before print-on-demand made publishing easy for anyone, there were four ways to publish a book in print. There still are. You can write a query letter to interest a traditional publishing company, pay a vanity publisher, hire a book packager, or self-publish. Before you decide to self-publish, what follows are the more traditional routes to book publishing and how they work.

Traditional Book Publishers

There are more than a few types of traditional publishers. There are the big publishers, such as Random House. Random House is one of the remaining Big Five, and companies such as this one are looking for the next blockbuster. They are not likely to be interested in a family's pictoral history. There are also smaller publishers, mostly niche publishers, such as Arcadia Publishing that specializes in local history books.

In order to get the attention of one of the big publishers, you may need a literary agent to make a pitch to the company for you. Writing a good query letter introducing yourself and your book may work with a smaller publisher. Most photo books, unless they include rare photographs that are of interest to the general public, will not interest a traditional publisher enough to offer you a contract.

Even so, if you have incredible photographs to show and can interest a publishing company, they will buy the rights to publish a version of your work (e.g. print, electronic, audio, foreign language, or all rights) in exchange for a royalty—a percentage of the sales price. Most publishing contracts are based upon the sales price rather than the retail price because so many books are sold at a steep discount to bookstores or book clubs.

When the book sells, the publisher is paid, and they will handle any returns. You will be paid approximately ninety (90) days after the publisher, to allow time for returns.

A well-known author can expect a royalty of about fifteen percent, a lesser known author about ten percent, and an unknown author or photographer something less than ten percent. For most authors, a small percentage of the sales price (your royalty) means you have to sell a great number of books to make any money. For most family histories, this is not likely.

A traditional publisher will have total control over the physical production, distribution, and sales. The publisher will choose the cover design. Oftentimes, they will choose the title. Most importantly, they will control the content through the editing process. As the author, you will start the process, but once you sign a contract, and the manuscript is turned over, the publisher is in control.

If your book needs revisions or corrections, that will take place only after the initial print run sells out. For many books, the first print run never sells out. (One advantage to self-publishing using a print-on-demand printer is that you can make revisions at any time.)

A traditional publisher will decide how long the book will stay in print, and how long marketing will continue. For many books, once the sales slow, the marketing ends. (If you self-publish, the book will stay in print as long as you want it to.)

Vanity Publishers

Please do not enlist a vanity publisher to "publish" your book and "market" it to potential readers. In reality, these companies are offering to take as much of your money as you are willing to give them, and do nothing for you that you could not do cheaper. It is best to avoid these companies altogether. That goes for some author services companies, as well.

Book Packagers

Book packagers offer the different parts of the publishing process as services a-la-carte. If you do not want to handle the book cover design, for example, you could hire one of these companies to do so for you. You sign a contract for a specific service at a specific price. Book packagers can be helpful if you do not want to learn everything there is to know about book production, but still want a professional looking book.

Author Services

Author services companies offer many of the same services that book packagers do, as well as editing and marketing. Some of the biggest print-on-demand printers also offer author services. CreateSpace (www.createspace.com and its author services company BookSurge, www.booksurge.com), Lulu (www.lulu.com), and Blurb (www.blurb.com), offer packages of author services, such as copy editing, eBook conversion, layout, and cover design.

Most of the time, you will be able to do for yourself most of what they are offering to do for a fee. A better solution may be to find a local person—a book packager—who can design a cover or typeset the book for you at a fee you can negotiate, rather than accepting a package price for more services than you want or need from an author services company.

Caution: Author Solutions (www.authorsolutions.com—the author services provider of Penguin Random House via its imprints AuthorHouse, Trafford, Booktango, WordClay, FuseFrame, PitchFest, Author Learning Center, Author Hive, Xlibris, Palibro, Inkubook, Partridge and iUniverse) had a federal class-action lawsuit filed against them in 2013 alleging that they have been cheating writers out of their royalties and charging outrageous prices for services—for years. What follows are the names of companies that have aligned themselves with Author Solutions. Please avoid these vanity presses: Archway (Simon & Schuster), Partridge (Penguin), Westbow (Thomas Nelson/Harper Collins), Balboa Press (Hay House), Abbott Press (Writers' Digest), Dellarte Press (Harlequin). Many thanks to David Gaughran, author of *Let's Get Visible: How to Get Visible and Sell More Books* for helping fellow writers avoid trouble.

Self-Publishing

The best option for most family photo books is self-publishing. You are the publisher. You are in control of the whole process. You decide what goes into the book and how it looks. You control who can buy the book if there is information about living people you do not want out to the general public. You control the contents and the process. You also do most of the work. Fortunately, printing technology and software to create book layouts and electronic files has made self-publishing not only possible, but relatively easy.

Now that you have a better understanding of the role of the publisher let us take a look at some of the nuts and bolts decisions about print production.

Book Printers

Please use a book printer, not the local copy shop. Producing books one at a time at the local copy shop is not only expensive, but most copy shops do not have the kind of equipment to create books with permanent covers—either softbound (perfect bound) or hard-bound. The local copy shop may be good if your manuscript will only fill a booklet (under 48 pages) rather than a book, and if you only plan to print a limited number.

To create quality softbound or hardbound books, there are two options—print-on-demand or offset presses. On additional note about printing full-color photo books is that they are much more expensive than printing a book with a black and white interior. For this reason, many full-color books are printed in Asia where the cost of color printing is substantially lower if you are planning to print more than a few books at a time. John Kremer, book marketing expert, has a good list of the top book printers by location here (bookmarketingbestsellers. com/the-top-250-book-printers-by-location/). If you are interested in having your book printed in Asia, you may want to look for a company that has a representative in the United States (or wherever you are located) so that the representative can deal with the rules of international shipping for you.

Offset Book Printers

Using an offset book printer has its advantages, especially if you can sell or give away a large print run. Ordering books in quantity will keep the price per book down. The downside is that you have to print and pay for a minimum number of books up front—often 250 or more.

Offset printing is best for books with custom sizes or books that require high-quality reproduction such as photography or coffee table books. High-quality, full-color books are often printed in Asia because the cost is lower, even with international shipping.

Print-on-Demand Book Printers

Print-on-demand (POD) book printers are exactly as their name suggests—you can print a single book when you need it, including full-color photo books. There is a wide variety of print-on-demand printers. The following is a representative example of what you will find.

Drag and Drop Photo Books

Most of the companies that used to process film into photographic prints are now able to process digital images into prints or photo books—Costco (www.costco.com), Walgreens (www.walgreens.com), WalMart (www.walmart.com), Shutterfly (www.shutterfly.com), Adorama (www.adoramapix.com), Mixbook (www.mixbook.com), Blurb (www.blurb.com), Snapfish (www.snapfish.com) and many, many others.

These sites use pre-made templates that gives the page backgrounds a theme, and online tools that allow you to edit, crop, re-touch, and rotate images. Most also allow you to add clipart and text. In most cases, you can determine the number of images on each page and are able to customize the size of each and their placement within the page.

These are very tempting sites to use to create a photo book, especially if you are in a hurry for an upcoming family event or holiday. They are also—usually—the most expensive option for individual books.

Lulu

Lulu (www.lulu.com) is a POD book printer that also offers author and marketing services. Their business model assumes that you, the publisher, have no experience, so their website will guide you through the process step by step. Anyone can create a printed copy of a book through Lulu. The only downside is that there is no quality control during the process, and some people—mostly those in the book industry—may assume that your book is amateurish if you publish through Lulu. If you are not worried about selling the book except to friends or family, then there is no need to worry about where you have your book printed. The ease of using Lulu's website is an attractive plus.

Lulu is one of the few POD book printers with privacy options. At Lulu, you can make the book available only to you or by private web link to only those people you allow to buy the book. Publishing privately is an attractive option for proofing books and for keeping books out of the hands of the general public if they contain information about living people. If your book is full of photos that would make your family members uncomfortable to have out there for sale online, publishing privately at Lulu may be a good option for you.

Lulu also has an online bookstore if you want to make your book available for sale. Lulu's catalog also appears in other major online bookstores' catalogs. Both

Lulu and the other bookstores will take a cut before you earn a royalty, if you print your book through Lulu but sell it through Amazon, for example.

At Lulu, your wholesale prices may be higher than at other POD printers. If you are selling the book to make money, investigate your options.

CreateSpace

CreateSpace (www.createspace.com) is Amazon's POD printer. They expect you to know a little bit more about the process, so the website is not as easy to use as Lulu. CreateSpace will have a staff person review your book before approving it. Your book will not become available in the Amazon catalog without approval. Gaining approval can be a hurdle if you have unusual page numbering or something that makes the staff unsure of the quality of the work.

The upside is that your book will be available at the largest online bookstore on the Internet, and your wholesale prices will be lower at CreateSpace than at Lulu. Amazon's reach is enormous, meaning your book will be available literally around the world if you print through CreateSpace.

Lightning Source

At the far end of the scale is Lightning Source (www.lightningsource.com). Lightning Source is an Ingram Company. Ingram is the largest book wholesaler in the United States, and selling through their catalog means access to 30,000 wholesalers, retailers and booksellers in more than one hundred countries around the world.

Lightning Source *only* works with publishers. They expect you have experience with the process.

At Lightning Source, you must have your own International Standard Book Numbers (ISBNs), unlike CreateSpace and Lulu—both offer free ISBNs. All books, including different versions of the same book (an eBook or a 2nd Edition) must have an ISBN. ISBNs are like the Social Security number for a book. ISBNs distinguish one book from another or a newer version from an older version. The benefit of a free ISBN is cost savings since a single ISBN costs $125.00. A package of 10 ISBNs costs $295.00; 100 ISBNs cost $575, and so on. The more you buy, the less they cost per ISBN. You can purchase ISBNs through the Bowker Company's Identifier Services (www.myidentifiers.com).

Note: If you use a free ISBN from your printer, that company will become the publisher of record, not you.

Lightning Source charges fees to establish and maintain each book in their catalog. There are also fees for every update or revision. In other words, you need a next-to-perfect manuscript and a properly-sized and prepared cover to use this service, unless you are willing to spend a lot of money in fees and proofs until you get it right. There is no hand holding through the process.

The upside to printing through Lightning Source is that your wholesale costs will be lower than other POD printers, and your book will be available to a vast distribution network of wholesalers, retailers and booksellers—including Amazon and Barnes&Noble.

Espresso Book Machine

The Espresso Book Machine (EBM) (www.ondemandbooks.com) takes print-on-demand a whole step further. They provide equipment to select locations allowing readers to choose a book and have it printed in about fifteen minutes while they wait. You will not find EBMs in every city, at least not yet, and in some states, there are few locations. EBMs offer some exciting possibilities, however. Think about creating a book with recipes or stories gathered during a family reunion and being able to deliver the book to family members a few hours later.

Print Production Basics

One of your first major decisions is whether to print the book in color or in black-and-white. The cover, of course, will be in full color since that will not cost you more, and color covers are standard across the industry. Color *interiors*, however, add significantly to the cost. At print-on-demand printers, if you choose a color interior, every page will be considered a color page, even if it only has black-and-white text on it. If the book is in color, it is color throughout. An offset printer may be able to insert color pages either as a section in the middle or select places throughout the book. Either way, the cost of full-color books is much higher than books with black-and-white interiors.

Since your photo book should consist mostly of images, one thing to consider is how costly the book may become based upon the number of pages. Consider that you may be able to create a 200 page, 8.5"x 11" book in black-and-white for around $7 wholesale. Whereas, a color version of that same book could run $80 or more. **Tip**: If you choose to include much history along with the photos, one way to keep the cost down is to give your family the stories in black-and-white and the photographs in full color as companion books. That way, you print the black-and-white book for $7 wholesale, along with a 20-page color photo book for $10 to $15—together, still cheaper than a full-color interior. If the photographs are going to tell the story, however, expect the higher cost of the book. It is an heirloom, after all.

Interior Files

All books have interior files and cover files. The interior file will contain everything from the title page to the index, including the images. You will set up your manuscript in the physical size of the final book, called the trim size. The paper will be slightly larger than the final size so it can be trimmed off neatly to give the book a finished look.

The most common trim sizes are 6" x 9," 7" x 10" and 8.5" x 11." You can create a book of nearly any size, but if you will use one of these common sizes, the production cost will be lower and your options for printers will be greater. Oftentimes, however, photo books look better in larger formats such as 8.5" x 8.5" or 12"x 12" or in landscape orientation 9" x 7," 10" x 8," or 13" x 11."

One additional consideration for full-color interiors is the paper. Color printed on standard, uncoated paper is fine for small images such as a logo, but photographs will always look better when printed on coated paper. Many print-on-demand printers offer full-color printing and photo-quality printing, and there is a difference. The difference is mostly in the quality of the paper and the density of the ink coverage. If you want stunning photos, choose the photo-quality option.

Choose a trim size based upon how many pages there are in the manuscript, and how large you wish to display the images. When you are ready to create the layout, you should have an idea of whether your book will run 50 pages or 500. Because of the cost of photo-quality interiors, you may want to narrow the project and create more than one photo book spread out over time, rather than one enormous volume.

Cover Files

You will not create your cover file until you have chosen the trim size, the binding, and have the manuscript ready because the number of pages will determine the spine width.

Most printers offer the following binding options:

Hardbound also Called Case Bound. Hardbound covers consist of thick cardboard pieces covered in material, glued or sewn to the interior at the spine. You will have the option of a plain cloth cover, wrapping the cloth cover with a dust jacket, or a full-color, glossy paper cover—such as a textbook.

Softbound also Called Paperback or Perfect Bound. Softbound covers consist of thick, paper cover glued to the interior pages at the spine.

Lay-flat. Lay-flat is a more expensive option than softbound, but best for workbooks or cookbooks that need to lay flat for easy use.

Each of the following binding styles is disliked by librarians and bookstore owners because they do not have spines, so the book must be removed from the shelf in order to read the title.

Saddle Stitch. Saddle stitch books are laid out in two-page spreads, folded in half, then stapled at the spine. Standard 8.5" x 11" paper becomes a 5.5" x 8.5" book, or an 11" x 17" paper becomes an 8.5" x 11" book. The covers are created from thicker card stock placed on the outside of the collated pages before folding and stapling. Saddle stitch is best for books under 48 pages.

Side Stitch. In a side-stitched book, pages are collated; loose card stock covers are placed on the front and back, then stapled on the left-hand side near the edge.

Spiral or Wire-O. These books look like a spiral notebook. One problem with spiral or wire-o is that every time the pages are turned, they rub against the binding. Eventually, the pages will tear from the book easily.

For a photo book, softbound or hardbound is best. Either looks professional, has a nice spine so you can read the title when the book is on the shelf, and lasts longer than spiral, wire-o, or old-fashioned comb binding which is expensive and does not hold up well over time.

Final Files

Most printers will accept Portable Document Format (PDF) files. Once you have your manuscript looking the way you want it to, save it as a PDF and send it to the printer. (More about the mechanics of saving PDF files in Section 4.)

Print Distribution Basics

To deliver a printed book to an interested reader, the book could be sold through a bookstore—a brick and mortar store or online. You could distribute them yourself by selling them on your own website; print a bunch and take them to a family reunion; ask interested family members to send orders to you; or, use an online print-on-demand service where buyers could purchase a copy for themselves. These are all easy options for distributing printed books to readers.

Selling books through a brick and mortar store is a little more complicated. Most bookstores order directly through one of the major wholesalers—Ingram (Lightning Source) or Baker&Taylor. To sell books to a chain bookstore, you must have an account with one or both of the major wholesalers. For a family-oriented photo book, however, chances are that the trouble you will go through to obtain an account will not be worth it.

There are exceptions. If you have extraordinary images, or images with widespread public interest, then traditional bookstore distribution channels may be an option for you.

Another exception is selling through a local independent bookstore. A local store owner may be willing to stock a few books bought directly from you, but expect this to be the exception rather than the rule. You may have more luck with a local museum shop where making small purchases from local authors is more common. Museum stores will purchase a few copies at a time, so give them an easy way to re-order.

Be aware of the expectations of booksellers. Wholesalers will expect up to a 50 percent discount, so they can make money and allow the end seller (the bookstore) to make a few dollars on the sale as well. You can probably offer a smaller discount to a local bookstore or museum shop, more like 20 to 30 percent if you are not using a wholesaler.

Then there is the matter of returns. Bookstores and wholesalers expect to be able to return books if they go unsold. Returns are an accounting hassle for you, not to mention that the wholesaler or retailer may send the book back years later, in no condition to re-sell, but expect credit for the return anyway. For small publishers, the only way around this is to sell books on a *non-returnable* basis. You may have to offer a bigger discount to induce the bookstore or museum shop to a non-returnable sale, but the greater discount is almost always worth not dealing with returns.

Electronic Publishing

Except for adult fiction, printed books still hold about ninety percent of the book market. However, people are reading more and more via dedicated eReaders and on other electronic devices such as tablets. On tablets, readers use an application (app) to display the book as the dedicated eReaders do. As smartphones, tablets, and other mobile devices become more widely used in schools and offices, electronic books will become even more popular. Electronic books are cheaper, mobile and easier to store.

Currently, there are three primary formats for electronic publishing—PDF, MOBI, and EPUB.

Portable Document Format (PDF)

Creating a PDF does not require a publisher or a distributor. PDF is a file type developed by the Adobe Corporation that solved cross-platform problems between computers. Before the PDF, sending a file to a person using a different operating system (PC or Mac) or software (Word or Word Perfect) meant that the recipient could not open or read the document.

You can convert almost any file to a PDF, and almost every computer comes with the free Adobe Acrobat Reader pre-installed. If your computer does not have Acrobat Reader, download it free from Adobe (www.adobe.com). PDFs can be opened and read on most electronic devices including tablets.

One upside to PDFs is the ease of creation. Most word processing and page layout software will save their files to PDFs. Saving to PDF keeps the page formatting exactly as you designed it. Everything will stay in place—the text, the pictures, and the captions.

A downside is that documents designed using 8.5" x 11" pages are easy to read on a computer screen or iPad, but may be almost impossible to read on a smaller device such as a mini-tablet or a phone. The pages are a fixed size, more like viewing a photograph than reading a text document. A better option for smaller devices is to use a format that allows the text to reflow, such as MOBI or EPUB.

MOBI and EPUB

Where electronic publishing gets a little more complicated is in the creation and distribution of different formats for different devices. There are two primary formats for eReaders or apps that imitate eReaders—Kindle's proprietary format MOBI and the EPUB format used by many other devices. Acting as your own publisher for these formats is not impossible, but not simple either.

Publishing for Kindle

The Kindle is Amazon's dedicated eReader. To publish for Kindle, use the Kindle Direct Publishing (KDP) service (kdp.amazon.com). You will be able to upload a Word document or a PDF, and Amazon will convert it to their proprietary MOBI format. Amazon will handle all sales and distribution. Readers will make their purchase through Amazon and download the book to their Kindle or a device with a Kindle app.

Amazon pays you a royalty based upon the book's retail price. In 2015, any book with a retail price under $9.99 will generate a 70 percent royalty, whereas books priced at $10.00 or higher receive a 30 percent royalty.

One nice feature of Kindle books is their ability to sync across devices, meaning that readers can switch from their Kindle to their tablet or smartphone and sync the files to maintain their place in the book.

Publishing for Other eReaders

While most word processing software will create a PDF, you may need special software to create an EPUB file. Since so many devices are using this format, it may become easier to create an EPUB in the future. If you have a Mac, Pages software will create EPUB files. Adobe InDesign will create an EPUB file on a PC, but the software is expensive. Microsoft Word will allow you to save your manuscript as an HTML file, and then you can use the free Calibre software (calibre-ebook.com) to convert an HTML file into an EPUB.

If you create your own EPUB files, download Adobe's free Digital Editions software (www.adobe.com). Use Digital Editions to preview how the book looks before sending it to readers or elsewhere for distribution.

Electronic Production Basics

Electronic books, like printed books, need an interior file and a cover file, but there are differences in how the files must be prepared—sometimes big differences.

Interior Files as PDFs

Setting up your manuscript for a PDF is almost the same as setting it up for print production. You can set the interior up as two-page spreads, so that the reader experiences the book the same way they would if they were reading a printed version, or you can set it up as a single page document without right-hand or left-hand pages. Single pages allow the reader to keep a single page on the screen that will make it easier to read on a device such as an iPad.

You can use a word processor or page layout program to create your PDF file, or you can use a presentation program such as PowerPoint or Keynote for the Mac. Word processors have the best spell and grammar checkers, but presentation programs may give you greater control over combining text and images. The slide sorter view, for example, lets you move information around much easier than cutting and pasting in your word processor. Page layout programs (albeit the most expensive software option) will give you the greatest control over both text and images.

Interior Files as MOBIs or EPUBs

Preparing a manuscript for conversion to MOBI or EPUB is, in some respects, easier than laying out and formatting a PDF for electronic or print production. Electronic books must be simple, and without a lot of complicated formatting because the look of an electronic book is controlled largely by the reader. The reader can adjust the type size to suit their needs so the text must re-flow within the eReader's window.

While it is possible for you to create a MOBI or EPUB file yourself, it may be easier to let an eBook aggregator or distributor create the file so that there are no glitches when the file is read by electronic devices.

Cover Files

While it is not necessary to include a cover file with your electronic book, many eReaders will show the cover in the device's catalog, and most eBook outlets will show a thumbnail. Make sure your title is readable in a small thumbnail.

Electronic Distribution Basics

How electronic books are distributed depends upon the format.

Distributing PDFs

Distributing a PDF is simple. You can send it directly to the reader in an email. Fortunately, PDF files can be optimized which makes the file small enough to send even long manuscripts with photographs and illustrations by email.

Another option is to post your PDF online for readers to download for themselves. You could send interested readers a link, or they could use a search engine to discover it. You could also create a website and post your PDF behind a password so that only paying customers can access it.

One downside to *selling* your book as a PDF, however, is limiting distribution to paying customers. There are tools that allow you to mark copies with the name of the original buyer so if the book is widely shared, you will know who made it available. Other tools allow you to lock the PDF from printing or to password protect the file. Practically, however, once you distribute your book in a PDF format, it may be re-distributed without your knowledge.

Distribution for the Kindle

Amazon distributes Kindle books. You can publish your eBook directly through their distributor CreateSpace (which also handles printed books) (www.createspace.com), or Kindle Direct Publishing (kdp.amazon.com), if you plan to publish only in the Kindle format. Right now, Kindle holds a majority of the eBook market through either its dedicated reader or through the Kindle app available for tablets or smartphones.

Distribution for Devices Using the EPUB Format

Hundreds of different devices use the EPUB format. If you can create an EPUB file, you can distribute the book yourself, much the same way as you would a PDF file (above). There are also hundreds of distribution outlets for EPUB books including:

- iTunes (www.itunes.com)
- The Android App Store also called Google Play (play.google.com)
- Google Books (books.google.com)
- Kobo (www.kokobooks.com)
- Smashwords (www.smashwords.com)
- Gumroad (gumroad.com)

These online bookstores sell electronic books, acting as a wholesaler between you and the end user.

Rather than dealing with hundreds of online bookstores, consider using an aggregator. Aggregators charge a fee, but they will prepare your manuscript for distribution across multiple platforms making sure the file passes the standards tests for different devices. They will also prepare the file for the many apps that mimic eReaders such as the Nook app or the Kindle app.

Aggregators will handle sales through the different electronic book outlets, take a percentage as their sales commission and pay the rest to you as a royalty. The following are all eBook aggregators:

- First Edition Design Publishing (www.firsteditiondesignpublishing.com)
- Bookwire (www.bookwire.com)

- Ingram (www.ingramcontent.com)
- INscribe (inscribedigital.com)
- Smashwords (www.smashwords.com)
- BookBaby (www.bookbaby.com)

Distribution of Other Electronic Files

Services such as Gumroad (gumroad.com), allow you to upload your electronic file(s) to their servers. Gumroad accepts audio, video or zipped bundles, if you have more than one book available or want to include an audio file along with your book file. To sell your book, place a link on your website taking viewers to Gumroad to buy it. You price your book; Gumroad keeps a percentage as a hosting and processing fee; they pay you the rest. In essence, Gumroad is taking care of the credit card processing and electronic delivery. Once the item is paid for, the buyer will receive a download link.

Distribution to Groups

If you want to sell books to an organization in quantity, for example, you can use Amazon's Whispercast service (whispercast.amazon.com). The organization will create an account and send an invitation URL to its members. If the member accepts the invitation, the organization buys a copy for that person. After the member receives the book, Amazon charges the organization's credit card for the sale. This would work for a family reunion, by pre-selling books during the reunion, setting up a bank account with a debit card on behalf of the group and using the funds collected to pay for books through Whispercast.

Global Distribution

One of the biggest advantages to publishing electronically through one of the major distributors such as Amazon's Kindle Direct Publishing (kdp.amazon.com), or Barnes & Noble's Nook Press (nookpress.com), is that they will make your eBook available to people across the globe. There is no negotiating of foreign rights or dealing with a foreign publisher to distribute the book on another continent. If you have family members across the world, publishing electronically may be a good option for you.

Distribution by Gift Card

Enthrill Books (enthrillbooks.com) enables you to use a pre-activated gift card allowing the recipient to download your book either in the EPUB or MOBI format. You could take the pre-activated cards to a family reunion, for example, to sell or give away to your family members.

Distribution to Libraries

One final consideration is placing your book with the major genealogical collections across the country and into the local libraries where your family once resided. While most libraries still focus on print books, they are coming around to the idea of purchasing licensing rights for eBooks. Most of the time, family histories or genealogies (including family-specific photo books) are kept in non-circulating collections, so the electronic format would allow the library to lend the book. OverDrive (www.overdrive.com), is one of the leading digital distributors of electronic books to libraries, schools, and some retail outlets. If you are interested in selling your eBook to libraries, check out the publisher services on their website.

Online Publishing

For those of you who may want to make your book widely available and are not interested in selling it, publishing online may be a good option. There are a couple of ways to do so. You can use an online book publisher (Google Books), or you can act as your own publisher by using online publishing tools such as blogging software, website builders, social media or on a genealogical website featuring family trees.

The difference between an online book and an electronic book is how it is delivered. Online books and electronic books are both in an electronic format. An online book stays on a server somewhere where readers can use a web browser to access the book via the Internet. An electronic book is more likely to be distributed to a reading device such as a Kindle, Nook or smartphone.

The upside to publishing online is that anyone with Internet access can find and read your book. Many of the options below cost nothing to set up and use, although, you are completely at the mercy of the host as to whether your site stays up and running. If the company folds, your free site folds with it. Another option is to pay for your own website which will give you more options for the look and feel of the material or whether you want to sell the book rather than give it away. But, you must continue paying the hosting fee or the site will come down and your book with it.

The following are options for publishing a book online:

Online Book Publishers

Google Books is one of the only online book publishers I have found to date, meaning that they sell books meant to be read via the Internet using a web browser. Google Books allows readers to choose between PDFs formatted exactly as the publisher formatted the book, or read through a proprietary browser platform that presents the book in side-by-side pages as if reading a printed book. Google's browser-based software also gives readers the option of reading the book like other dedicated eReaders. The reader can change the type size or the font, and the book text will reflow. If you want to publish a book through Google Books, sign up through their Google Play Books Partner Center (play.google.com/books/publish/).

Amazon offers something similar allowing readers to purchase a book for their Kindle, also allowing them to access the book from a web browser through the Kindle Cloudreader software (read.kindle.com). The experience of reading a Kindle book online is similar to reading from the Kindle device itself.

Publishing a Book by Blog

Blog is short for web log. Blogging software allows publishers to post new content easily and quickly. If you can use email, you can blog. The process is similar. You will use a headline to alert the reader, and the body text to tell the story and display images.

The difficulty of publishing a book on a blog is organizing in a way that the reader understands what to read in what order, and keeping the segments short enough to avoid scrolling (and scrolling and scrolling).

Publishing a Book Using Social Media

Facebook (www.facebook.com) is the most popular social media site right now, although it has not always been, and may not be in the future. The appeal of Facebook is that it is so easy to connect with other people (family members) interested in reading your material. The downside of using something such as Facebook to deliver your book's content is that each post can be only so long, shorter, even than blog posts. You will be delivering your book in little dribs and drabs using small web-ready images. Facebook may be a better place to obtain additional images from family members, more so than playing host to your finished book. (You will find more detailed information regarding publishing by blog or social media in *Set Yourself Up to Self-Publish: A Genealogist's Guide.*)

Publishing a Book on Your Own Website

If you create a website to publish your book, you can install blogging software such as WordPress, or more traditional HTML coding using any number of HTML editors (website building software) such as Adobe Dreamweaver (www.adobe.com).

If you create your own website and use an HTML editor to build it, you will have complete control over how the site looks, and how you will organize your book as web pages.

Publising a Book Using a Wiki Platform

Wikis are user-generated content that can be edited directly using an ordinary web browser. A wiki is a great opportunity for collaboration with family members to keep family information up to date, but it is also an opportunity for malicious users to spread misinformation or to delete a lot of hard work. The power and the bane of wikis is the ability of anyone to contribute.

Publishing a Book with a Genealogy Service

Neither the paid genealogy services Ancestry (www.ancestry.com), or MyHeritage (www.myheritage.com), nor the free service FamilySearch (www.familysearch.com) (or any of the other genealogy-based search sites) were designed as book publishing platforms. Many offer tools to attach stories and photographs to individuals within an online family tree. Publishing your book in this way is similar to publishing on a social media site—short snippets rather than a beginning-to-end book.

Note: FamilySearch, Ancestry, and MyHeritage have book or booklet publishing options that use your online tree to create printed books. When investigating the process, I found that the cost was much higher than using a print-on-demand printer, and the options for what to include or exclude was a bit clumsy, at least at this point. If you are going to create a one-of-a-kind photo book, it is worth the effort to use a dedicated book printer.

Online Production Basics

If you publish online, preparing your manuscript is relatively easy. Although, how you prepare it depends upon where you are going to place it on the Internet. Let us start with Google Books since they are the exception to the rule, and then we will look into making your book into blog posts or web pages.

Files for Google Books

If you publish online through Google Books, you can upload both a PDF version and an EPUB version, so the reader can choose whether to view the book exactly as you have it laid out, or as flowing text they can control through Google's browser-based platform. PDF and EPUB are the only two file formats Google Books accepts for upload. They will also accept a printed book and scan it for you, making it possible to create a new eBook out of an older, out-of-print title.

Google Books uses thumbnail-sized cover files in their online catalog.

Files for Blog Posts

While you can organize your material as a complete book on a blog, you must organize in a way that lets readers know how to follow the stories one after the other, and split the manuscript into short segments (posts) to keep scrolling to a minimum.

Each post requires a headline and body text, similar to composing an email. Blog posts can include images and captions. You can also add keywords to categorize each post so that readers can find the blog using a search engine.

Readers familiar with feed reader programs can subscribe to your blog so that they are notified every time you create a new post.

You can use your book cover image as a part of the blog's header so that it is always visible no matter which post the reader is viewing.

Files for Social Media

Publishing to a social media site is similar to publishing to a blog. Posting to a blog or social media keeps your short snippets in one place with the latest post at the top. The older posts will move down as the new posts appear.

On social media, if you create a page (sometimes called fan page) dedicated to your book, readers can come to that page to see everything you have posted, similar to visiting a blog, but if readers are "following" your page (i.e. they have "liked" it), then the snippets will be delivered to the reader through the newsfeed on their own pages.

For each post, use a headline to catch the viewer's attention as they skim their newsfeed (the posts coming in). Place the text in the body, and add images. Some social media platforms allow you to caption each image, and "tag" the people in the image. Tagging is similar to adding a keyword to the image. It helps people find the image using the search feature on the social media site, or by using a search engine.

Use your book cover image in the header area or as the profile image so that every time you post, the book's cover is shown in the little icon next to the post. Facebook uses square profile images, and book covers are longer than they are wide, so you may have to add a bit of white space on either side of your book cover image to make it square. Otherwise, it could be cut off at the top and bottom when displayed.

Files for a Website

Creating your own website gives you a lot of flexibility for how and what you make available to readers.

Web pages can hold text, images, video or audio files and contain links to other resources on the Internet. To publish your book as a website, use an HTML editor to create a page for each story or chapter and navigation links to help the reader move from story to story logically.

Keywords are used on web pages the same way they are used on blog posts to help the search engines find the web page. HTML editing software and most website building tools online offer a way to include keywords in the metadata for each page.

Use your book cover image in the website's header, or alongside the text on the home page.

Files for a Genealogy Service

Most genealogical websites where you can build an online family tree have a way to attach stories to individuals or groups.

Ancestry provides two ways to attach stories to people in your family tree. One method is to use the story view settings. Ancestry uses the documents you have linked to the person to suggest a storyline, and gives you the option of adding text and photographs to the story view page. Another option is to add stories directly through the media gallery section where you can also add images, video or audio.

The process is similar on FamilySearch. You will add stories in the "memories" section of your family tree where you can also add a picture.

At MyHeritage, each individual in your tree has a page where you can add biographical information and media files (photographs) or links to video files.

Cover files are a little more difficult to place at one of these online options, unless you want a book cover image attached to an individual.

Copy and Paste Text Cleanly

The easiest way to prepare text for any online option is to copy and paste from your word processor. However, many word processors add code for formatting features such as margins, fonts, font size, bold or italics. These codes do not always translate cleanly to email, blog posts or websites. Word processors use an 8-bit environment for formatting, while many of the tools of the Internet use a 7-bit environment which can cause conflicts. What you can end up with is unexpected characters in your text, mostly where you expect punctuation to be.

For example, this is what happens when a quote is copied from a Word document into an email:

From Word: "Jacob's intended return ..."
Copied into email: "Jacob@s intended return ..."

One way to avoid these unexpected ASCII characters is to copy the text into a plain text editing program such as Notepad first. Notepad will remove all formatting, leaving a plain text (.txt) version of whatever you are copying and pasting. The plain text version can then be used in an email, a blog post or a website without any unexpected characters surfacing.

Create Web-Friendly File Names

Tools of the Internet also prefer standard filenames. So, file names that are acceptable on your local computer may contain unexpected characters when posted online. For example:

Local file: Jacob Wilson's will.pdf

Online becomes: Jacob%20Wilson%20s%20Will.pdf (depending upon the server settings)

For clean file names, avoid punctuation except for periods and use under-scores for spaces. Either of these file names would be fine, for example:

Jacob.Wilson.Will.pdf
Jacob_Wilson_Will.pdf

Online Distribution Basics

If you publish online, you have largely determined how the book will be distrib-uted to the reader—on a blog, a website or within a social media platform. You do not have to distribute it; the readers will come to the book. You need only take the steps necessary to help readers find the book online—good, descriptive key-words, great content, and a willingness to get the word out.

☙ॐ

What is the easiest way to prepare a book to distribute to family members at the least cost? That would be a PDF. As long as the PDF is designed for easy reading on the screen, the book can be distributed by email. For some family members, a PDF is perfect. If they are used to reading on screen or a large format tablet such as an iPad, they will appreciate the PDF. For other family members, print will always be preferred.

What, then, is the easiest way to prepare a book for sale? The easiest way is to create an eBook and use an eBook aggregator to convert it to the different electronic formats for you. There is a fee to have an eBook aggregator prepare and submit your manuscript, but for those family members who are used to a dedicated eReader, this option will delight them.

Publishing a book online and in print are a bit more challenging than pub-lishing PDFs and eBooks.

Publishing online has organizational challenges, but most options are with-out cost. Online publishing has the risk of all other electronic products—obso-lescence. If the company hosting your website folds, or the social media site be-comes unpopular, or your blog is lost in a server crash, the book is lost.

The best, most permanent way to preserve your images is to publish in print. Your family members will appreciate a printed book. A book printed today, given the technology and materials, should last one hundred years or more. If pre-served well, a modern book will last much longer. In the event of natural or per-sonal disaster, giving a few copies of your book to the major genealogical libraries around the country will preserve your images for generations to come.

Chapter 5

The Right Tool for the Right Job

To make your way from idea to finished book, using the right tool for the right job will save you time and frustration.

In a perfect world, you would use an organizational tool to set up the table of contents and organize your notes, a word processor to draft your manuscript, an image capture program to scan documents and other printed materials, an image editor to crop, size and alter images, a page layout program to typeset the book so that it reads and looks its best, and backup tools to keep your manuscript and image files safe from disaster.

In general, organizational tools are not the best place to format text correctly, word processors are not the best place to lay out book pages, and page layout programs are not the best word processors.

Realistically, you may not want to invest your time and money in all of this software. You may not need to. What you do need is an understanding of how to make your photographs look their best plus the rules of readability for books; and either, the willingness to learn how to create a layout, typeset the text, and prepare images in the software you already own, or recognition that the software you have will not do the job well. If the latter is the case, you can engage professional help or invest in software better suited to the job.

Organizing

In the preliminary stages, you may want software to keep you organized. Scrivener (www.literatureandlatte.com/scrivener.php) is a powerful organizing tool to gather your notes, pictures, video clips, or thoughts. It is available for both PC and Mac.

If you use an outline, the left-hand panel shows your outline in a menu that you can use to rearrange files, and expand or collapse depending upon what you want to see while you are working. You can split files into pieces to create a more detailed outline.

If you organize in a more visual way, you can see your notes, organized on a cork board. If you want to keep your sources attached to each note, you can do so either in the body of the text or off to the side in a panel designed to document source material.

At any time, you can move notes from one place to another using the drag and drop features in the cork board or outline, helping to organize your information into a cohesive whole.

Other organizing software includes: Microsoft OneNote (www.onenote.com) and Evernote (evernote.com). Both of these organizing tools have the advantage of being available on your desktop and by app on mobile devices with the ability to sync files. I use these apps to add notes or ideas when I am out and about, but when I am in the office writing, I use Scrivener to organize.

Word Processing

With most books, at some point, you would want to move your notes from an organizing tool into a word processor. With a photo book, much depends upon how much text you wish to include with each photograph. You may want to put the photograph into context, or tell a story about someone in the photograph, or how you came to possess the photograph. At the very least, each photograph (or page of photographs) should have a short caption. Another option is to allow the photograph(s) to fill the page completely, and add narrative information about the images on the opposite page, or in the back of the book as endnotes.

Whether you are at the stage to add formatting, or you are still writing and want to collect your material chapter by chapter, a word processor is a better tool than organizing software to create a manuscript.

Word processors are ideal for creating eBooks. Unfortunately, most word processing software falls short when creating layouts and correct typesetting for print books because they lack the sophistication to create the best-looking pages.

Word processors often hyphenate incorrectly or add space between words to avoid hyphenating that can create rivers of white or blank areas through the type. Word processors do not have nearly the kind of control over how tight or how loose text is typeset that also can result in dense or dark areas of text on the page. Most word processors do not have as much control over margins, columns and text wrap around images, as page layout programs do.

Unfortunately, page layout software can be expensive, so you may opt to layout and typeset your final manuscript in your word processing software. If you do, be prepared to learn about the advanced features. Fortunately, some word processors have helpful time-saving features to create a table of contents, an index, and footnotes, for example.

There are numerous word processing programs available including:

- Microsoft Word (office.microsoft.com)
- Pages for Mac (www.apple.com)
- Word Perfect (www.wordperfect.com)
- OpenOffice Writer (www.openoffice.org)
- LibreOffice (www.libreoffice.org)
- Google Docs (docs.google.com)

Microsoft Word has become the standard among book designers and packagers, professional editors, some eBook aggregators, and online resellers. For book designers and book packagers, Word files can be imported directly into more sophisticated page layout software without much trouble. For editors, Word has a "Track Changes" feature that allows you to see and accept or reject an editor's changes. Most eBook aggregators prefer Word files because they can convert the file for the requirements of the different eBook readers easily. And, some online resellers will accept Word files from which to create print and electronic books.

Page Layout

There are many options for printing photo books, including using the templates available on many photo book printing websites where anyone can go to create a quick book of their vacation photographs or holiday images to share with friends or family. In this book, I would like to give you a few more options for creating your own layout while still using an online print-on-demand printer.

When typesetting print books, you will achieve the best results from a page layout program. The two major powerhouses are:

- Adobe InDesign (www.adobe.com)
- QuarkXPress (www.quark.com)

Pages for the Mac (www.apple.com) was designed as a word processor but has many of the same features as the best page layout programs.

Page layout programs are designed to put the finishing touches on book-length manuscripts using the same tools professional typesetters use. These programs also can handle full-color books and, for the time being, are best for converting word-processed text into good looking eBooks in the EPUB format used by many eReaders. Creating good photo eBooks can be a challenge, however, because it is difficult to both size the image to look its best on a variety of different screen sizes while maintaining enough resolution so that the image looks good on larger screens and keeping the book's file size small enough for download.

PDF is another popular electronic format, and page layout programs create beautiful PDFs with settings to create the appropriate file sizes and quality for printing, emailing or posting online. Creating your own PDF eBook is not only possible, but may be the best solution if you wish to distribute your photo book electronically to be read on large-format tablets or on a computer screen.

The biggest advantage to using a page layout program is the control you have over where items are placed on the page in relationship to other items, the ability to create precise text formatting styles (rules) for different needs, and the flexible layouts possible with master pages with different grids for different page styles.

The sophistication of these programs is a big step up from even the best word processors. Unfortunately, most page layout programs come with both a hefty price tag and a hefty learning curve. For some projects, using a book designer or packager to take your final manuscript from as good as a word processor can do, to as good as a New York publisher could do, may be a better tradeoff than buying and learning a page layout program. For most people who want to preserve heirloom photographs, you will be able to create a stunning photo book without any professional help.

Image Capture

There are two ways to turn a printed photograph or document into a digital image—you can photograph it, or you can scan it. For items such as photographs pasted into a scrapbook, heirloom objects or photographs with textured surfaces, re-photographing the item may give you the best results.

For most flat items, however, scanning will give you a good digital image. Producing a good, print-ready scan will save you time and effort later.

There is more information about scanning in Chapter 8: Scanning and Optical Character Recognition.

Image Editing

The best way to prepare images in the correct physical size and resolution is to use an image editing program.

There are hundreds of image editors, including online tools, free downloads, apps for mobile devices, pre-installed software, and those designed for professional photographers. One of the best is Adobe Photoshop. For most people, the consumer version called Photoshop Elements (www.adobe.com) will do everything you need to complete your book project.

If you have many photographs to process or catalogue, consider Adobe's Lightroom software. This software has editing features that allow you to make the same change across a number of photographs. For example, if you have images that all need to have color correction because they have begun to fade, you can create a setting in Lightroom that enhances the photographs the way you want, and then you can apply that filter across to photographs you choose even if they are in different file folders. Lightroom also allows you to "tag" photographs and rate them which makes searching for every photograph you have of an individual or place simple. Adobe offers a combination package for of Photoshop and Lightroom for photographers through their Creative Cloud subscription service (www.adobe.com).

Another handy use for image editing software is to caption your photographs so that the caption stays with the photograph no matter what. In most image editing software programs, you will use a feature called "canvas" to add a bit of additional real estate to the photograph. For a caption, you would add white space at the bottom so that you can add your caption.

Illustration

While it is possible to create a book cover in a word processor, an image editor or a page layout program, to create the best-looking images and type, you may want to use illustration software, also called vector editing programs. The most popular among graphic designers is Adobe Illustrator (www.adobe.com).

There are many others available, including:

- CorelDraw Graphics Suite (www.coreldraw.com)
- Xara Designer Pro (www.xara.com)
- Inkscape (www.inkscape.org)

Illustration programs are another case where the cost of buying the program (and the time required to learn it) may be better spent hiring a cover designer.

Utilities and Backup

While you are writing, scanning and editing your images, make backups—frequently. You never know when your hard drive will crash, or some other calamity may come your way. One way to create on-going backups is to use one of the cloud services such as:

- Carbonite (www.carbonite.com)
- MyPCBackup (www.mypcbackup.com)
- Mozy (www.mozy.com)
- SugarSync (www.sygarsync.com)

If you keep good backups and something happens, you can always retrieve the most recent backup once you are up and running again.

If you also want to share files with family or editors, think about using a file sharing service such as:

- Dropbox (www.dropbox.com)
- Hightail (formerly YouSendIt) (www.hightail.com)
- Box.com (www.box.com)

- Google Drive (drive.google.com)
- Microsoft OneDrive (onedrive.live.com)

These services are perfect for sharing copies of your manuscript or images, even if the files are large. Do not keep your only copy on one of these services, however, because anyone who shares the folder with you can delete items.

The most secure place to keep backups is in the cloud, or on a portable hard drive, stored away from your home in a safe deposit box.

⇛⇝

How many or how few of these tools you utilize is up to you. You may find that the right tool for the right job is easiest. Or, you may prefer hiring someone to handle the tasks you would rather not tackle. Thankfully, most photo books are successfully published without spending a king's ransom on software or professional help.

SECTION 2

The goal in this section is for you to review your images, scan them so that they are ready for use, and gather anything else you need before you begin writing narrative, captions or laying out the book.

Everyone should:

- Identify your target audience—the people for whom you are writing the book.
- Conduct an image review.
- Read the chapter on scanning and optical character recognition.
- Put your citations in order if your book includes a longer narrative with documented research.
- Read the tips for project management.
- Make completing book project a priority by scheduling time on your calendar to devote to it.

Baby Steps

If you planning to use a drag-and-drop photo printer, scan your images at the right size for printing, fix any that need repairs, and organize them so that your time online will be efficient.

Next Steps

If you are planning a more custom photo book with images and captions, follow the Baby Steps and conduct another round of research to gather any images you may be missing.

Giant Leaps

If you are planning a longer narrative to showcase a few historical or extraordinary photographs, follow the steps above and plan an additional round of research to gather the social history and historical context to help you write the narrative.

Even though it may seem that I am suggesting you retire and devote your life to writing your book, I am not. I want you to be realistic about the preparation phase, however, because it can take longer than the writing.

Because this section has so many tasks, there are additional Baby Steps, Next Steps and Giant Leaps within some chapters.

*In this section, when I refer to characters, I always mean real people—ancestors—not fictional characters.

Chapter 6

Identifying Your Target Market

Your target market—who you are creating the book for—matters. According to *Elements of Style*, "The true writer always plays to an audience of one." To keep your perfect audience in mind as you write, place a photograph on the wall or near the desk as a constant reminder.

Having a clear idea of the people who will appreciate your book will influence what to include and what to leave out. If you choose the best images and write enough about them to meet your audience's needs and expectations, you will naturally answer their questions.

You also may choose to *leave out* images if they would be embarrassing to living relatives. That is not to say that you should shy away from images of what actually took place, only that a touch of tact may be in order when choosing images.

Who is Your Audience?

Your family, of course, is the natural audience for your book. Your immediate family, perhaps some extended family, even distant cousins may be interested because of their relationships with people in the book. You also may have photographs that will appeal to a more general audience.

Even though the images should primarily satisfy the curiosity of your core audience—your family—most books have more than one natural audience.

Genealogical Researchers

In addition to your family, consider other genealogists who are researching your family as a collateral line. Or, if you have unique photographs of an area during a specific time period, genealogists may be interested in your book to help them with their research or writing their own family stories.

Local Historians

There may be researchers or hobbyists interested in the era or area shown in your photographs, especially if you have rare photographs of local people.

The General Public

Your images may appeal to the general public if they are representative of a generation's experience during WWII, for example.

Museum Shops

Although most family photo books are not sold commercially, if you have images that would interest local people, then a museum shop may be interested in selling your book.

Libraries

While many libraries are happy to accept a donation of your book, to convince the library to buy a copy, show a significant tie between your family and the library's location or region.

Bookstores

Bookstores are great places. As a bibliophile, I love bookstores, but the pressure on bookstores is to move inventory. Unfortunately, photo books, even those with broad, general public appeal, are a risk for bookstores unless you, the author, or the photographer is well known, or the subject of the images is popular. Unless you can generate traffic into the bookstore, do not count on bookstores to sell many of your books. There are ways to entice interested readers through the bookstore door, but that discussion is later in Section 5: Getting the Word Out.

While you are researching and writing, consider what your target market(s) may need to get the best experience while reading your book.

What Does Your Audience Need?

The goal while writing is to spend your energy making the book the best it can be, given the time you have to finish the research and write the book. Give the reader everything he or she needs to understand the images and their significance to your family.

Subject Matter

How many images you include and how much information you use to describe them will depend upon the level of detail you desire and how much research and writing you are willing to do.

Format

The format or style of a photo book, typically, puts more emphasis on the photographs than on the narrative. That said, you may choose to include a chapter-length narrative for each photograph. The format is up to you.

Documentation

Documentation is not absolutely necessary in a photo book, however, there may be researchers who will want to recreate your research steps and they will use your evidence to evaluate the credibility of the book if you are showing family relationships through the photographs. If you are creating the book solely for the enjoyment of your family, you could skip the documentation or you could choose a format that is easier to accomplish than one of the more rigorous or formal genealogical styles.

Images

Granted, a photo book is all about the pictures, but you may want to include images other than photographs such as maps or illustrations.

While you may know exactly where photographs were taken, your family may not. Giving the reader a map may explain a great deal.

Illustrations can help readers imagine skills, places or events they are unfamiliar with, such as what a typical inner-city tenement looked like, how cattle were branded, or how machinery was used to create textiles, even if the illustration is only representative of your experience. Think of how many kids have never used a rotary phone.

Index

Unless you are creating the book solely for the enjoyment of your family, an index is indispensable. One of the first things your family members are going to do is turn to the index to see whether or not their pictures are in the book. Genealogical researchers will turn to the index to see if the line they are researching is represented. Additionally, librarians hesitate to stock books without indexes unless they are fiction.

While you are gathering images, researching and writing:

- Could an explanation help the reader appreciate the photograph more?
- What does the reader need to gain a complete understanding of what is happening in the image?
- How much detail is needed to make the reader feel as if they are experiencing what the people in the photograph are experiencing?
- For those who may want to do additional research based upon your book, what level of documentation will be the most helpful?

What Will You Need to Explain the Photographs?

The next step is to figure out what *you* will need to explain anything about the photographs that may be unclear to the readers, or what information to include that the readers may appreciate having.

Characters

How much you will describe about the individuals in your photographs is up to you. You may choose images that tell the whole story, or you may wish to include a bit of biography about the people shown.

One of the best pieces of writing advice I have ever read is this:

> The story is not what happens; it's to whom it happens.
>
> **—Peter Rubin and Gary Provost**
> *How to Tell a Story: The Secrets of Writing Captivating Tales*

Rubin and Provost have it exactly right. There is no reason to keep reading if the reader does not care about the people. If you will include biographical information, your biggest challenge may be to learn enough about the people pictured to describe what kind of characters they were—not just what they did or how they did it—but how they handled triumphs and struggles, and what that says about them as people. Of course, your images may tell that story without any words.

Description

Are there aspects of your images that could use explanation? Will readers wonder where the photograph was taken? Should you go farther than merely naming the people in the photograph? If you show an heirloom, for example, should you include an explanation of how long it has been in the family, where it came from, or where it was made? How much beyond the images you include, is up to you.

Detail

If you include descriptions or biographical information, the credibility of your book will depend upon the details—historically accurate details.

❧❦

Your next step is to conduct a research review. A research review will help you organize what you already have, and develop a plan for gathering what else you may need before you can begin writing or assembling the book.

Chapter 7

Review Your Photographs

The purpose of a review is to discover and organize what you have, but more importantly, to create lists of what you do not have. Depending upon what type of photo book you are planning, you may need to find photographs you are missing to complete a composite image or a section of the book, or you may find that you will need some additional research to identify people, places or events. You may even want to add some genealogical, social or historical research to help explain your photographs. Much depends upon the project. This exercise will help you to form a publishing plan focused solely on the photographs and information you need for this book and not to wander into other interesting projects.

For now, take a look at the photographs you have. If you are starting from the beginning, and have not organized your photographs or scrapbooks, keep reading. You may be surprised by what you do have.

Baby Steps

Decide upon your project and search for only the photographs you will need for this project. If, for example, your project is to show your Christmas letter and the photographs from each Christmas from the time you married until now, then once you have gathered the letters and photographs, you can skip ahead to the next chapter to learn how to digitize the images for your book.

Next Steps

Take a look at everything you have and figure out a way to organize it. My method is to organize by nuclear family group so that the children's photographs will remain within the folder of their parents until they are adults—then they get their own folders. I also have a few folders by topic. My father's Marine Corps photographs are together in one folder and all cemetery photographs are together by cemetery, for example. This method works for me. You may find other methods work best for your collection of photographs.

Giant Leaps

Analyzing what you do have should also illuminate what you do not have, but would like to so that you can start asking other family members if they have the photographs you would like.

Getting Started

One issue you may run into is that the further back in history you go, the fewer photographs you will have. By the time you get to your great-grandparents' generation, there may be few indeed. A photo book is a great way to showcase the rare photographs, even if they bear the tears and scratches or other scars of time.

For more recent generations, you may have too many photographs from which to choose. In this situation, use the critical eye of a photojournalist to pick out the best photographs. Photojournalists look for *the* photograph that sums up the story and often it is the emotion in the picture that makes the difference.

Sometimes the best photographs are the portraits, but oftentimes the most revealing photographs are candids. Look through your photographs for family members at different ages; photographs that help distinguish siblings (height, weight, hairstyles, paired or group photographs); and photographs of biographical details such as lifestyle, hobbies, pets, profession, home life, room arrangements, celebrations, or travel.

As a matter of courtesy, leave out any photographs of sensitive subjects or embarrassing situations. For some relatives, it is bad enough that a photograph exists, but to include an embarrassing photograph in your book may be a step over the line.

Leave out photographs that are badly over- or underexposed, and those with distracting backgrounds unless you are willing to alter these photographs digitally to make them usable.

While you are evaluating your photographs, make a list of what you *do not* find, as well. Are there heirloom objects that should be photographed under studio conditions to look their best? Are you missing a picture of one of the siblings? Do you have wedding photographs for each married couple? Are there decades between pictures of some individuals? Do you have a school photo from each year for each sibling? Do you have yearly holiday or vacation photographs?

The process of sifting through photographs serves two purposes: one is to choose photographs that best fit your project, the other is to compile a list of photographs you want, but do not already have.

Chapter 8: Scanning and Optical Character Recognition has advice if you need to alter photographs in your possession digitally. Chapter 9: Developing a New

Research Plan has tips for obtaining permission to use stock photography or historic photographs, having photographs taken by a professional, or taking new photographs yourself.

If you have more than just modern photographs to organize, you may need to do some detective work to identify the people, era, location and events.

Identify the People

One situation we all find ourselves in is looking at photographs of people we once knew but cannot recall their names, or we have inherited photographs from an earlier generation in which there are people we do not recognize at all. One reason to create a photo book is to pass along precious family photographs to other members of the family, another is to preserve the memories of the people in the photographs. To do so, you should try to get names for each person pictured and identifying unknown people in photographs can be a challenge.

The following are sources to help identify who and what are in your family photographs:

- *Family Photo Detective: Learn How to Find Genealogy Clues in Old Photos and Solve Family Photo Mysteries* by Maureen A. Taylor, (n.p., Family Tree Books, 2013).
- *Forensic Genealogy* by Colleen Fitzpatrick, (n.p., Rice Book Press, 2005).
- *Uncovering Your Ancestry Through Family Photographs* by Maureen Taylor, (Cincinnati, OH: Betterway Books, 2000).
- *Unlocking the Secrets in Old Photographs* by Karen Frisch-Ripley, (Provo, UT: Ancestry Publishing, 1991).

One way to begin organizing is to start with the photographs of the people you do recognize and further categorize those photographs by year or by era.

Identify the Era

Often you can identify the era in a photograph by identifying what type of photograph you have. For example, the cabinet card was popular between the years 1866 and 1906. There is a very good article by David L. Miskin entitled "Everything You Ever Wanted to Know About Your Family Photographs" online (genealogy.about.com/library/authors/ucmishkin1a.htm).

Another clue may come from the back of the photograph. Photographers often stamped their names or the name of their photography studio along with the city and state on the back of the photograph. A quick look through local city directories may give you the correct era for the photography studio.

53

Clothing and hair styles are another way to date the age of a photograph. Costume or fashion catalogs, advertisements in newspapers showing fashions and hairstyles guides can help pinpoint the era. Check out the many boards on Pinterest (www.pinterest.com) devoted to era fashions and the Costumer's Manifesto (www.costumes.org) a wiki site dedicated to period costumes for the theater. There are also hundreds of books and academic articles about period clothing, many of which specialize in a geographic area, because clothing styles differed by era and location.

Identify the Location

Take a close look at what is visible in the background of the photograph such as buildings or houses and their addresses, store or street signs, or other evidence of transportation such as street or railroad crossings. Many of these clues can lead you to an exact location.

Identify the Event

Before the era of the cellphone where everyone carries a camera at all times, most photographs were taken for a reason, either to record people or an event. Identifying the event taking place in a photograph can sometimes help to identify the era, the location and the people, as well.

Identifying photographs can be difficult but also rewarding. You may discover new clues about your ancestry in your photographs.

Create a Timeline

One way to help place your photographs in the correct era and location is by creating a timeline of known family events. And conversely, looking through your photographs may help you build a timeline of events you discover in the pictures.

Arranging your photographs in order along a timeline is similar to telling stories by creating arcs from a timeline. Think of story arcs as episodes of a television show. Writers often tell the longer story by stringing together shorter stories where one event comes to a conclusion followed by a new event. At the same time, ideas or themes will carry through the shorter stories to provide continuity for the longer story. Timelines help writers see the story arcs. They may work the same way for you as you are sifting through your photographs.

To create a timeline, I use an Excel spreadsheet because I can add columns for information that does not fit neatly into any one category. A spreadsheet is a simple visual way to expose gaps where you are either missing information or missing photographs. The act of typing out each event in my timeline also makes me stop and analyze what I have and what I may be missing.

If you are using software to keep track of your genealogical research, you may be able to create a timeline within the software. Family Tree Maker, for example, has a function that shows family events in a timeline. To create a comprehensive timeline for an individual, include not only the major milestones for that person, but also each family event such as the birth or marriage of children, since (more than likely) the individual participated in those events.

The following are websites where you can create a timeline:

- TimeToast (www.timetoast.com)
- Tiki-Toki (www.tiki-toki.com)
- Dipity (www.dipity.com)

If you are not aware of the book *In Their Time: A Timeline Journal for Placing Family Events into Historical Context 1000-2076* by Roger L. Dudley, take a look. His book chronicles events in history with room for you to record what your family was doing at the same time.

While there are not quite as many mobile apps that create timelines, there are a few. Check out:

- iTunes (www.itunes.com)
- Android App Store also called Google Play (play.google.com)

Write a Bit

While you are identifying the people and places in photographs, write a short bit about each. If nothing else to keep track of the steps you have already taken to identify who and what is in the picture. If you planning to write a longer piece to accompany the photographs, this exercise is similar to a good warm up stretch before running. You do not need to worry about the quality of the writing at this point. Even if you write only a synopsis of each photograph, you will be writing and giving yourself a quick reminder of what each photograph contains that will be useful later.

There are good tools for recording little bits of writing so that you can not only keep track of them, but rearrange them easily should you like to combine them into a longer piece. In particular, I like the following software:

- Scrivener (www.literatureandlatte.com/scrivener.php)
- Evernote (www.evernote.com)
- OneNote (www.onenote.com)

OneNote and Evernote also have application versions that you can download to a tablet or smartphone so your notes are available to you even when you are away from your computer.

Beyond the Photographs

There may be images you would like to include that are not, strickly, photographs such as documents or source materials, illustrations, maps, art or heirloom objects belonging to your family. As a part of a greater project review, consider the following to include along with your photographs:

Source Materials

Most family histories include document images of one type, or another and depending upon your project, they could be included in your photo book, as well. If you have been researching your family for a long time, you probably have more documents than you could use for this book. The challenge is choosing those documents that will be the most meaningful or will help tell the intended story in the most convincing way.

Be on the lookout for records in your ancestor's handwriting—a recipe card in your grandmother's handwriting or a signature, for example, may be more meaningful than an event recorded by a clerk.

Consider including these types of records as images: land records that have hand-drawn lot lines; wills and inventories; birth, marriage, christening, or death records; pension records; passport files; ship's passenger lists—essentially anything interesting for the reader to see.

Illustrations

There are times when an illustration conveys a clearer message than either a document or a photograph. The following are a few examples:

An Ancestor Chart. If you want the reader to see who descends from whom quickly, a multi-generation ancestor chart may be the easiest way.

Timeline. A timeline is an effective way to show small bits of information in a logical way. You could show the birth of each child or a military unit's participation in different battles, for example, using a timeline.

Diagrams. An architectural drawing, for example, may help give readers an idea of what a typical house would have looked like. I particularly enjoy artists' renderings of what a place may have looked like, or how buildings may have been constructed in the past. The floor plan of an ancestor's home would help the reader gain a sense of how large (or small) the home was, and where everyday activities took place.

One caution about using illustrations for the sake of having something to look at on the page—adding ClipArt is tempting because it is easy, but not, perhaps, what is best. Beautiful line art published in 19th century newspapers, books or magazines is now in the public domain. It is worth your time to find a good image to illustrate an old farming technique, for example, or to have a good image created by an artist rather than settling for a low-quality image.

Maps

Maps are an easy way to help readers get their bearings. Context maps show the reader what part of the state or country you are referring to in a story or are pictured in other images. The map of Kentucky shows Bath County up in the northeastern part of the state. The second map shows Caldwell County in relation to Bath County on the same map.

County map showing Bath County, KY

County map showing Bath and Caldwell Counties

Road map showing directions for readers to follow.

A map can also help the reader find a location to visit. The topo map shows the roads leading to the cemetery, marks where the cemetery is, and shows the topography—all helpful information for a visit.

Maps help describe movement from place to place as you would if you were describing a battle scene, for example. A battlefield map would help the reader visualize where the opposing forces met, how far troops had to go from one battle to the next, and so on.

The possibilities for including maps are nearly endless: plats, roads, historical, political, battlefield, migration, topographical, economic, climate, coastline, survey, nautical, soil, trails, and so on. If you cannot find a map of exactly what you need, you can create one using Google Maps using the My Maps feature (mapsengine.google.com). Google Maps has a generous Terms of Use agreement that includes creating and sharing individualized maps with proper credit. Make sure to read the Terms of Use carefully before you include a Google Map in your book, however.

Art and Objects

Look at the artwork and heirlooms you have and make a list of the items in the possession of other family members. When approaching family members for information about heirlooms, be clear about your intentions—that you want to get a good photograph so that readers can see what grandmother's china looked like—not that you have any designs on the object(s) yourself. The same advice goes for asking to use rare photographs or portraits.

Artwork and objects deserve a special mention because these items should be photographed not scanned, so they will display well. You will find information about photographing these items in Chapter 9: Developing a Research Plan.

Images from Social History

Genealogical research establishes relationships. Social history research reveals details about daily life. Items and sources you have already may contain evidence of your family's social history—*how* they lived and worked.

Think about the typical things you do in a day. How would your ancestors have done the same things? How did they shop? Could they have sent a letter? How much was a stamp? Was there a Post Office? What did they have for breakfast? Did breakfast consist of things already in the cupboard, or did they have to go to the hen house to gather the eggs? It is a lot to think about, but answering some of these questions will give you good ideas for other images to include. Be on the lookout for the following:

Personal Papers. Letters, diaries, journals, recipe cards, scrapbooks, greeting cards, birth announcements, wedding invitations or funeral cards. Look for anything that may have been written, compiled or saved as a remembrance.

Newspaper Clippings. Look for obituaries, birth, wedding or engagement announcements, feature stories or advertising. Advertising also can be a quick, visual way to get ideas of what fashions and prices were like during the era. You may find newspaper clippings loose or within other bound volumes such as bibles, photo albums or scrapbooks.

School Records. Gather up anything school related, such as report cards, diplomas, academic achievements, group activities, club or sports awards, theater or music programs, personal or class photographs, and yearbooks.

Business Records. Look for anything that may indicate how you or your ancestors were employed or conducted business, such as employment records, pay stubs, account books, store ledgers, client lists, professional guides or books, licenses or certificates.

Military Service. If you or your ancestor served in the military look for service records, discharge papers, uniforms, commendations, medals, photographs, or identification papers.

Religious Records. Religious institutions were often the place where ceremonies were recorded, such as baptisms, confirmations, weddings, deaths or burials. You may find a certificate of the event. Also look for bibles or other religious texts, evidence of religious education, religious magazines or bulletins, general magazines or newspapers.

Association Records. If you or your ancestor ever joined an association, look for handbooks, costumes, awards, jewelry, rules or bylaws, group photographs or membership lists.

Court Records. Look for court rulings or judgments, lawsuits, probates, divorces, and civil or criminal cases.

Administrative Records. Locate any papers filed with a government clerk or other administrator such as deeds, taxes, licenses, voter or auto registration.

Collections. Are you or were your ancestors collectors of things, such as stamps, coins, spoons, salt and pepper shakers, images, statuettes or photographs? There is almost no limit to the things people collect. The story of how you came by each object could be interesting, as well.

Enthusiasts. Are you or your family members fans? Did you keep photographs of stars, autographs, tickets, posters, playbills, albums, memorabilia, or sports jerseys?

Ephemera or Memorabilia. Ephemera is a catch-all term for items that were meant to be temporary such as tickets, menus, playbills, posters, or advertising. Memorabilia is a slightly larger category that may include items such as snow globes, travel posters, postcards, souvenirs, reunion books, mugs, or t-shirts.

Any of the above items could help tell the story of your family through images.

Historical Photographs

There may be instances where a historical photograph may be needed. For example, if you do not have pictures of the town your grandparents lived in, you may want to contact the historical society of that area to see what they have available. Think about places where using a historical photograph would benefit your book project. There is advice in Chapter 9 for finding historical photographs.

Take Care of the Housekeeping

If your plans include giving away copies of your photo book for the enjoyment of family members only, you can skip this section. But—while it is possible to create a family photo book without citing a single source, if your book contains genealogical information, then a well-documented family photo history will be more respected and can be useful to other genealogical researchers. If you are willing to go the extra mile to make your photo book a useful genealogical tool, then as a part of an overall project review, put your citations in order, guard against any inference of plagiarism and gather any permissions and usage fees you may need to pay in order to use materials belonging to others.

Citing Sources

Create good citations as a part of your project review. Decide how you will cite each piece of factual information in your book. Include the name of the article, book, image or document, and the location where you found it so that other researchers can weigh the strength of your sources and recreate your research steps, if necessary.

I do not recommend waiting to create citations until you are ready to add footnotes or endnotes to your book. At that point, the task will seem daunting. It is better to figure out what method you want to use now, and stick to that method as you write and perform additional research. There is no need to decide whether you will include your sources as footnotes or endnotes yet, as long as you have the citations ready to work with when you start writing.

I understand that the mere mention of the Elizabeth Shown Mills book, *Evidence Explained*, sends some family historians into fits of pique, but she offers a way to document every conceivable source type systematically. Friend, fellow genealogist (and a good gentleman of Kentucky), Kirk Woosley Patten, likens formal citations to setting a formal table. He explains that "once you understand where everything goes, you never have to guess which utensil to use." I agree, but I also shudder at the thought of having to correctly pick out the lobster fork. Formal citations may cause you the same anxiety.

There are ways around the fear of formal citations without compromising the scholarship of your book.

Thankfully, many of the online genealogy websites where you will find documentary evidence also give you the citation information. Take a look at how the top genealogy sites—FamilySearch, Ancestry, and Fold3—provide citation information. Each cites sources in a slightly different way, but you have all of the information you need to cite your sources properly.

The two major formulas for proper source citation are *The Chicago Manual of Style* or *Evidence Explained* by Elizabeth Shown Mills.

The Chicago Manual of Style type:
1. 1800 U.S. Census, Second Census of the United States, New York, Essex County, Crown Point, pg 192-A, line 7, Daniel Smith household; NARA microfilm 1804, roll 1.

Evidence Explained type:
1. Daniel Smith household, p. 192-A, Crown Point, Essex County, New York; Second Census of the United States, 1800, vol. 2, New York: Clinton-Green Counties; Manuscript Schedules of Decennial Population Census, 1790–1870. Records of the Bureau of the Census, Record Group 29, National Archives, Washington, D.C. [Evidence Explained (2007), p. 238].

Here is a third option.
2. **"beguiled ... rifling around in the past"**: Alice Munro, *The View from Castle Rock* (New York: Knopf, 2006), p. 347.

I found this example in David Laskin's book, *The Family*, (New York: Viking, 2013), p. 342. The book is well documented. He and his publisher have chosen to place their source citations in endnotes rather than in footnotes, and although they do not strictly follow either formal style, it gets the job done.

There is software as well as downloadable templates that make creating good citations easy. If you have not discovered the software *Evidentia*, now may be the time. This software leads you through the process—first choosing your preferred style as either *Evidence Explained* or *The Chicago Manual of Style*, then giving you a template in the chosen style for most of the common sources used to document a family history. There is also a way to create a template for any additional sources that do not fit the existing templates.

If you are determined to create citations in a unique way, the following are the basic elements necessary for a good citation:

- Who created the source
- What the source is
- Where the source was created
- When the source was created
- How to find the source (where the source is held or where you saw it as a digital image)
- The form (original, a copy such as a microfilm or a digitized original)
- Why the source is useful

For a complete explanation of these elements, consult *Mastering Genealogical Proof*, by Thomas W. Jones. Consult Robert Raymond's article, *Citation Baby Steps*, in the FamilySearch wiki online for more information about why effective citations are necessary.

Plagiarism and Copyright Reminder

Avoid using another writer's words—no matter how beautiful they are or how tempting they are to repeat. This goes for another photographer's photograph, as well.

Facts and ideas cannot be copyrighted, but the way they are expressed belong to the author from the minute the words are recorded. The same rule applies to images. The most common form of plagiarism is inadvertent. If you repeat more than three words in a row or use words in a distinct combination or with a distinct emphasis copied directly from another author, you must give the author proper credit.

When it comes to photographs, the principle is the same. The person who took the photograph controls the rights to the photograph. This can be tricky when it comes to creating a family photo book while respecting a photographer's copyrights because the copyright holder alone has the right to copy, distribute, display in public or create derivative works from the original.

The place where this issue comes up most often is in school photos, where a professional photographer or studio took the photo and sold you the prints. Owning a print does not give you the copyright to the image. You can locate photographers at the Photographer's Registry (www.photographerregistry.com) to obtain permission to use a photograph.

Practically speaking, however, including school photographs in a family photo book with limited distribution will not likely be discovered nor will action be taken against you in court because it will be difficult for a photographer from years ago to show the financial loss he or she has suffered if you include your children's school photos in your book. You should, however, make an attempt to gain the photographer's permission.

Note: Writing a family history or creating a family photo book without trying to make money does not absolve you from plagiarism or copyright violations. Give credit where credit is due and ask permission to use written words, images or illustrations that do not belong to you. A good source for information about copyrights and genealogy is Judy Russell, the Legal Genealogist (www.legalgenealogist.com).

Permissions and Usage Fees

You may encounter repositories or collections that require permission to transcribe or display images of source materials in their possession. The terms of use and fees vary from repository to repository, so it is important to check before you make an image or a transcription an integral part of your book.

Oftentimes, permissions are nothing more than citing your source in a particular way acknowledging the repository or collection. In many cases, if you explain the nature of your family photo book and that you are not planning a commercial run of thousands of books, you may be able to get fees waived.

As you are reviewing your photographs and as you expand your research in the next round, gather any permissions you may need, and keep a good record of any fees that you may need to pay. As you work through the project, you will be able to evaluate whether it is worth the fee to include the image or source.

❧ ❦

A review of your photographs should be fun. There are no rules about how much you need to do each day or each week as long as you keep the project moving forward. If you have a trunk full of photographs, start with a few dozen. Accomplish what you can in an hour and come back to the rest later.

And write. When you evaluate a photograph, write a little bit about it. When you find a great image, write about it. Google grandma's china pattern, then write about it. Put a picture on Facebook, write a little about it, and ask your cousins to comment. Write about what you see, what you do not, and the questions it may raise that you would like to answer later.

The biggest problem I see with people who are starting a book project is becoming overwhelmed. It is easy to do, even for an experienced author. If you are busy with other activities and only have fifteen minutes a day to devote to the project, so be it. Do your fifteen minutes and go on to other things. Those fifteen minutes will add up over time.

If you make out a plan, and put the pieces of your plan onto your calendar, you greatly improve your chances for getting what you intend to accomplish, actually accomplished.

This is the time for making good notes about what you know for sure, how you know it, and where any research must go before you begin putting the book together.

At the end of your photographic review, you should have:

- A list of photographs you want to use for this project
- A timeline if it is helpful to identify people and events in photographs
- A list of sources
- A list of permissions you may need
- A list of items from your family's social history
- A list of historical images you would like to obtain
- A list of the items or images you want to ask your family about
- A list of photographs you do not have but would like to
- Simple, written summaries of each image you already have

In the next chapter, you will learn about scanning so that you can digitize your images in the size and resolution you will need for your book project.

Chapter 8

Scanning and Optical Character Recognition

Images are the heart and soul of a photo book. It pays to begin by learning about your scanner and scanning software. You will save a lot of time and effort making your images ready for print if you get a good scan from the start.

Scanning Basics

From the scanner's point of view, there are only three types of items it can scan— reflective items (photographs or documents), negative transparencies (film negatives), or positive transparencies (slides). Because the scanner will treat each of these types differently, you may need different software settings or different equipment to obtain the best scan.

The goal while scanning is to create an image large enough to look good in print, at the size you want to display the image. Once you have the largest scan you will need, you can scale, downsample or resize the image for other uses such as a website, an electronic book, or to share on social media.

Scanners

There are many different types of scanners including dedicated flatbed, all-in-one, photo, film, slide, hand-held, and microfilm/microfiche. Each has advantages and disadvantages.

Dedicated Flatbed Scanners

For most book projects, a dedicated flatbed scanner is what you need. The major scanner manufacturers such as HP, Epson, Canon or Xerox (among others) include software, most of which will work for your book project. Some dedicated flatbed scanners are designed to scan photographs primarily, so the software may include Digital ICE (digital image correction and enhancement). Most photo-priority flatbed scanners allow you to make corrections to the image as it is scanned.

Not all dedicated flatbed scanners are equipped to scan transparencies, either film negatives or slides. Transparencies require a dual light source and an adapter to hold the film or negative during scanning, allowing the light source to shine through the transparency. Because of the small size of the transparency (usually one inch square or less), the software must be able to scan at much higher resolution to obtain a print-ready digital image. (More about resolution shortly.)

Film or Slide Scanners

Dedicated film or slide scanners have no glass between the light source and the transparency to prevent distortion. These scanners also use a cool light source to keep from warping the film or slide, and the software included will be capable of high resolutions. Some of these scanners have a feeder for 35mm film strips or a stacking tray for slides. If you have older, large-format negatives, you will need a flatbed scanner with adapter trays to hold those negative sizes.

Hand-Held Scanners

Hand-held scanners (or wand scanners) are convenient, but often it is difficult to produce a good scan if your hands are not steady or the object is not perfectly flat.

One hand-held scanner I like, however, is the FlipPal (flip-pal.com). This mini-scanner was designed with the researcher in mind. It is small, light-weight, and is approved for use in repositories such as the National Archives. Even though the surface area of the FlipPal cannot scan a full piece of standard U.S. paper in a single scan, the software that comes with the FlipPal has a stitching function to put documents back together after they have been scanned in pieces. The one disadvantage to the FlipPal is how little control you have over making corrections as the scan is being made. It is a trade off—the ease and convenience of being able to scan photographs or documents where you find them, versus producing the best scan possible. Better to obtain the image while you can and make corrections in your image editing software later.

Microfilm/Microfiche Scanners

You may run into a microfilm or a microfiche scanner while conducting research. Many Family History Centers and libraries across the country have them. It may be more convenient to save your scanned images as PDFs while you are researching because they are easy to read on your computer later using the free Adobe Acrobat Reader software. If you know, however, that you want to use an image of a document, obtain a higher resolution JPG (.jpg) while you are at the library. Take both. Look for the settings in the scanning software to change back and forth from JPG to PDF.

Most word processors and page layout programs will not treat a PDF the same way they will a JPG. Most will not allow you to place a PDF directly into a document. You will need an image editing program to convert the PDF to a JPG, PNG (.png) or TIFF (.tiff).

All-in-One Scanners

For those of you who own 3-in-1 or 4-in-1 scanners (scan, copy, print, fax), the scanning software that came with the machine may be fairly rudimentary. Dedicated flatbed scanners tend to come with better software including:

- SilverFast (www.silverfast.com)
- VueScan (www.hamrick.com)

You may purchase this software as stand-alone products. You may find that once you have better software, an all-in-one will do what you need it to, as long as you do not have transparencies. In my research to date, I have not found a 3-in-1 or 4-in-1 scanner that includes a transparency adapter.

Resolution

First, let us be clear about some terminology. You may see the acronyms dpi and lpi and ppi used interchangeably. They are not exactly the same, however. Dots per inch (dpi) is an old printer's term that refers to the number of horizontal dots per inch in a halftone. If you look closely at a photographic image in a pre-digital-era newspaper, you will see the dots used to make up the photograph. Printing dots was a clever way to simulate the effect of a solid image. Commercial printers used the same technology to produce magazines, maps or brochures.

Lines per inch (lpi) is another way to measure the number of dots per inch in a halftone, although this is a vertical measurement. The more lines per inch, the sharper the image. Magazines have more lines per inch than newspapers.

Pixels per inch (ppi) is the proper way to describe resolution in the digital era. If you zoom in to a digital photograph closely enough, you will be able to see each pixel. Pixels are square, whereas dots are round. The higher the number of pixels per inch, the higher the resolution in the image, and the better it will look when printed.

What resolution you need depends upon the physical size of the image you want to display, and how you will display it.

Scan high and use low, meaning that you want a scan that is as big physically—in inches—as you will display in print. Most books are (physically) 8.5" x 11" or smaller. If you subtract room for margins, about the biggest image you will need is 8" x 10." If you go with the print size for a coffee table book, you may need a larger image—as big as 13" x 11" for an interior page with a full bleed and even larger for a cover (up to 30" x 12" or bigger).

For print, the resolution must be at least 300 ppi for photographs. Line art (think handwriting in a document) may look better at 600 ppi because the edges of the lines will be crisper.

Many of the older photographs you will encounter may be physically small. It was not until the 1990s that photography became so much cheaper. Today, you can buy a poster-sized print for less than what a small school portrait cost in the 1940s.

Take a 1" x 1.5" slide or school portrait as an example. In order to create a proportionally equivalent 8" x 12" digital image at 300 ppi, the final file size must be 2400 x 3600 pixels (8" x 300 ppi and 12" x 300 ppi). If you are scanning a 1" x 1.5" slide, in order to end up with a file at 2400 x 3600 pixels, you will need to scan at 2400 ppi (1" x 2400 ppi = 2400 pixels wide and 1.5" x 2400 ppi = 3600 pixels long).

A common pre-1950s photograph size was 3" x 4.5," so let us use that as an example. If we want to use a photograph that size in print at 6" x 9," then we will need a final file size of 1800 pixels x 2700 pixels. In order to achieve that resolution, you must scan at 600 ppi (3" x 600 ppi = 1800 pixels wide and 4.5" x 600 ppi = 2700 pixels long).

If you are planning to acquire images from a stock photography company, a library or an archive, ask for the image resolution needed to print at 300 ppi in the physical size you want for the page or the book cover.

There may be other uses for your photographs at much lower resolution, such as an eBook, to email to cousins, to post on social media sites or your online tree. As long as you start with an image large enough to look good in print, scaling down is easy with good results. Scaling up is not. An image that has been scaled up may look fine on the screen because your computer screen can only display an image at 72–96 ppi. A scaled-up photograph may look fine in your word processing program viewed on a screen, but pixelated or blurry when printed in a book.

There is also a difference between scaling a photograph and stretching it. Your word processing program will allow you to take an image, insert it into the text, and then adjust the display size by pulling the corners. Pulling the corners is not scaling the photograph; it is stretching it. Stretching causes even worse results in print than scaling the image up to a larger size.

Scaling a photograph means opening it in an image editing program and changing the physical size of the image. You will achieve far more consistent results on the press if you scan the image to the correct size first, and then place the image into the layout in the correct size and resolution.

File Size

Do not over-scan your images, either. To keep the file size of the final book manageable, create images at a size that will look good in print, but not any bigger. In other words, scan your image so that you could print an 16" x 24" photograph to give to a cousin (the biggest use you may have for the image), but adjust it down proportionally before placing it into your book layout.

To adjust the image down proportionally, determine the final size you want the image to be on the page, for example 3" x 3.75," and use your image editing program to make the physical size of the image smaller.

What you do not want to do, is place the largest size image into your manuscript, and squeeze it into its final size by dragging the corners. Dragging the corners will make the physical size smaller, but it will not alter the file size. If your original image is 8" x 10" at 300 ppi, it will have a physical size of 2400 pixels x 3000 pixels. If you squish those pixels closer together to make them fit into a 3" x 3.75" space, your resolution will go up from 300 ppi to 800 ppi (2400 pixels divided by 3" = 800 ppi and 3000 pixels divided by 3.75" is 800 ppi).

Print publication requires a final image resolution at 300 ppi. Use your image editing program to reduce the physical size of the photograph to 3" x 3.75" which is a proportional reduction, while maintaining the resolution of 300 ppi, giving you a final image size of 900 pixels (3" x 300 ppi) x 1125 pixels (3.75" x 300 ppi).

Color Depth

Color depth affects file size. The greater the color depth, the more color possibilities there are and the larger the file size. A black-and-white image (e.g. a printed document) has only 1 bit of color depth because there is only one color—black. The other color, white, is the paper color. A black-and-white photograph is made up of shades of black—an 8-bit black-and-white file would contain 256 shades of gray. A 24-bit color file could contain up to 16.7 million colors and so on up to 36-bit and 48-bit files.

Scanning a photograph to display on the side of a bus, would need as much color information as possible because the image is so large, and too little color information can cause banding rather than smooth transitions between shades.

Many of the newer scanners offer greater than 24-bit depth. The biggest difference between 24-bit and 48-bit scans is in the file size. Reserve the 48-bit setting for scanning negatives and slides. Anything you want to scan for a printed book (and even less so for an eBook or digital file) can be scanned at 24-bit color depth and look great. There is no need to over-scan color depth.

Color Density

To achieve the blackest blacks and the whitest whites—the greatest possible dynamic range for color in your images—you may want a scanner that captures the greatest image density, not necessarily the greatest bit depth. Be forewarned, however, the higher the image density, the higher the cost of the scanner, and realistically, unless you are planning a high-end, glossy photo book printed on the best digital presses in Asia, the end results on the page will not be any better.

Color Space

Color space matters to some printers for some print jobs. Chances are good that you will not have to mess much with the color space during your book project, but, just in case, here is a quick explanation of what color space means.

RGB

Computer monitors and other digital screens use the RBG color space (red, green, blue). RGB is also fine for printing photographs. RGB is preferred for images in eBooks that will be displayed on digital screens. The most common file format for RGB images is JPG. When you are scanning photographs, it is acceptable to scan them as RGB images and save them as JPGs.

CMYK

The CMYK color space (cyan, magenta, yellow, black) is necessary to use an off-set press and print in full color. Cyan, magenta, yellow and black are the four process colors that are combined to create full-color images. For most books, you do not need to worry about the CMYK color space. It is acceptable to leave your images in their original RGB color space when creating your final file. Let the printer convert the images to CMYK based upon the equipment they have, to generate the best results.

Grayscale

Become familiar with the grayscale color space. For books with black-and-white images in the interior (forget the covers for right now, almost all covers will have full-color), convert your images to grayscale before you place them into the layout. Another reason to do this is to see how the image will look when printed in black-and-white. Not all color images make good black-and-whites. If there are not enough shades of gray, the finer details will be lost.

Convert black-and-white originals to grayscale. It is possible to scan directly into grayscale, and some scanners have good grayscale settings. Most of the time you will achieve better results if you scan black-and-white photographs in full color, and then use your image editing program to convert the image to grayscale.

Bitmap

The bitmap color space is one that you may use, but infrequently. On occasion, you will find that a document or line drawing is easier to read if scanned as a bitmap. The bitmap color space only contains black and white; there are no shades of gray. The scanner will force each pixel in the image to be one color or the other.

Sometimes, especially if there is a noisy background on a document, the type or handwriting is clearer when scanned as a bitmap image.

File Formats

Digital image file formats are either compressed or non-compressed. A non-compressed format will retain the most information and will create larger file sizes than a compressed format.

TIFF or RAW

Two non-compressed formats are TIFF (or TIF) (.tiff or .tif) and RAW (.raw). RAW image files can be especially large because they are not compressed in any way. To compare, an image taken in my 16 MP (megapixel) camera and saved as a TIFF is about 5 MB (megabytes) in size, whereas the same image saved in RAW format runs 16 MB or more. Saving images in the RAW format is an option in high-end cameras. Some scanning software will create RAW files, but unless you are planning to use your image on the cover of a high-end magazine, there is no compelling reason to create RAW files while you scan.

JPG

The most common file format for photographs is JPG (or JPEG) (.jpg or .jpeg). JPG is a compressed file format, and yes, you will lose information every time you open, alter and save the file, somewhat like making a photocopy of a photocopy. But, unless you alter the file hundreds of times and then blow the photo up to something large enough for the flaws to become obvious to the naked eye, do not worry about whether you scan and save your photographs as compressed or uncompressed files. Save them as TIF or JPG, whatever is easiest for you to use with your image editing software.

Producing a Good Scan

Before you begin scanning, clean the glass on the scanner. Unless there are smudges, compressed air or a good microcloth will do the trick. If there are smudges or fingerprints, use a good glass cleaner. Read the instructions for your scanner to make sure an alcohol-based glass cleaner is safe. Then, spray the cloth, not the scanner glass and clean the glass often. Small specks of dust will show up in the scans (magnified if you are scanning film or slides) and it takes much more time to fix the dust particle flaws in your image editing program, than it does to eliminate them from the scanner.

Do not damage originals in order to scan them. Do not cut them or try to make repairs, and please *do not* clean the photograph unless you know what you are doing. Any effort to alter the surface of a photograph can damage or destroy it. If you are in doubt, seek the help of a photo restoration company. If you have delicate photographs, it is always safer to re-photograph, than to put them on the scanner exposed to a strong light source.

Photographing a Photograph

The trick to photographing a photograph is to use a macro setting on your digital camera that allows the lens to be close to the photograph while keeping it in focus. Fill the frame with the photograph to take as large an image as possible.

Keep the angles consistent so the photograph does not become distorted in the digital image. Place the photograph on a level surface (wall or table) and set the camera up to shoot straight on. If the camera is angled in any way, the original photograph will not look square in the new image. You can fix distortions later in your image editing program, but you will save a great deal of time if you take a good photograph to begin with.

If your old photograph has curled or has warped, introduce a little humidity before unrolling it. I have had good luck with my own photographs by steaming up the bathroom and taking the photograph into the bathroom away from the faucet where the hot water is running. I have only tried this on modern photographs (less than 50 years old). I would not attempt this on any photograph made before modern fixatives were used. If you are at all in doubt, take the photograph to a photo restoration company for help before you begin. Never try to force a photograph to unroll. Once the emulsion on a photograph cracks, you cannot undo the damage.

For photographs that uncurl easily, placing a piece of non-glare glass over the top may help to hold it down while you photograph. Even non-glare glass can yield reflections, though, so watch for flares from light sources such as lamps, overhead lighting or windows.

If you are not a steady hand, use a tripod. In fact, a tripod with a scientific arm that allows the camera to point straight down, is the easiest way to obtain great digital images of photographs or documents.

Scanning Slides or Film Negatives

Before you scan slides or film negatives, use compressed air to clean them. If you remove a slide or negative from a plastic film sleeve or run a microcloth over it, static electricity can attract even more dust. Be careful not to use the spray air too close to the slide or negative because of the moisture that comes from the spray.

Scanner Software

Get to know your scanner and its software. Locate the feature that allows you to change the physical file size and resolution while scanning. It will not take you long to be able to calculate what you will need to achieve a 300 ppi resolution for images at the maximum size you will display them in your book. Remember to scan high, use low. It is better to create an image that is bigger than what you will ever need and scale it down to fit the page, than to scan an image too small and scale it up to size.

Some scanning software features will correct image flaws while scanning. Some software has good automatic settings for color, contrast, brightness, sharpness, and saturation or neutralization. Others do not. Experiment with a few flawed images to find out what your software is capable of correcting well.

Save Time Scanning

Most scanning software allows you to preview the image before you scan it. In the beginning, this feature will save you a lot of time having to look back and forth between the scanning software and your image editing program to make sure you captured the image you wanted in the scan. After a time, especially if you are scanning the same types of items that are also the same size, you may be able to skip the preview to save time. The trick is to keep similar items together, the black-and-white photographs, for example, or the images with fading tints.

While it is tempting to place as many photographs on the plate as possible and scan them all at once as one big photograph, avoid this. Not only will you spend more time turning them into separate photographs later in your image editing program, but the scanner will take readings across many different photographs which will give the automatic correction settings a difficult time determining what should be corrected. The results are often bad scans.

Some scanning software allows you to batch scan everything on the plate with separate settings for each item. This feature will save time because each object on the plate is being analyzed and scanned individually.

The straighten and flip settings can save time. Even if you place a photograph on the plate perfectly, closing the lid may cause it to move. Allowing the scanner to straighten the photograph will save time. Same for flipping photographs—especially flipping slides and film negatives. It can be difficult to slip the slides and film strips into the holders exactly the right way each time. Look at the preview, and then let the scanner turn the image right-side up or flip it on the vertical axis to make the scan match the direction of the original.

Photographs

While it would seem that scanning photographs will have fewer challenges than other types of material, it all depends upon the type of photographs you need. If you have the time, consider scanning everything you have and creating backups on external hard drives or DVDs just in case. You never know when originals will be lost or damaged.

Older photographs that have curled over the years can yield Newton Rings when scanning—distortion caused when there is distance between the photograph and the glass. If a photograph is particularly delicate, taking a new photograph of the old photograph is always safer than putting it on the scanner and exposing it to an intense light source. If you cannot re-photograph the item, look for a studio photographer who has the right setup and lighting to do so.

Occasionally, scanning a black-and-white photograph in full color will leave tinges of yellow, cyan or magenta in the picture. You can use your image editing program to eliminate unwanted tints. Or, try scanning in grayscale to see if you achieve a better result.

If your book will contain only black-and-white images, it may take some experimentation not only with your scanner, but also in your image editing program to make each photograph look its best when printed in black-and-white.

It was popular for a time to print photographs on textured paper so that they looked more like a painted canvas. These photographs (mostly from the 1970s) can be a challenge to scan because the texture can cause shadows on the scan. Taking a new photograph may be a better option.

Matte prints often scan with fewer streaks or glare than glossy prints. Modern glossy prints are not as difficult as older glossies mounted on thick paper, such as those from instant cameras such as Polaroids. If you see streaks in scanned images from glare off the glossy print, taking new photographs may be easier than fixing the digital images.

When a digital image is printed on uncoated paper, such as what will be used on the interior pages of your book, dot gain (ink absorbed by the paper) causes photographs to become darker than expected. You may need to lighten the shadows and mid-tones of photographs in order to make them look their best in print. This is true whether the photographs are in black-and-white or color.

One way to create a digital image from a slide is to scan it; another is to project it onto a screen and photograph it using a digital camera. While the projector version works quite well for images that will be shown on a computer monitor, often the result in print is flat, soft or dark images that do not look as good as if you had scanned the slide directly. If a slide is particularly important to you and you cannot produce a good scan, print the slide at the size you need for the book, then scan the new photograph. Printing slides is an expensive option, however, if you have more than a few vital slides.

Documents and Illustrations

For the most part, documents and illustrations (line art) are easier to scan and achieve good results, than photographs. Line art such as lithographs look best when scanned at 600 to 1200 ppi to keep the edges and lines crisp. Many of these images will be black-and-white, so scanning as bitmaps (BMP) that forces the image into black-and-white, may give you the best results. If the line art is in color such as a logo or sign, scan in at least 24-bit color depth to keep gradients smooth. Scanning at lower bit depths may cause banding in the colored areas.

One challenge may be the paper the item is printed on, however since thin paper can allow printing on the reverse side to show through. If bleed through is a problem, one option is to photocopy the originals using light settings to lessen what shows through, and then scan the lightened photocopy using settings that make the document darker.

Using Optical Character Recognition

Most scanners come with optical character recognition (OCR) software. While it may be tempting to OCR documents or passages from printed sources so that you do not have to transcribe each and every one, be careful with the results. The software works best with printed, standard font text (nothing script-like or hand-writing-like) in point sizes between six (6) (very small but still readable) and 72 (about 1 inch high) on laser or inkjet quality print or better.

Mocavo (www.mocavo.com) the online genealogy search engine, is experimenting with OCR that works on handwriting. They are the first, and they have not perfected it yet. You will not find commercially available scanner-based OCR software that can help you with handwritten documents just yet.

No matter how sophisticated your OCR software, you must proofread the results. It is difficult for the software to tell the difference between a "1" that looks like an "l" that looks like a "]."

The easiest OCR programs to use are those that let you correct the copy while the software is creating the text. Many of the best programs show the image in one window with the text results in another window side by side so that you can look at the original as you edit.

If your scanner did not come with OCR software, OmniPage (www.nuance.com/for-individuals/by-product/omnipage/index.htm) consistently receives high accuracy ratings and is easy to use.

Maps, Newspapers, and Memorabilia

If you have maps, newspaper clippings or memorabilia, such as a theater program that was printed using halftones (bunches of little dots rather than a solid image like a photograph), you may have some challenges when scanning items printed on older presses.

Halftones may create moire patterns (common in black-and-white images from newspapers) or rosette patterns (common in color images due to the CMYK colors used on the press). The result of scanning may be images with irregular areas, or areas that are much darker or lighter than other areas.

A special feature in some scanning software allows you to de-screen as you scan. Software that comes with a de-screening feature will have the following settings for different types of print: art print (175 lpi), magazines (133 lpi) and newspapers (85 lpi). You will achieve the best results with the setting closest to what was used to create the original image on the press. Sometimes de-screening can soften an image too much. Sharpening can help restore the edges.

If your software does not have a de-screening feature, try scanning at a 45-degree angle. Turn the object so that it is not straight up or down (90 degrees), but at an angle (45 degrees) on the plate. Another option is to scan at twice the size you are planning to use in the book, and then downsize the image so that the dots or dot patterns are not so obvious.

Objects

It is much easier to photograph objects, such as heirlooms, against a neutral background than it is to scan them. It is almost impossible to make a teacup look good sitting on a scanner. Instead of scanning dog tags, a uniform, needlework, or a picture in its frame, take a photograph.

For less than $50, you can buy a small studio lighting kit that sets up as a two-foot square box, with neutral backgrounds of several different colors, a couple of lights, and a table-top tripod. For around $200, you can buy a similar studio lighting setup to photograph larger objects such as quilts or furniture.

Art

Photograph artwork rather than scan it, especially if the art is in a soft media such as pastels or charcoal. Pencil sketches can smudge. Oil paintings or watercolor paintings can be a challenge because of the texture of the paint or the unevenness of the canvas.

Film Negatives and Slides

The biggest issue with scanning film negatives and slides is cleaning them before you scan to minimize the dust and particle debris in the digital image and scanning at high enough resolution for your planned use.

A standard 35mm negative is not square. It measures approximately 1" x 1.5" or at a 2 x 3 ratio. If you want the digital image to fill an 8.5" x 11" page, you will need a digital image of 2550 pixels (8.5" x 300 pixels) by 3300 pixels (11" x 300 ppi). So, the resolution for a 1" x 1.5" 35mm film negative is 2550 ppi. The ratio of standard American paper at 8.5" x 11" is not quite 2 to 3, however, so your scan at 2550 ppi will be perfect across the 8.5" top, but too long for the 11" length. Even when you adjust for the margins, cropping may be necessary. If you are thinking about printing from your digital image and want a good 12" x 18" print, scanning a 35mm negative at 4000 ppi will work.

Curled filmstrips can result in blurry scans. If necessary, the individual negatives can be cut and mounted into slide mounts, but once you cut the negatives, they can no longer be printed at a standard photo lab. You will need a specialty lab that often charges more. If you are going to cut a filmstrip, make prints first.

Scan film negatives with the emulsion (duller side) down. The emulsion side should be closest to the glass on a flatbed scanner. You can tell if you are looking at the emulsion side if the film numbers along the edge are backward.

Before you scan slides, check to see if your scanning software has adjustments for different slide types. Kodachrome slides, for example, should be scanned on a Kodachrome color setting for best results. If you have no idea what type of film was used to create your slides, you may have to play with the color adjustment settings to create the best digital image during the scan.

Tip: Although it may be tempting, once you have finished scanning, never discard the originals. Newer scanners may do a better job in the future, and digital images can be lost or become corrupted.

Enhance, Repair, Retouch

Even if you achieve great scans, you may want to open each image in an image editor to take a look close up. Before you place any image into your layout, fix flaws, sharpen softly-focused images, adjust the contrast, or crop to enhance the composition. Repair damage from bends, breaks or mold on the surface. Restore the faded color. Fill in the scratches and correct over- or underexposed areas.

There is controversy surrounding editing or enhancing images that alters *in any way* the historical accuracy of the image, because you are using the image to tell a family history which should be historically accurate. Having said that, there is no reason not to repair or retouch photographs so that they look their best.

When does restoration become alteration? That is a matter of opinion, but I think it is fine to use a little grain reduction to make a person's skin look smooth and beautiful, or to remove red-eyes, or to whiten teeth. It is fine to crop an image to enhance the composition, or to merge two images to create a more complete picture of what a place looked like. I know I am stepping into controversial waters here, but it is acceptable to remove distracting elements from the picture even if it alters the historical accuracy of the photograph a bit. I am not advocating that you digitally cut out your ex, or blur the face of a family member you do not like. Oftentimes, however, amateur photographers take pictures without paying attention to the background, resulting in images that appear as if a telephone pole, for example, is growing from a person's head. I find it historically acceptable to remove the telephone pole.

There are many options for editing your digital images. Most computers come with simple image editing software pre-installed. There are also many websites or photo sharing sites that offer image editing tools. Some of them, such as Pixlr (pixlr.com) or Picasa (picasa.google.com), have impressive features. There are also apps by the dozen for tablets or smartphones that edit, enhance or create funky artwork from digital images. Another option is to buy a stand-alone image editor such as Corel PaintShop Pro or Adobe Photoshop (the full version is pricey, but Photoshop Elements, the consumer edition, is not).

Before you alter any digital image, make a copy and keep the original scan in a safe place. Work off the copy in case you make an alteration that you regret.

This book is not the place for a complete primer on digital image restoration. Consult, *Digital Restoration from Start to Finish* by Ctein or other works on digital photography repair and retouching.

Anyone can learn to make simple adjustments to damaged photographs. If you are not interested in learning how to make complex repairs, a photo restoration firm can make your damaged images look almost new. Save this step for the images that are so faded or so broken that fixing them yourself may be nearly impossible without a lot of investment in time and effort, because digital restoration can be expensive.

Final File Preparation

The first step in the final preparation of your digital images is to create a backup that can be stored somewhere safely off-site. A backup drive, a flash drive or a DVD can be given to another family member, or stored in a safe deposit box. It breaks my heart every time there is a natural disaster, not only for the lives that are lost or endangered and the property destroyed, but for the memories that cannot be recovered in a tangible way.

At this stage, you may not be ready to choose the final images for the book. You may have far more images than what you could possibly use, so the next step is to implement an organizational system that makes sense—not just for this book project, but for future projects.

For some, naming each digital image with the subject and approximate year will make sense. I have too many photographs to spend my time naming each image individually. I would rather keep folders within folders. I keep images of families together, meaning that pictures of children will appear in the parent's file folder, but once the child is an adult, he or she receives his own folder. I organize by last name, then first name so that the file folders alphabetize well. I also keep dated folders of events such as vacations or holiday celebrations so that there is a folder for each family Thanksgiving by year, for example.

I also keep originals in folders and work only from copies. I give my copies different file names with an indicator of what type of correction I have made. As an example, a file that has been color corrected will have its file name changed from IMG2036.jpg to IMG2036cc.jpg. That way, the files still alphabetize together, but I can tell without having to open the file which is the original and which has been altered.

Consider adding borders to keep images with light skies, for example, from fading into the page, or adding photo corners to make the images look like they are in a scrapbook. There is no need to apply any final touches, however until you are ready to place the images into the page layout.

Share

While you are scanning, share with other family members. Sharing will build interest in the book and may encourage family members to reciprocate with their photo treasures.

Send a few interesting images by email, post them on Facebook or Twitter, or add them to your family tree online. If you have a smartphone, send a few by Snapchat or Instagram. Create a few albums or slideshows at websites such as Photobucket (photobucket.com) or Flickr (www.flickr.com).

Sign up for one of the multitudes of online picture sharing sites such as Snapfish (www.snapfish.com), Shutterfly (www.shutterfly.com) or DotPhoto (www.dotphoto.com). Then send an announcement that you have created a photo album for family to see or order copies.

Create interesting gifts for purchase on sites such as CafePress (www.cafepress.com) or Zazzle (www.zazzle.com). If you are planning a reunion, photo gifts are popular.

You can even design fabric using photographs at websites such as Spoonflower (www.spoonflower.com) or Fabric on Demand (www.fabricondemand.com).

Learning a few simple techniques for scanning your images will give you an abundance of options for how to use them, and will guarantee the images will look their best in your book.

≈৶৶৻৶≈

If you find yourself overwhelmed by the prospect of scanning an abundance of family photographs, film negatives or slides, you may want to engage a scanning company to help you.

Working with a Scanning Company

Contact one of the many companies listed on the Memory Preservation Coalition's website (memorypreservationcoalition.org). The coalition is a non-profit group dedicated to helping individuals preserve, protect and archive documents and photographs.

One idea I particularly like is having a scanning service come to you. Scangaroo launched this idea. The company has since been acquired by Gen-Arc Digital Estate Scanning (www.gen-arc.com). They use mobile scanning labs to come to your home so that your important photographs, documents, scrapbooks or video never leave your possession. They also offer cloud-based digital asset management meaning you can store your family documents and photographs so that they can be shared with generations to come (assuming the company stays in business).

Another option is to contact FamilySearch about their Worldwide Photo Scanning and Preservation Initiative. The Mormon Church has teamed up with Kodak and E-Z Photo Scan (ezphotoscan.com) to equip a few of their Family History Centers, their central library in Salt Lake City as well as a center in Riverton, UT with high-speed, high-resolution scanners. Look for one of their "photopalooza" events or find out whether the Family History Center in your area offers photo scanning.

There are also local companies who can scan photographs, or convert older forms of analog film into modern digital video. A company that specializes in memory preservation, however, may be better than the local photo shop.

National Archives Standards

Before you hire a scanning company, ask whether they follow the guidelines prescribed by the National Archives for handling your photographs or delicate documents. You would not want an item damaged by careless handling.

File Size and Format

Make sure you have the images scanned at the largest size you will need to make a reprint or to include in your printed book. You may have images of different sizes to scan, so if you want all digital images large enough to create a full-page image in your book or a large photo reprint, be specific about that requirement.

Be clear about what file format (JPG or TIFF) you need. Most scanning companies will return files as JPGs. Unless you have a compelling need for TIFF images, JPGs will work for a printed book, an eBook, and any use you can think of online.

Bound Items

Ask about scanning photographs that are glued into photo albums. Photo albums often require special handling in order to scan, so these items may cost more. If your photo albums are bound or such that they will not lay flat on the glass for scanning, ask whether the company could re-photograph, or whether they have the kind of equipment used to scan open books. Book scanning equipment may be better for the uneven surfaces in a scrapbook than a flat, plate scanner.

Slides and Film Negatives

Ask about scanning slides and film negatives. Make sure the slides or film will be scanned at a resolution high enough to create a digital image large enough for your biggest need. Often slides and negatives are scanned at a standard 4000 dpi resolution which will yield an image of 3622 pixels by 5320 pixels for the average slide that measures 23mm x 34mm. This image size is large enough to produce a photograph of 12" x 17" at 300 dpi, which is large enough for most book projects unless you are planning an oversized coffee-table book.

Video Transfer

You may have other media that you want made into digital images or transferred to a modern DVD—VHS, VHS-C, 8mm, Hi8, Super8, mini-DV or other formats.

Most film- or tape-to-digital video transfer is done at a standard resolution, and the transfer is done in one piece—the length of the original film to a single video clip.

If you need still digital images from your video, work with the technician to create a list based upon time stamps. You also may need to ask for frame-by-frame images over several seconds in order to obtain the best still from video where the subjects are moving. Obtaining multiple images may cost a bit more, but is more likely to generate one usable image than a single attempt.

If you need stills at higher resolution, that process is more difficult because the film must be marked and stopped in order to adjust the resolution upward. The technician will likely make the complete transfer, then rewind the film and start and stop at each place where you requested a digital still from the film. Again, this may cost a bit more, but if you need a high-quality, high-resolution digital image from a family video, it may be worth the money.

Restoration or Retouching Services

Ask about photo retouching services. Most scanning companies offer basic re-touching services, and some offer advanced retouching services for photographs that are badly faded or damaged. For most old photographs, even a bit of dust and scratch removal, color correction, sharpening, saturation adjustment or over- or under-exposure correction is well worth the trouble and expense. Much of this, however, can be done in your image editing software. If the photograph requires extensive digital restoration, such as fixing tears across people's faces, or removing color shifting caused from mold, expect to pay more. If the only photograph you have of one of your ancestors needs major restoration, the cost may be less important than having a restored, usable image.

Write a Formal Proposal or Contract

Write a formal agreement detailing the work you want to have done, the cost, when you are to deliver the items to the company (or the date the company's scanning equipment will come to you), and when the scanning will be complete. Include the file type and how the images will be given to you—thumb drive, external hard drive, archival DVD, through a file sharing service, or in permanent cloud storage that you can access at any time.

❧❧

The primary goal for scanning is to create a digital image large enough and at the correct resolution to look good in whatever format you plan to use it. Once you have a print-quality digital image, you can reduce the image size for other uses such as sending by email or posting on the Internet. A secondary goal is to preserve the photographic memories and documentary evidence of your family. Preserving your images is important, but try not to let the task of scanning sideline your book project. For those of you with hundreds or thousands of images to scan, it could.

Chapter 9

Developing a New Research Plan

In this round of research, gather as many images as you need to tell a complete story. You may want to gather images to place your family in historical context, or you may want to include images showing the social history of how people lived in the place and era.

Why go beyond the images in your personal collection and gather images from social and local history? Because books with accurate details are more respected, and the next generation may have no experience with some of the things that were very familiar to the generations that came before them. Very few children today have ever heard of Jiffy Pop Popcorn, and their parents may be unfamiliar with bobby socks or poodle skirts, and their grandparents may not remember flappers or why they would have gone to a speakeasy. But many of your ancestors did. Using images from the era when your family members lived will help tell a more rounded story of what it was like "way back when."

Baby Steps

Ask family members for any pictures you would like to have but do not—a complete set of school pictures, wedding pictures from each couple, candids from family events, and so on.

Next Steps

Do a bit of social history research to find out more about what it was like to live at different times in history. You may want to pick out a few important dates and focus on those. Take the year your parents were married, for example. You may want to find out what courtship was like for them, what the number one song was for the year, the most popular movie (if there were movies), what fashions were popular, or what the price of ordinary things were such as bread, milk, a suit of clothes, shoes, a house, and so on. Look at the major headlines for that year. Search for photographic collections of that era. Look for collectors of items popular at that time—everything from cars to household items.

Giant Leaps

If you plan to write more than captions about your photographs, use this round of research to gather whatever you are going to need to tell the story behind the image(s).

The rest of this chapter contains tips for images you may want and where you may find them.

Before You Begin the Next Round of Research

Let us step back to the book project for a moment to make sure you have a clear idea of the scope of the project, because you will not want to spend time gathering images or researching elements that you will not use for this book.

Do you have a clear vision of the project? Are you showcasing one family or many families? One generation or a timeline across multiple generations? Will you organize around themes?

You may or may not choose to write an introduction, or a preface explaining what images are contained in the book. Ask yourself whether the person looking through the pictures will be able to discern who, what, when and where the photographs were taken from the captions alone, or whether more explanation is needed. Try not to get too bogged down by expanding the project unnecessarily. In this round of research, gather enough material and images to fit this project.

Preliminary Organization

Even a collection of the most fantastic images are better off if well organized. Look at the following ways to organize a photo book. These suggestions may give you a few ideas, not only for how to let your images tell a story, but for what else you may need to research in order to tell the story well.

Chronologically

Organizing from the past to the present makes the most sense to readers because it follows a natural timeline—the images are shown in the order they were taken. That does not mean that you have to place every image into a rigid timeline. You may want to dedicate a page, a few pages, or a section to showcase a single member of the family, returning to an earlier time to begin a new section for other members. The first child in the family, for example, may have a series of photos from birth through graduation together, followed by the next sibling, and the next. That type of organization would not fit a rigid chronology, but would follow a rough chronological organization overall.

Organizing chronologically may make the most sense, for example, if you are creating a chronicle of events as they happened. For example, showing images of letters home from a soldier at war on the facing page with a map of where the letter was written, or what action was taking place at the same time would create a powerful combination of images.

By Family

You may want to organize by family if more than one generation is represented. In other words, you could keep the photographs of the children with their parents until they are old enough to have a family of their own, and any subsequent photographs of those people could be grouped into sections of their own, or into another book.

You could represent your genealogical research in images following one of the more traditional ways a genealogy is organized such as a:

Surname Line

This style would start with a daughter (the last to use the surname in your family) and proceed back through the generations with each male as far back as you have traced using photographs and documents to show the line backwards in time.

Ancestor Line

This style is similar to a surname line but would follow the path from the present to a particular ancestor in the past (a president, a Salem witch, or a Revolutionary War ancestor, for example) without regard to the surname. Instead, it would follow the path back to a particular ancestor.

Nuclear Family

This style (described above) could include a chapter (or section) for the parents, plus a chapter for each child where the images are shown together when the second generation are children, but separately once the second generation reaches adulthood. Once you reach the third generation, it may be easier to create separate books.

By Topic

Showing your family photographs by topic can be fun. Do you have photographs of different generations on their bicycles, playing sports, or on vacation? Could you group the school photographs together—grandma, her children and grandchildren at graduation, or in the early grades? Do you have photographs of similar traits such as freckles, or buzz cut hair?

Showing "then and now" photographs by topic can be fun as well. Vacation photographs from Disneyland forty years ago next to a modern trip, or Grandma's kitchen next to Mother's, uncle's first car next to his nephew's and so on.

An underlying theme or central idea can help pull the different images together as a more cohesive story.

Randomly Organized

I understand the temptation to organize randomly because it takes less planning than any other style of organization. That kind of idea could work, for example, if you are showcasing an artist's best work over a lifetime. They images would not necessarily have to be shown in the order that the paintings were created, but there would be an underlying theme or topic—all images of an artist's work, not merely random images of that person's life.

It is not necessary to determine what organizational style you will use for the final book while you are still gathering images or while there are still holes in your research. Thinking about how you could organize may generate additional ideas, however.

Timeline Events

Take a look back at your timeline. Do you have images of each of the major events you wish to depict in the book? In many cases, what you lack is something simple such as you have a graduation photograph for each of the siblings but one and that final photograph is a mere phone call away.

While you research and gather images, keep your timeline up to date. As you discover new information, it is much easier to update the timeline(s) as you go, rather than trying to organize an even larger pile of information later.

Adding Images of Social History

Social history is more about *how* people lived rather than where or when. The following are categories of social history you may want to think about because they may inspire you to find images or take new images of items you still have in the family, such as:

Heirlooms. What items do you, or other family members have that belong to your family? Household goods? Books? China or silver? Jewelry? Watches or clocks? Clothing or quilts? When you imagine yourself at your parents or grandparents homes as a child, are there things you remember about the things they had you would like to show in the book?

Household Items. Some of the rarest items in Americana museums are the everyday household items or utensils because so few still exist. Everyday items were used, worn out or broken and thrown away. I will admit, that not too many people will want a photograph of the olive refrigerator or stove common in 1970s houses, but looking at images of those items may bring back great memories of family time in the kitchen.

Home. Think about the different homes your family lived in. What type of houses did your family have? How were the houses built and by whom? What type of furniture did your family have? How big was the house? What was the floor plan? How was each room used? Did the house have plumbing and electricity? Was there central heat? Did they use fireplaces or stoves to heat the house? What type of fuel was used? Unfortunately, many people do not take photographs of the insides of their homes, and back when photography was expensive, photographs were reserved for portraits. You may want to find or take images if the houses still stand, or find images representative of what the insides were like.

Ethnic Heritage. Even though America is the world's great melting pot, many of us maintain pieces of our ethnic heritage. Look for ethnic differences in language, customs, cooking, clothing, music, theater, building styles and the way holidays or other special occasions are celebrated. Are there images you would want to include to represent your ethnic heritage?

Customs. Does your family follow customs for big life events such as births, marriages, or deaths? Would you want to show those customs in images?

Beliefs. Religion, superstition, education, politics and social standing influence beliefs. Are there images representative of your family's beliefs?

Education. Most people have school pictures from each grade, but do you have pictures of the schools? How about images of report cards or diplomas, playbills from school performances, or images of athletic events?

Employment or Profession. Photographs of people at work are a bit rarer than photographs of kids at school. Much of our work history is represented by items such as business cards. Do you have images of the places family members worked or how they worked?

Entertainment. Most people have images from family vacations, but how about other leisure activities such as music, games, sports, or theater? Did your sister keep a poster of her favorite teen idol on her wall? Did your brother have an autograph of a major league ball player? Did your grandmother have a favorite television show? Does your grandchild have a favorite toy? Think about all of the ways we entertain ourselves to see if there are entertainment images you would want to include.

Holidays. Most families take photographs during holidays, but how about images of some of the finer details? Do you have images of the Thanksgiving table, or closeups of the china that is only used on holidays? How about an image of your grandmother's glass Christmas tree ornaments or your family's menorah? Think about the items you display during holidays.

Neighbors. Do you have images of close neighbors or friends? How about group activities such as neighborhood gatherings or ball games?

Neighborhoods. How about images of the neighborhood? If you do not have images from long ago, how about creating a neighborhood map showing where each of your close neighbors lived and who lived there?

Animals. Are pets a part of your family? Or perhaps your family has work animals such as horses?

Clothing. One of the funniest Facebook polls I saw recently asked people what item of clothing they still had from High School—and a surprising number of people still had items such as rock concert t-shirts, go-go boots, jeans, bell bottomed pants, sweater dresses and much, much more. Clothing styles can bring back great memories.

Transportation. How did your family get around? Did you take the train for vacations or the station wagon? Do you have images of each sibling's first car? Does your wild uncle ride a motorcycle or fly a plane?

Cooking. These days taking food photos is somewhat routine given the number of apps showcasing food. Think through the whole process of cooking at your home. Do you have images of favorite dishes, utensils, your everyday dishes, or your best china? How about pictures of the kids helping out?

There is a lot to think about in terms of social history, but learning about these things will help you better depict your family's everyday life in images.

Where to Locate Social History

To study social history, you will use many traditional genealogical sources. To gather rich, detailed information consult eyewitness testimony—through interviews, diaries, journals and letters; expert research found in academic books and journals; museums where artifacts of daily living have been preserved; and memorabilia or ephemera—those items meant to be used and thrown away.

Manuscript Collections

Use WorldCat (www.worldcat.org) and ArchiveGrid (beta.worldcat.org/archivegrid/) to locate manuscript collections with letters, diaries, journals or other community history appropriate to your research. Many archives with manuscript collections also have images.

Every archive is different. Some archives keep only original sources created by governmental institutions while others keep personal papers. It pays to search major and local archives.

Scholarly Articles

Journals address nearly every historical niche, and the people who write articles for these journals are experts in their fields. You may find the physical journals at your local university and some public libraries. Most universities have access to JSTOR's online collection (www.jstor.org). Often, scholarly articles will include images of items representative of a historical niche with information about where the photograph was taken or where the item is housed.

Museums

One of the best ways to experience how people lived during a certain era is to visit a historic house, living or open air museum of that time. There, you can get a feel for the size of the living space, items that were in the home and, in some cases, the land that surrounded the home. Museums of all types are good places to take new images of historical artifacts.

There are museums for nearly every type of living space from ships that transported people to the new world, to tenements in the inner city, to sprawling plantation homes. The trick is to find one from the right era, in the area where your family came from since building styles varied so greatly from place to place.

Another way to experience an era is to attend a re-enactment. Re-enactors pride themselves on their ability to create exact replicas, and they often create temporary museums using items such as Civil War-era tents filled with era-appropriate items.

Collectors clubs and their events are another source of temporary museums. There are collectors clubs for farm equipment, automobiles, costumes—name it; there are people who collect it. When they gather together to show off their collections, you will have an abundance of objects to look at, and enthusiastic experts to answer your questions.

Inns and hotels are additional sources of period information. Think of these structures as working museums. Some have been restored to their original look, although most have modern conveniences such as indoor plumbing and electricity. In order to restore their buildings accurately, however, many inn owners have become experts in period furniture, building techniques and other information in which you may be interested.

Look for specialized museums if you want to get an idea of how people worked. There are too many types of specialized museums to name them all here, but consider some of these possibilities: school house, transportation, medical office, agricultural, newspaper office, courthouse, mining, and railroad depots.

Art museums may be a source for landscape paintings that could show you what an area looked like before photographs were available. Art is are also a source of images of period dress or events, such as battle scenes.

A good source for finding historical museums is the *Directory of Genealogical and Historical Societies, Libraries and Museums in the U.S. and Canada*. If your local library does not have a copy, ask that they purchase it.

Many museums, if they do not also have a full library, have a collection of books and journals to help the staff answer questions about their collection. These highly specialized collections could save you countless hours of research. Ask if the museum has a working bibliography of their books and journals, or a list of their archival items. Make an appointment with the staff member who has expertise in what you are researching. He or she may know of additional sources or images that would be of interest to you.

Ethnic Associations

Use the search engines to find associations or journals that honor your ethnic heritage. Some have active memberships and websites devoted to the history of immigrant populations and the customs that make each culture unique. Many ethnic societies maintain libraries, archives, museums or photographic collections, as well.

Neighborhoods

Look for a history of your family's neighborhood. You may find that archaeologists or field historians have studied the area. You may find a neighborhood association that maintains a website, or that has historical information about the neighborhood. If the neighborhood been declared a historic district, there may be more information on the neighborhood at the local planning board or preservation society. The National Park Service maintains a database of buildings on the National Register of Historic Places (nrhp.focus.nps.gov).

Religious Institutions

Houses of worship are not only rich sources of original documents, they often keep a local library for congregants that may include more than religious texts. It is common to find histories of the institution written on anniversary dates, such as centennials, sesquicentennials or bicentennials.

Search Engines

Use the search engines to find niche sites to help answer specific questions or locate specific images. Try searching for "coal mining images in 19th century Pennsylvania" or "1970s fashions." You never know what you may find. Check out demonstration or re-enactment videos on YouTube; hard to find books on Google Books (book.google.com) or the HathiTrust (www.hathitrust.org); and the incredible collection of digitized images at the Library of Congress.

Specialty Books

Many modern specialty books are full of social history such as cookbooks, travel guides, business or industry histories, histories of events or tragedies, and institutional or neighborhood histories. The two largest publishers of this type of material are:

- Arcadia Publishing (www.arcadiapublishing.com)
- The History Press (www.historypress.net)

Publishers Global (www.publishersglobal.com) Publishers Global has a directory of publishers by subject including military and history publishers.

eBay

eBay is a rich source of ephemera and archival material. I never know whether to be sad or glad when archival items come up for sale on eBay. I guess it is better that the material be sold to a collector who will preserve it, than not. Search for items on eBay that may pertain to your family, the area where your family comes from, or the era you are researching. If you cannot afford to purchase the item(s) of interest, perhaps the seller would give permission to use their photographs.

Setting up an eBay email alert is simple and helpful to ongoing research. Create a free eBay account and sign in. In the big search box enter a term you are interested in (e.g. horton family new york) and hit search. Click on the button at the top of the results labeled "+ Follow this search." Your search terms will be saved, and you will have the option to receive a daily email showing you the results.

One of the challenges of investigating the social history of your family is not in how hard it is to find it, it is how easy it is, and how much of it there is. I could easily become distracted on Google Books or eBay for days. The best advice I can give you is to avoid the temptation to become a collector. Use the tools above to answer specific questions or locate specific images, rather than an excuse to go fishing or collecting.

Including Images of Historical Context

Placing your family in historical context is about placing them within their communities and any historic events that may have influenced their lives.

Images of Locations

Location images can help "set the scene" for a story or for other images. Think about the time period and your family members would have seen every day. Can you name the landmarks they would have known—the lakes, hills, waterways, springs, public buildings, business districts, and neighborhoods? Can you find images that will show what the community was like then? How far apart were the neighbors? What were the weather and the terrain like? The biggest challenge when using images for historical context, is not, for example, to picture the New Orleans of today, but to picture New Orleans as it was when your family was there and when any other photographs were taken if you are using them concert with the historical photographs.

A more general discussion of where to find location images is in a later section. The following are a few ideas for location-specific images other than historical photographs.

County Histories. County histories are a good place to look for images. Early county histories may have good lithographic prints that are in the public domain because of their age that may show the area long ago. More modern county histories may have images whose dates span decades and often give credits to let you know who owns or holds the image, such as a local historical society.

To find county histories, search the online catalog of a library in the area. Most library catalogs allow you to search either by keyword or subject. Using the subject category may return a better list. Google Books (books.google.com) and the Internet Archive (www.archive.org) are also good sources of early county histories available to read online or for download.

City Directories. City Directories often have street maps, and are a good resource to find out what businesses were operating in what years, and who your family's neighbors were at different times. While it is easier to find a city directory for larger towns, some directories include the rural areas nearby. Ancestry.com has a good collection of digitized city directories, although many thousands are available on microfilm through:

  • The Family History Library (www.familysearch.org)
  • The American Antiquarian Society (www.americanantiquarian.org)
  • The Library of Congress (www.loc.gov)

Bird's Eye View Maps. Bird's eye view maps were popular in the 19th and early 20th centuries. Bird's eye view maps will give you an idea of how the town was laid out, what buildings were prominent, and the terrain. The best sources for these maps are:

- The David Rumsey Map Collection (www.davidrumsey.com)
- Art Source International (rare-maps.com)
- eBay (www.ebay.com)

Fire Insurance Maps. Starting in 1867, the Sanborn Company made fire insurance maps of more than 12,000 cities and towns to help insurance companies assess the risk of insuring buildings. The Sanborn maps are a top-down view of each property and will give you an idea of what each building was constructed of and how many structures were on the property whether each was a house, barn, carriage house, garage, or even a structure as small as a coal bin. There are many digitized Sanborn maps available online, and major universities and libraries also have collections of these maps.

DVD Extras. Although you should not take images from a movie extra, watching the extras is one way to see for yourself what a location looked in years past. Modern day filmmakers often go to great lengths to achieve historical accuracy in their films, and many times the DVD extras will describe their research or how they created different aspects of the film. If a film was set in the area you are researching, watch the DVD extras, as well as the commentary tracks, for background information.

Images of the Home

There are many ways to include images of your family's home or homestead—as exterior, interior, floor plans or location images.

Interior Images. In addition to seeing images of the community, your readers may be interested in more intimate details, such as what the family's home was like. How was it furnished? Did they read by candlelight or oil lamp? Were there rag rugs on the floor and quilts on the beds? Was there a fireplace or a furnace? *Houses and Homes: Exploring Their History* by Barbara Howe, Delores A. Fleming and Ruth Ann Overbeck is an excellent study of the role that homes play in local history. Unfortunately, people rarely take photographs of the interiors of their homes, so you may not find an actual image among your photographs. You may find representative images of interiors and exteriors in the collection of a local historical society, library or archive.

Exterior Images. You may have a photograph, or you may want to find a photograph representative of the architectural style in the area if the home no longer stands. *A Field Guide to American Houses* by Virginia Savage McAlester and Lee McAlester is a good overview of what homes looked like in different eras.

Floor Plans. You may find representative floor plans in the following publications. Beginning in 1846, *Godey's Lady's Book* published house plans, and *Ladies Home Journal* offered early Frank Lloyd Wright home designs for $5. Sears, Roebuck and Co. sold entire houses as kits to build. You will find back issues of these magazines and catalogs at major libraries. There are more modern floor plans available online through sites such as Architectural Design (www.architectural designs) or Floor Plans.com (www.floorplans.com).

Maps. Deed, tax, and homestead records along with plat maps can help pinpoint where your family's home was. If the actual house no longer stands, look for personal accounts, photographs, or a historic home museum representative of homes in the area (or the era) to gather images and more detailed information. If the house still stands, consider using a modern map showing the location.

If you find a legal description using the Public Land Survey System (Range, Township and Section) and need to plot a location, here is a site for doing so: Earth Point Tools for Google Earth (www.earthpoint.us/TownshipsSearchByDescription.aspx).

If your land description uses the metes and bounds system, you may want to purchase one of the many software programs available to help you plot out the property. Cyndi's List has more than a dozen software programs listed for both Windows and Mac. Or, here is a website that will generate a map for you using metes and bounds data (genealogytools.net/deeds/index.php).

Fortunately, there are many places that have good map collections. Check with the major universities (e.g. Harvard and Yale), large libraries (e.g. Newberry Library and the Free Library of Philadelphia) and the local college or university in the area you are researching.

The following is a list of good historical map collections online:

- Library of Congress Maps Collection (www.loc.gov/maps/)
- David Rumsey Map Collection (www.davidrumsey.com/)
- Perry-Castaneda Library Map Collection at the University of Texas (www.lib.utexas.edu/maps/)
- American Geographical Society Digital Map Collection (collections.lib. uwm.edu/cdm/landingpage/collection/agdm)

There are easily searchable modern maps at:

- MapQuest (www.mapquest.com)
- Bing (www.bing.com)
- Google (www.google.com)

Each has fairly generous Terms of Use that allow you to capture a screenshot of a map and reproduce it elsewhere as long as you are not using the map, itself, for commercial gain. Check the terms on the site before you spend too much time gathering maps as screenshots.

Google, Bing and MapQuest each offer street maps, topographical features, and satellite views. All three offer directions and information about local services such as restaurants, hotels, and local attractions.

Google and Bing offer GPS coordinates and closeup views—Google calls it Street View, Bing calls it Bird's Eye and Streetside. These features are helpful in determining what exists at a location currently. Not all areas are updated by Bing or Google frequently, so looking at the date watermarked on the map will give you an idea of how long ago the view was captured.

Google allows you to sign in to your Google account and create maps with your own map points, to save or share by email. They also offer developer tools to create your own maps and place them on your website or blog. The Community Walk feature allows you to create a map with personalized points, and add photos, videos, and comments.

Images of Work Life

The place where people spend a great deal of time is at work. Details of your family members' work lives may be as interesting as details of their home lives. Did they work on farms or in factories? Did they own the business or were they employees? What products or services did the business sell? Who were their customers? What was it like to spend a day or a shift in the workplace?

Specialized, living, or open air museums may be the best way to experience what it was like to work as your ancestors did. If the museum has docents or re-enactors, see if you can spend an entire day doing what people of the era did. Rent a costume and wear what they wore. Try your hand at operating the machinery, pressing the linen or cooking the meals. An living museum is also a good place to take modern photographs of museum items.

Profession. Look to the census for information about your family members' professions, including the manufacturing censuses. For images, look to scholarly articles or collector's clubs for images of the items that would have been in the workplace long ago, such as bottles in a 19th century drug store.

Business Promotional Items. Look to the newspapers of the era for ads touting your family members' businesses. Search a local archive for items with company's logos and sales brochures, or a local museum or collector's club for examples of product packaging.

Other Important Places

In addition to your family home(s) and workplace(s), consider a little research on the places where family members went to school, shopped, attended religious services or other public buildings in the community that would have been frequently visited, such as the local courthouse.

Images of Events

Most family events such as birthdays, weddings or holidays are well represented in photographs within the family's collection. But other local, regional or national events may have affected your family.

Local Events. Events that affected your ancestor's local community likely affected your ancestor. Local events will more likely come from local newspapers covered in the next section.

Regional, National or World Events. The following are good, general sources to help you gather information and occasionally images about world, national and regional events. *The Genealogist's U.S. History Pocket Reference: Quick Facts & Timelines of American History to Help Understand Your Ancestors* by Nancy Henderson (San Diego, CA: Family Tree Books: 2013). *In Their Time: A Timeline Journal for Placing Family Events into Historical Context, 1000-2076* by Roger L. Dudley (Denver, CO: Warfield Press, 2013). Eyewitness to History (www.eyewitnesstohistory.com) is a good source of first-person accounts. They describe themselves as "History through the eyes of those who lived it." *New York Times* TimesMachine (timesmachine.nytimes.com/browser) has digital issues of the *New York Times* from its beginning in 1851 until 1980, although you have to be a subscriber to the newspaper. Some libraries have subscriptions to this database through ProQuest.

Sources of Historical Images

There are an abundance of sources for historical images. To use them in your book, however, they must be in the public domain or you must obtain permission from the copyright holder to use them.

You also need to find images that are of sufficient size and resolution to use in a book project. While it is easy to locate images by using the "Images" feature on a search engine, the Internet is not the best place to find digital files with resolutions high enough to look good in print. For print production, you need an image at 300 ppi at the size you want to display it. You will need a higher resolution image than most of what you will find on the Internet because websites use images that have been down-sampled to 72 ppi for quick retrieval and display.

You can, however, use search engines to locate collections that contain the images you want, some free from copyright restrictions, others require a fee.

Locating Photograph Collections

Use the "Images" feature on a search engine to locate an image. Bing has an interesting feature on its Images page called "Image Match." By clicking on an image, then using the Image Match feature, the search engine will list other places online where that image exists. In many cases, you will be able to find the desired image in different sizes and resolutions.

Sources of Royalty Free Images

The following are websites where you may find photographs or illustrations free from copyright restrictions so that you can include them in your book without permission or fees. Proper attribution, however, is a must.

Library of Congress Photographs. Each image within the pictures collection at the Library of Congress (www.loc.gov/pictures/) has an indicator of whether the image has any known rights restrictions. The images in the American Memory Project within the Library of Congress are gathered from other collections, so be sure to check with the image's owner for permission.

Flickr: The Commons. Flickr (www.flickr.com/commons) is a photo sharing site that has a section of images that owners have agreed to allow others to use without copyright restriction. Flickr is also the host of many museum and archive photographic collections. Unless you find the image you want among The Commons, ask permission to use it.

Getty Images Stock Photos. While Getty (www.gettyimages.com/creativeimages/royaltyfree) mostly sells images, it has made a collection available without copyright restrictions. Please do not be tempted to use an image that is rights restricted, however, without paying for use. Getty is known for its hardball tactics to extract compensation if you use an image without permission.

Ancestry. Ancestry (www.ancestry.com) has a postcard collection consisting of thousands of images from around the world. Old postcards are a great source of location and event images. Be sure to read the Terms of Use information on the Ancestry website before including one of their images in your book.

Wikimedia Commons. Wikimedia Commons (commons.wikimedia.org) has millions of images without licensing restrictions contributed by the individuals who own them.

Again, proper attribution is a must.

Sources of Rights-Managed Images

Rights-managed images are those that you may license for use. The following are sources of low-cost, rights-managed images:

- Shutterstock (www.shutterstock.com)
- Dreamstime (www.dreamstime.com)
- MorgueFile (www.morguefile.com)

Historical Societies

Many local historical societies have photographic prints, slides or negatives in their collections that have not been digitized or cataloged online. The same is true of some local libraries. It pays to call and ask. Explain that you want the image for a family photo book. If the institution will not make the images available to you without cost, negotiate the fee. You may have to pay only for the staff time to scan the image for you. You could offer to help scan images in return for waiving a fee. What the historical society may lack is staff to scan their images.

Ideas for Images

The following sites have millions of images of everything imaginable. If you need ideas, consult one of these sites.

ClickAmericana. Click Americana (www.clickamericana.com) has images covering every decade from the 1820s to the 1980s. ClickAmericana has such a good collection of images that you are certain to get a few ideas, and the site encourages sharing to Facebook, Twitter or Pinterest.

Retronaut. Retronaut (www.retronaut.com) describes itself as a photographic time machine. Retronaut has partnered with museums and archives around the world to create this digital collection.

Mountain West Digital Library. Mountain West Digital Library (www.mwdl. org) is a portal to the image resources of several historical societies and universities in the western states.

Panoramio. Panoramio (www.panoramio.com) is a user-generated Wiki site where photographers post their images. Panoramio is a good resource for modern photographs of the places your ancestors once lived. Ask for permission. Often, the photographer is flattered that you want to use the image and asks only for proper photo credit.

The sites above are also sources for images of what places look like today, for people in period clothing; objects found in museums or full-color images of historic places. In fact, you may find better images taken with modern equipment, than historical photographs.

Newspapers

Newspapers can be a tremendous source of images. Early images were lithographs—made up of small lines and dashes. Later images were halftones made up of little dots. Either will re-produce well in a photo book with a little knowledge of how to get a good scan (see Chapter 8). Fortunately, many newspapers are already digitized which makes including those images even easier.

To find out whether there was a newspaper published in the town or area where your family lived, consult the U.S. Newspaper Directory, 1690-Present, found at the Chronicling America section of the Library of Congress website (chroniclingamerica.loc.gov/search/titles/). The Library of Congress also has a large number of digitized newspapers available. If you want to know more about a specific paper or about the early newspaper industry, consult *The History and Present Condition of the Newspaper and Periodical Press of the United States*, produced by the Census Office of the Department of the Interior. This book is available as a free download at Google Books (books.google.com).

The following free sites have links to digitized newspapers:

- The Ancestor Hunt (www.ancestorhunt.com/newspapers.html)
- Elefind (www.elefind.com)
- Google News Archive (news.google.com)
- Old Fulton New York Post Cards (fultonhistory.com/Fulton.html)
- Australia's Trove (trove.nla.gov.au/newspaper)

There are also many local or state-wide newspaper preservation projects. Consult the area's major universities as well as the state historical society, as they often either have original copies or microfilm copies of newspapers significant to the area. The Ancestor Hunt (www.theancestorhunt.com/newspapers.html) also has a state-by-state list of historic newspaper projects as well as helpful articles on searching historic newspapers.

There are several subscription websites devoted to newspapers where you can either search by name or keyword. The name search can be frustrating, especially if you are searching common names. Use the advanced search features that allow you to narrow the search by date and location. Use the keyword search, especially if your ancestor lived in a town near where the newspaper was published. Local newspapers often carried columns of information from surrounding towns as a regular feature.

The following are the leading newspaper subscription sites:

- Newspapers.com
- NewspaperArchive.com
- GenealogyBank.com
- PaperofRecord.com

One of the best features of the subscription newspaper sites is the ability to search across multitudes of papers. You may find obituaries, for example, in the newspaper where your ancestor once resided if you cannot find one in the town where he or she died. Letters home were popular especially during times when masses of people were leaving an area, such as during the many gold rushes or land giveaways. Keep the date ranges narrow to limit the number of results.

Charts

Generation charts or pedigree charts are good visual references for readers who are not familiar with different branches of the family. Generation charts show three or more generations at a glance. Most genealogy software will produce a generation chart at the push of a button. If you want to fancy up the chart, you can add photographs or background pictures. You could also use third party software designed to make elegant, detailed generation charts.

Another useful visual reference is a family group sheet showing a nuclear family—a couple and their children in the order in which the children were born. Genealogy software creates these charts, as well. The charts can be modified to show multiple marriages with all of the children (full and half-siblings), as well as the children's spouses. Family group sheets are another simple way for readers to see who belongs to the family at a glance.

Another option is to display your images in one of these familiar genealogical forms. In Section 4—Production, there are suggestions for how to do so.

Documents and Memorabilia

From your images review, you should have a list of documents and memorabilia you would like to include but do not have an image. The following are examples: an ornate marriage certificate; a passenger list showing the name of the ship, its captain and your family; a land patent showing a map of the property; or a document with an ancestor's signature on it. Signatures are fabulous, because they are so personal.

Some items are considered ephemera or memorabilia rather than documents, but are welcome in a family photo book, such as a letterhead from your family's business, a newspaper clipping, a funeral card, a playbill if your ancestor was in a show, a school report card, and so on.

The documents most handy for establishing relationships are not always the ones that readers will want to see in a photo book, even if they are mighty interesting to the person doing the research. What should make the cut for the book are those documents that help tell the story *and* are visually interesting. In fact, illustrations may be better than documents for that purpose.

Illustrations

There are times when an illustration is better than a photograph. Before photography, paintings were used to illustrate an event or to capture the likeness of a person. At ruins, for example, you are likely to find an artist's rendering of what a place probably looked like, since there may be no paintings or drawings from the era to show the place as it once looked.

There are times when a line drawing is better than a photograph to illustrate an event. Think about how you use maps online today. If you want to see what a place looks like, you may prefer the street view (a photograph), but if you need to drive there, a standard street map (an illustration) would be easier to follow.

There are rich sources of illustrations online. The key, again, is finding files with sufficient resolution to look good in print.

You may find an image that is out of copyright, such as a line drawing or lithograph from a 19th century magazine or book. The trick is locating an original and producing a good scan or photograph. There are stock photography companies that also offer line art free, but in most cases, you must pay to use the image.

Another option is to find an illustrator who can create original drawings. (See Working with an Illustrator below.)

Screen Captures

Screen captures are not an issue if you are planning to publish only in an electronic form. They can be an issue, however if you want them to look good in print.

Your computer, whether a PC or a Mac, probably has a screen capture feature. On the PC, press Control + Alt + PrtScrn, then paste the image into another program such as Word or Photoshop. Unfortunately, standard screen capture software does not always create an image that looks good in print because the software is only able to capture what is on the screen displayed at 72 to 96 ppi.

To obtain the best possible screen capture, increase the size of an image displayed on screen by zooming in (Control+Shift+[+] on a PC), which makes the image bigger on the screen when you capture it. Ideally, you will end up with a screen capture at a size large enough to create a 300 ppi image at the size you want for the book. For example, if you were to capture an image on screen at 16" x 12" at 72 ppi, that would translate into a pixel size of 1152 x 864. The largest 300 ppi image you could create from that pixel size would be 3.84" (1152 divided by 300) x 2.88" (864 divided by 300).

SnagIt (www.techsmith.com/snagit.html) has been the industry leader in screen capture for years. It has the most options for gathering screen captures from different sources such as websites or video, and the ability to edit and enhance captured images. The cost is around $50, but if screen captures are important to your printed book, it may be worth the purchase.

Taking New Photographs

There is no time like the present to take a few new photographs. Even if you do not use them in this book project, ask for updated photographs of the people in your extended family every so often.

Children have their pictures taken frequently, but adults have a nice portrait made only about once a decade, if that. Ask your family members to send you a recent photograph of each member of their families. They do not need to use an expensive portrait photographer. Plan a time when everyone can gather, and then find a friend or neighbor who can take a decent digital photograph. Take pictures of the entire family, as well as a few pictures of each person individually.

Asking for recent photographs can help open doors to other areas where you want help from family members or other researchers, such as information, stories, or old photos.

Heirlooms

Photograph objects that are difficult to scan. If there are heirlooms spread throughout your family that you want to show in the book, ask family members to photograph them for you (if you are not in the area to do so yourself).

Small objects, such as china or jewelry, often look best when isolated in a studio box with a neutral background and good, even lighting. Larger objects may have to be photographed in place.

Good lighting is key to good photographs. In most cases, opening curtains for natural light or placing reading lamps to shine on the object along with proper camera settings will be enough light to take a good indoor photograph.

Artwork

Artwork, like other objects, is difficult to scan—easier to photograph. The key to photographing artwork is to make sure the camera is lined up in a way that keeps the image square, so that you do not create distortions—either narrower at the top than at the bottom, or narrower on one side than the other. You can fix distortions in your image editing program, although taking a good photograph to begin with will save time.

Research the artwork or heirlooms you discover. Readers may be interested to know, for example, that a desk that has been in your family for 150 years was hand-crafted in New England and brought by train to Wisconsin. Or, that your aunt has a complete set of dinnerware popular in the 1920s, sold in dime stores.

Tombstones

Tombstone photographs are common in family histories and in family photo books as they are often the only remembrance available for some people. Internet sharing sites such as Findagrave (www.findagrave.com) and BillionGraves (www.billiongraves.com) have made it easy to obtain tombstone photographs from across the globe thanks to willing volunteers. Ask permission before using someone else's photograph in your book, and give proper photo credit if you do.

Location Photographs

While it is interesting to see historical photographs or paintings that show an area as it looked in the past, there are some instances in which a photograph of what a place looks like today would be appropriate as well. If you have both a modern and a historical photograph, consider creating a side-by-side composite for comparison. Search the website What Was There (www.whatwasthere.com). It pairs historical photographs with Google Maps to get a few ideas.

While You Are on a Research Trip

If you are taking a research trip, schedule enough time to take an abundance of photographs. Digital photography is cheap, so shoot away. You may not use all of them in this book project, but they will be available to you or other family members for future projects.

Bracket Your Shots. Most digital cameras will allow you to alter the speed or the aperture from shot to shot. Some cameras do so in a three-shot burst. By bracketing, the camera will use different settings to alter the amount of light in the photograph. By bracketing, you are likely to take at least one usable shot from the three-shot group without having to alter it in your photo editing program.

Take Establishing Shots. The best example I can give of this is to take a picture of the sign at the cemetery entrance, and then a few shots of the view within the cemetery to give readers an idea of what the landscape is like. In a town, take a few photographs of the landscape as you come into the town, and a few of the town square and surrounding neighborhoods.

Take Encapsulating Shots. An encapsulating shot is a complete picture. At a grave site, take a photograph of the entire stone. In the town square, take a shot of the whole courthouse.

Take Close-ups. On tombstones, take close-ups to make sure you can read names and dates when you get home with the photographs. Taking close-ups will also remind you to look carefully at the entire tombstone from all sides, so you do not miss anything. In town, take photographs of any historic markers. Shoot close enough so that you can read the marker when you return home.

Take Both Vertical and Horizontal Shots. You will not know how a photograph may fit best into the book's layout until much later, so shooting from both directions is helpful.

Panoramas

Panoramic photographs sometimes tell the story better than a single photograph can, and they are easy to create. If you want readers to experience how wide open the family homestead was, how close together the homes were on your family's street, or where buildings were in relation to other buildings, panoramic photographs are the way to go.

There are many image-editing programs, such as Photoshop (or Photoshop Elements) that will stitch together different shots to create a single image. It can be tricky, however, to stitch together two historical photographs if the horizon lines or focal distances are different. Editing prior to stitching can help.

If you are taking new photographs to create a panorama, overlap the shots by about thirty percent. Do not change the focal distance while you are shooting the series, and try to keep the horizon line at the same position in the viewfinder as you shoot. If you are not a steady hand, a tripod can help with this.

For panorama purposes, I shoot a scene first going from left to right, and then repeat the series going the other direction. Sometimes, shots taken going one direction come out better than the other.

Most people take photographs according to long-established personal habits. We shoot from the same standing position, from the same distance, from the same angle or from the same direction (e.g. horizontal). Your book may be more interesting, however, with a few out-of-the-ordinary photographs. As you are taking new photographs, think about ways to alter your tried-and-true habits.

Family photo books satisfy the curiosity. Your family members may be curious about what their ancestors looked like, and what their homes, land or businesses may have looked like. Use as many images as you think you need to tell the story in images. Leave out images if they are included solely to document facts and not very interesting to look at. Seek out instead, memorabilia or ephemera that helps define the era, or maps to help readers understand where the photographs were taken. If the book grows too big, you can always split it into more than one volume.

Asking for Help

You should have an idea of what additional images you want and what you may need help with—either from family, other genealogical researchers, volunteers, or perhaps the professional assistance of photographers, illustrators, or companies who will help you make your images look their best.

Help from Family

Ask family members for any images that you think they can contribute to complete your book. Determine who has the heirlooms. Locate the photo albums and scrapbooks. Find out who still has stuff.

Social Media

It is amazing how many cousins you can rustle up on Facebook, Twitter, or LinkedIn. Use the message boards on sites such as Ancestry.com where other researchers may be working on the same family lines.

Private messaging features allow you to send a message that is only between you and one other person, more like sending an email than asking a public question. Privacy settings allow you to determine who will see the comments you make or the questions you ask. Even so, be careful how much information you share about yourself online.

Although you can post photos to most social media sites, there are dedicated photo sharing sites such as:

- Flickr (www.flickr.com)
- Shutterfly (www.shutterfly.com)
- DotPhoto (www.dotphoto.com)

Some photo sharing sites will let your family members download the digital images or order prints for themselves. Encourage family members to use the photographs you have shared. Holidays or family reunions are a good time to make use of the images. Besides, you may find your images coming back to you through talented or creative cousins in the form of scrapbooks, additional photo books or other photo-inspired gifts.

If you are not familiar with how social media can be used for genealogy, the National Institute for Genealogical Studies (www.genealogialstudies.com) offers a course in *Social Media for the Wise Genealogist*, or consult Drew Smith's book, *Social Networking for Genealogists* (albeit a bit dated, having been released in 2009), or Thomas MacEntee's eBook, *Staying Safe with Social Media: A Guide for Genealogy and Family History*.

Help from Strangers

Reference librarians are my favorite "complete strangers" to ask if I need help with research. Volunteers and historical societies are my favorite "complete strangers" to ask if I am looking for images.

Historical Societies, Museums, Archives and Libraries

Many of these institutions have photographs within their collections that they are willing to let you use within a family photo book. Others require credit given according to their rules, and still others charge a fee for use. Oftentimes, if you are not planning a commercial run of thousands of books, you can get these institutions to waive their usage fees. You may still have to pay to have the image digitized or sent to you.

Social Media

Mobilize an army of photographers or researchers at the click of a mouse using social media. Throw out your question about an image on one of the big genealogical blogs and see if one of the blog's authors can answer you, or put you in touch with someone who can. See if a museum or historical society that may have the image you are interested in has a Facebook page.

Photo Sharing Sites

There are helpful photographers on Findagrave.com, Flickr.com or Panoramio.com. Oftentimes, a credit for taking the photograph is enough for the photographer to give you permission to use their photo.

If you cannot find exactly the right photograph online, sometimes you need only ask. If you want a photograph of a school, for example, you may find a helpful stranger associated with one of the websites above, willing to make a trip over to the school to take the picture. The staff at the local library or historical society may also know of a volunteer willing to help you.

For the best results, be specific about what you want. Explain that the photograph will be used in a printed book, so you need a high-resolution image. If you need a photograph of a building with enough clear blue sky above it to accommodate your title and subtitle, say so. Ask for both horizontal and vertical images if you do not know yet what you need for the layout. You are more likely to receive exactly what you need if you are specific when you ask.

After getting what you need from a helpful volunteer, a nice thank you goes a long way. (This applies to family members as well.) Send a hand-written note or a small gift card for someone who has gone the extra mile for you.

Help from Experts

If you are conducting additional research on your photographs and need help identifying something with a photograph, or if you need an expert's help in locating an image of something specific, they tend to be most helpful if you can sum up succinctly what you need and why, to get on and off the phone quickly, or to come to the point in a few paragraphs in an email.

If you need more than a quick question answered, schedule an interview. You must tell the expert why you are consulting them and what type of advice you need before they will agree to an interview. Most experts, will not allow you to waste their time dithering about. Prepare a list of questions before you make the call. You never know, the expert may be available right then if you are ready to go. Other experts may prefer you to send the questions ahead of time or to answer by email.

Expert advice can be invaluable and can cut your research or your search for an image down dramatically. He or she may know of other resources available or other authorities who could help. Most experts in their field know which books are the definitive guides and which are best to gain background information. They should be aware of image collections as well. An expert should be able to explain the jargon common to their field of expertise to you in an easy-to-understand way.

Some experts will give you quick answers freely; others may charge for their time. Others may turn you over to a research assistant. With any expert you hire; it is worth the effort to negotiate. To get the best deal possible, it does not hurt to have a good counter-offer ready, or something that would suffice, say ... a nice meal. You will not know until you ask.

Working with a Photographer

You may need photographs for the book that you are unable to take for yourself, obtain from family members, or from a helpful local volunteer. In this case, hire a photographer or license a photograph taken for other commercial uses.

Find the right photographer for the job. If you want a group picture of the entire family or candid photographs taken during a reunion, find a portrait photographer—someone who specializes in people pictures.

If you need location photos, look for someone who shoots photographs for advertisements in the area. That photographer may have images not previously sold to clients that he or she would make available to you, for a nominal fee or photo credit. If the photographer has to go somewhere on your behalf, however, be prepared to pay for their travel time as well as shooting time.

Studio Photography

If you need good studio photographs of your heirlooms, consider using a professional. A commercial photographer should be able to shoot objects in their own studios, or take their equipment to a location if the heirlooms are too fragile or too big to be moved to the studio.

Portfolio

Before you hire, ask to see a portfolio. Many photographers have their portfolios online, so you may be able to find exactly the right photographer before placing a call.

Fees

Ask about fees and whether they include travel, time at the location and any cropping or alterations before the photographs are given to you. You will not need prints unless you want them. Portrait photographers expect to make their money on packages of prints, although many photographers are willing to take a higher event fee in exchange for giving you the digital images outright.

Most event photographers will charge for the time they spend at the location, not by the number of images they take. Be clear about this, however. You will not want to pay for time and two hundred images you cannot use, just because the photographer took them. You also do not want the photographer to limit the number of photographs taken. Even with a good photographer, one-quarter to one-third of the shots taken will not be great photographs.

File Type and Resolution

Most photographers today shoot in resolutions much higher than what is needed for print production, so resolution should not be an issue. Ensure, however, that the photographer will deliver images in the largest resolution and size you need. In most book projects, that is the book cover image.

Location Images

If you want location shots, give the photographer the names of local landmarks. A good photographer will know to take shots from different angles, but it does not hurt to be specific. If you want a blue sky in the background in order to put your title in that space, say so. If possible, show the photographer a book cover with an image similar to what you want, so the concept for your cover is clear.

Capturing an Event

If the photographer is to capture a family event, be specific about the images you want. Give the photographer a schedule of activities and a list of the people you want to be photographed. You may need to provide a spotter—someone who is familiar enough with the family to point out who is who on the shot sheet.

Consider asking for establishing shots—shots of the location where the event is taking place. Ask for close-ups as well as group shots, candids as well as staged or portrait shots.

Make sure the photographer is familiar with the event location. Schedule a site inspection with the photographer to discover any lighting issues, obstacles or distracting backgrounds to avoid.

Deadlines

Set clear deadlines. Unless you have an upcoming family reunion where you would want the photographer to be present, wait until the manuscript is nearly finished to send a photographer to take location photographs for you. The only exception to this rule is if the time of the year makes a great difference to the quality (or subject) of the images. If you want a clear shot of a building, for example, you may want the photograph taken in winter.

Copyrights

Do not make a big issue about copyrights unless you are willing to pay more to make the photographer give them up entirely. Negotiate the uses you want for the photographs instead. If you plan to use the photographs for more than your book project, obtain the rights for other uses—on your website, in your eBook, on a family reunion t-shirt or journal cover, on photo souvenirs, and any other use you can think of. It is unlikely that a photographer will deny you any extended uses of photographs of your family. But, it does not hurt to be thorough.

Note: If you have permission to use a volunteer's photo for your book (from sites such as Findagrave or Panoramio), but want to use it for some of the extended uses listed above, ask permission from the photographer for those uses as well.

Payment

Ask about any extra charges, so there are no surprises and clarify how you are expected to make payment and when. Half of the total fee is common for a down payment to secure the booking, with the final half due upon delivery of the photographs. Ask about album fees, overtime charges, or any special handling of the images not included in the quoted price.

Cancellations

Cancellations can be problematic. If you have to cancel, be prepared to pay at least part of the photographer's booking fee unless you cancel well ahead of time. Unfortunately, there may be a reason for the photographer to cancel. To protect yourself, require that the photographer has a similarly qualified backup colleague to fill in, in the event of a cancellation, or that he or she pay any additional charges you may encounter in order to hire someone at the last minute.

Write a Formal Proposal or Contract

Use a formal proposal to indicate the photographs you want and how you want them delivered to you—on a thumb drive, an external hard drive, an archival DVD, or through a file sharing service. Make sure deadlines, and dates of events are clear. Include all prices and payment terms. State what uses the photographer is allowing you, and be specific about what happens if either you or the photographer cancel.

Working with an Illustrator

Working with an illustrator is a bit different than working with a photographer. Because of the artistic nature of the work involved, illustrating often takes far longer than taking photographs. If you want one-of-a-kind illustrations, build extra time into your publishing timeline.

Hire the right illustrator for the job. Illustrators have their own styles, although many illustrators can work in different media, such as pencil, pen and ink, or watercolor. Some illustrators create only computer-generated images. Find a style that you prefer, and then choose an illustrator who can create the images you want. Use the same illustrator throughout the book so that the style is consistent.

Portfolio

Ask to see a portfolio. Many illustrators have their portfolios online, or they can point you to other books they have illustrated. The illustrator may have worked on a book that is available commercially, and has an online preview.

Fees

Ask about fees and be specific about the size and resolution of the digital images you need. A professional illustrator should be able to advise you how their artwork will look best in a print publication, whether by scanning the originals or photographing them. There may be additional fees if the illustrator must engage a studio photographer to create a digital image of their art.

Deadlines

As with hiring other professionals, be specific about what you want and make your deadlines clear. Ask for a set price per illustration, and inquire about any extra charges, so there are no surprises. Clarify how you are expected to make payment and when. Illustrators often require payment in installments as the illustrations are in progress, rather than half before and the balance after an event as you would pay a photographer.

Copyrights

Copyrights may be a more complicated issue with an illustrator than with a photographer. Because of the time it takes to create illustrations, illustrators may not be as eager to give up their copyrights. Negotiate any other uses at the same time you negotiate for your book. You may wish to use the illustrations on social media, on your website or in an electronic book. If you have a reunion coming up, you could use the illustrations on giveaway items such as t-shirts, tote bags or mugs. Negotiate the rights to use the illustrations in other ways or at least leave open the possibility for uses in the future.

Cancellations

If you must cancel, be prepared to pay at least part of the fee unless you cancel well ahead of time. If the illustrator cancels, you can expect a full refund of any fees you have paid. In your agreement, ask that the illustrator pay any additional fees you encounter as a result of his or her cancellation if you are up against a deadline to finish the book.

Write a Formal Proposal or Contract

Use a formal proposal to indicate the illustrations you want and how you want them delivered to you—on a thumb drive, an external hard drive, an archival DVD, or through a file sharing service. Make sure deadlines are clear. Include all prices and payment terms. State what uses the illustrator is allowing, and be specific about what happens if either you or the illustrator cancel.

eLancers and Freelancers

One place to find an illustrator online is to use one of the freelance services, such as Elance (www.elance.com), oDesk (www.odesk.com) or Freelancer (www.freelacer.com). At any of these sites, you will find illustrators listed under designers or graphic design and the person you hire may be from another country. You post the project details and your budget. Freelancers will bid on your project. You accept a bid from the person who offers the best price and has the portfolio you think is best. You will be able to see their ratings from other clients before you choose. They do the work. You approve the work or ask for revisions. They submit final versions, and you pay them through the website, not directly. The sites will take care of the funds transfer and any taxes that apply.

Another place to find freelance illustrators or photographers are at local schools. There are plenty of high school or college students who want to build their portfolios, and who may work for a recommendation or fees far less than a professional would charge.

Working with a Professional Historian or Genealogist

There are times when it pays to hire a professional historian or genealogist to help you finish your research. Although there is some crossover between the work that professional genealogists and historians do, before you hire someone make sure you have the right type of professional for the job. Genealogists tend to focus on establishing relationships, whereas historians tend to focus on location-based research.

Initial Consultation

The initial job consultation should be free. A phone call of 30 minutes or more is not unusual, but you should have your homework done before you call. In some cases, you may need to describe the research problem in detail in order to get a professional researcher's opinion of what it will take to obtain what you need and how much that may cost.

Portfolio

Ask to see examples of their previous work, and check the researcher out online at their personal website, and on social media sites. If there are no testimonials listed, ask for the names of a few previous clients. Look for credentials and certifications. In the U.S., membership in the Association of Professional Genealogists (APG) is a good indication of their experience. In the UK, look for membership in the Association of Genealogists and Researchers in Archives (AGRA).

Deadlines

Be clear about your expectations and deadlines. State how many hours you agree to pay for and the completion date for the work. If the researcher must travel to a repository, be prepared to pay for their time even if they do not find anything.

Fees

Fees vary greatly and you can negotiate. Shop around and get a sense of the going rate for researchers in the area. Clarify how and when you will make payment(s).

Ask about additional fees for copying or the use of a digital camera at different repositories. The researcher will expect you to cover these expenses. Spell out fees for travel. Expect to pay a retainer, and have the researcher explain how the retainer will be applied to the balance.

Research Report

Expect a full research report and that the researcher will maintain the copyrights to the report. If you want to use any part of the researcher's report in your book, obtain permission. Then quote and adequately attribute the researcher.

Digital Images

If you want the researcher to obtain digital images of documents or other evidence, explain the digital image size and resolution needed.

Where to Find a Professional Researcher

The Association of Professional Genealogists (www.apgen.org) has a database of genealogists for hire by location or specialty. They also have a good checklist for hiring a professional genealogist, (www.apgen.org/articles/hire.html). You will find the code of ethics members agree to abide by on their website.

Progenealogists (www.progenealogists.com) is Ancestry's official research firm. You can get an estimate online and talk with a researcher before agreeing to hire anyone. Genlighten (www.genlighten.com) lists researchers and their specialties such as record types or repositories they will search.

You may find freelance research historians among the members of the American Society of State and Local History (www.aaslh.org) or the Society of American Archivists (www.statearchivists.org). Your local historical museum may also have suggestions.

The following private firms have employees who may take on freelance jobs:

- History Associates (www.historyassociates.com)
- History Factory (www.historyfactory.com)
- Historical Research Associates (hrassoc.com)

At the end of this round of research, you should have most of what you need to compile the book. If your book consists mostly of photographs with captions, read the tips on project management in the next chapter, but then you can skip ahead to Section 4—Production to begin organizing the layout.

If your book contains additional research about the images or a narrative to accompany them, writing and research are a cyclical process. There may be times when you will need to return to research momentarily in order to flesh out important details.

Hopefully, you have been organizing information and images as you have been researching so that you have all of the following:

- A list of images (physical and digital) in folders by person or subject
- Timelines if they will help you put the images in order
- Written notes about each source along with full citations
- Notes and images from your social history research
- Notes and images from your historical context research
- A list of any remaining holes or outstanding items

❧❧

It is time to leave the comfort of research for a time, and start the process of writing. Do not worry. Like golf, you can take a few practice swings before you are expected to make it count. Just in case you are worried about staring down a blank page, the next chapter is full of tips to keep the project moving forward.

Chapter 10

Project Management

Most people experience a bit of anxiety when beginning a new project, and the prospect of having to stare down a blank page may seem daunting. Do not let it stop you. In this chapter, you will find project management advice, and if you have been writing about your images or other sources containing social history or historical context, you already have some bits and pieces started. In other words, you conquered the blank page without even knowing you had.

Before You Begin

The following is a bit of collective wisdom from books, editors, and writing courses to give you a lift before you begin the real work of compiling your photographs, preparing them for print, and writing about them if the project warrants it.

Give Yourself a Round of Applause

Not everyone is willing to undertake a project as big as a book, so congratulations. If you are still reading this book, then you have more tenacity than most people out there who will never get beyond the idea that they will create a photo book ... someday.

Discover What Motivates You

It is not enough to start a book project; you must complete it if anyone is to benefit from it. Focus on how much your family will appreciate learning about their history and seeing the photographs. Know that your ancestors would be proud of the lengths you have gone to preserve their memories. Know that your precious photographs will not end up in the dumpster after you are gone, because there will be a book showcasing them sitting on the shelves of family members and, perhaps, libraries across the country.

Analyze What Makes You Doubt

If you are inexperienced, you are not alone. There are few genealogists or family historians who have created even one photo book, so you are in the same place as most others were when they began. What is the worst that could happen? Nobody dies from a less-than-perfect book. There are no lives on the line. If you finish your book and are unhappy with it, there is always an opportunity to fix it. That version can be a practice run. The next version will be better.

Set a Schedule

To finish your book project, you must devote time to it. The most common advice in the writing community is: "butt in chair." That pretty much says it all. You must *choose* to complete the project and be there to do so. If you complete one page a day, at the end of the year, you will have a 365-page book. You do not have to work in marathon sessions. You can work for fifteen minutes a day or one hour a week.

One caution, however. If you leave too much time between when you work on the book, you may spend most of your time trying to remember what you doing when you left off and what you had planned to tackle next. Schedule your dedicated book time close together to get more actual work done. Continuity is important to keep the project moving forward.

Just Say No

For many, a cloud passing over is excuse enough to abandon work on a book for some other task or activity. You may have to tell the people in your life that when you are working, they are responsible for entertaining, or cooking, or cleaning, or driving—themselves. The withdrawal symptoms (for you and your family) will subside eventually.

Do Not Wait for Inspiration

You cannot wait for the right inspiration or perfect conditions if you expect to complete your book. There will always be laundry to fold, kids to pick up, and additional research that may be interesting. If you wait for perfect conditions, you may as well wait for perfect weather—72 degrees and sunny with a slight breeze blowing gently from the east, but not enough to rustle your papers or muss your hair. You cannot wait for a miracle either—nor a flash of genius—nor divine intervention.

Be Careful Who You Ask for Advice

Think twice about showing your manuscript to friends, family members and particularly to other family historians or genealogists. I wish it were the case that everyone was not only *capable* of offering beneficial advice, but also *willing* to offer constructive criticism. Jack Bickham hits the nail on the head in his book, *The 38 Most Common Fiction Writing Mistakes (And How to Avoid Them)*, when he explains, "There are know-it-alls and know-nothings. If your work is good, many of them will be jealous. If your work is bad, few, if any, of them will know how to point out your mistakes in a constructive manner."

If you need a photo restoration company to fix the flaws in your older photographs, or an editor to help you with the text, hire a professional. If professional help is not in the budget, ask for a volunteer who has learned the ins and outs of photo editing who could teach you, exchange manuscripts with another genealogist working on a photo book, join a genealogical society where you can get constructive feedback from other people who have similar experience, or seek the advice of creative scrapbookers who have experience with page layouts and clever captioning.

Food for Thought

Every book project involves decisions about what to include and what not to include. You have done much of this already by how you guided your research. The following are a few more questions to ask yourself before you begin compiling your photo book.

What Do You Want Your Readers to Know?

By the time the reader finishes the book, what is it you want the reader to understand about your family? Will you be able to convey everything you want in images? Or will you need stories or an explanation to make your meaning clear?

Is there Something You Want Readers to Do?

You may want family members to contact you, continue your research, dig their own photographs out of the attic, or gather for a reunion. If there is something you want family members to do as a result of reading the book, how will you communicate that?

How Will You Handle Sensitive Images?

Not every family has a simple, straightforward past, and not every image conveys a clear, well-meaning message. How much of what you have discovered do you want to reveal? You have an obligation to accuracy, but not at the expense of the feelings of living people. What happened a century ago is fair game, but revealing hurtful or potentially embarrassing, private details about a living relative is not, especially if you have an unflattering photograph to illustrate the point.

How Will You Handle Hearsay?

Most families have legends or stories that have been passed down. Some may be the "God's honest truth," so to speak. Others have been altered and changed over time and have little resemblance to what actually happened. Others are wishful thinking. You may let your reader know what you have been told, and what you have been able to find to confirm it (or not). Dispelling a popular legend may cause disappointment among some family members. Are you prepared to handle their disappointment?

How Will You Deal with Speculation?

If there are relationships you cannot prove, or if your family's involvement in events is uncertain, how will you let the reader know that you are speculating? It is acceptable to let the reader ponder the possibilities. It is not acceptable to imply a connection without proof.

Managing the Project

Any project that has a multitude of "moving parts" can become bogged down. The following are suggestions for keeping your project moving forward.

Schedule When You Are at Your Best

Try not to fit your book project into scattered, unpredictable little pockets of time. Put the project on your schedule at a time when you are at your best and able to focus. If you are a morning person, for example, trying to stay up an hour later to work on the book may not be the best way to spend that hour.

Do not schedule yourself to the point where you are exhausted either. Down time is necessary. If you find that you are spending every spare minute working on the book, re-prioritize so that you have time for breaks and time for the book.

Commit to a Don't List

Manage the distractions, whether they be the phone, the kids, the laundry, Facebook or Twitter. Make yourself a list of don'ts—things you will not do during your scheduled project time. The most common excuse given for not finishing projects is unproductive tasks intruding on the business at hand.

Put multitasking in your list of don'ts while you are at it. Trying to be productive on multiple projects at once often nets poor results for all.

Organize Your Work Space

Nothing bogs a book project down faster than having to stop to search for something "vital." Before you begin compiling the book, take whatever time you need to organize your images and any accompanying text into easy-to-locate folders.

Break the Project Down into a Simple Outline

Start by creating a simple outline of the tasks that need to be accomplished. The following is an example of how your task list could look:

Chapter 10: Grandma and Grandpa Wilson Get Married

> Scan wedding photos (4), repair flaws and discoloration
> Write captions identifying each individual
> Request a photograph of their wedding venue ca 1900 from the local historical society
> Caption: Other family members married there too
> Write a small caption about the minister
> Photograph Grandma's wedding tiara (Aunt Mimi has)

An outline gives you a simple overview of what needs to be done, so you can prepare a schedule that makes sense for the tasks.

Create a Checklist

Use your outline as a checklist. Mark off what you have done and what remains. If it makes more sense, reorganize your checklist into similar projects even if they occur in different parts of the book. For example:

Saturday 1 hr	Scan and repair sepia photographs of: Grandma Wilson's wedding (4) Grandpa Wilson's blacksmith shop (1) Grandpa Wilson's military photos (3)
Tuesday 15 min	Write captions for Grandma Wilson's wedding photos
Saturday 1 hr	Properly size photographs for Chapter 10 Grandma Wilson's wedding portrait (10 x 10) Wedding party (10 x 4.75) Wedding carriage (4.75 x 4.75) Wedding tiara (4.75 x 4.75) Wedding Chapel (10 x 10)

Estimate the Time it Will Take

Expect that everything will take longer than you think it will. Even the best book project managers can underestimate the time it can take to complete a project as long and complex as a book.

I set deadlines because they keep me on track. I also like the flexibility of being able to reschedule some tasks. If I have an hour scheduled for a task that only takes fifteen minutes, I add in another more difficult task in the remaining time. I also like to give myself an out—on occasion. If I am feeling tired or overwhelmed,

I keep a list of "brainless" activities that I can accomplish without a lot of thinking that must be done to complete the book, anyway.

Be cautious with your "happy" tasks. We all have tasks we like more than others but if you burn up all of your happy tasks, then you are left with only the "must do" stuff. That can put a damper on the rest of your schedule. Balance out the difficult or rigorous with the fun or "brainless."

Question Perfectionism

I am all for producing the best book possible, but if you consistently find yourself repeating the same task, or going over the same section again and again, put it aside and work on something else for awhile. Perfection can be an excuse to avoid finishing the project.

Keep the End in Mind

Every task you accomplish contributes to the whole, but sometimes it is hard to see the book when you are looking over a long checklist. Put a picture of a full bookshelf up somewhere you can see while you are working to remind you that someday your book will be proudly displayed on the shelf alongside others.

Celebrate the Milestones

Look at your task list and set a few milestones among the tasks. When you finish the first full-chapter, celebrate. When you finish all of the book's front matter, celebrate. Give yourself permission to do something nice for yourself at each of the milestones. And reserve a really big bear hug, a nice dinner out, or a day at the spa (ball park, ski slope, cabin—whatever tickles your fancy) for the day you finish the book.

❧❧

The only way to go from idea to book is to keep the project moving forward until you finish. Schedule the time and commit to it. If you feel overwhelmed, pick a different aspect of the project temporarily. Come back to the part you left behind when you are feeling more refreshed.

Chapter 11

Organizing Your Images

If you read writer's guides or attend writer's workshops you will hear terms such as vision, focus, and structure. All of these terms imply "the bigger picture." Once you can see the big picture, you can organize your images into an outline.

Vision

Now that you have examined the images you have in your own collection and added to them during the latest round of research, you should have narrowed your vision from what is possible to what is practical based upon what you have. You should be able to state your vision for the book in a short paragraph. For example: "The book covers Grandma Betty's life from 1912 to 2000."

Focus

Focus should describe the main characters and the events depicted. For example: "Grandma Betty was born in Red Bud, Georgia, on a farm, the second of five children. She attended school until age 16 when she became a teacher. She married at the height of the Great Depression and raised six children of her own. Her younger brothers went off to war in Europe and the Pacific while her husband Don, an engineer, built ships at the Navy yard two-hundred miles away. The 1940s are a time of kids, and school, and worry. The 1950s and 1960s are full of grandchildren. By the 1970s, Betty and Don are retired and traveling. In the 1980s there was a 50th wedding anniversary, and a family vacation. The 1990s were full of great-grandchildren. Don died in 1998, and Betty in 2000."

Structure

The structure is more concrete and describes the organization of the book—what happens and when. Using the example above, here are a couple of ideas of how to organize the images, using the organizational structures described in Chapter 9.

Following the example, these are the main events:

- 1912 Betty is born
- 1928 Betty becomes a teacher
- 1932 Don and Betty marry
- 1935, 1938, 1940, 1944, 1946, 1950 children are born
- 1941 the war begins
- 1945 the war ends
- 1956, 1957, 1960, 1962, 1968, 1970 children marry
- 1975 Don retires
- 1975, 1977, 1980, 1984, 1985, 1990, 1993, 1995 major trip dates
- 1998 Don dies
- 2000 Betty dies

Chronologically

Organizing a photo book chronologically one way, and probably the most common way, to organize. If you organize chronologically, time is the unifying factor. The book will follow the outline above with new elements introduced as they occur, so a more detailed outline for 1962 could be:

- April, Don becomes Regional Manager for American Ships
- May 16, Lisa marries Robert Moore
- June 11, Bob and Carol welcome baby James
- August 10, Don and Betty celebrate 30 years together
- November 22, Thanksgiving with the whole family

By Family

Organizing this same book by family means that the dates of each event are less important as who is participating in them. Here is the same example organized by family:

- Betty and her siblings
- Betty and Don - the parents
- Don and Mary and their children
- Lizzie and Steve and their children
- Hope and Will and their children
- Lisa and Bob and their children

...

- Betty and Don - the grandparents

By Topic

Organizing by topic is another way to group events. Here a part of the same example organized by topic:

The War Years

- December 7th, 1941
- Don works at the ship yard
- Robert serves in Europe
- Betty raises kids on ration coupons
- Ellis serves in the Pacific
- VE Day
- Homecoming

Create an Outline

From the last round of research, you should have all of the following:

- A list of images (physical and digital) in folders by person or subject
- Timelines if they will help you put the images in order
- Written notes about each source along with full citations
- Notes and images from your social history research
- Notes and images from your historical context research
- A list of any remaining holes or outstanding items

By now, you should have a good idea of how you want to organize your images. What remains is to determine how the images will work together within a page layout, and how much text should accompany each image. I find the process of layout the book easier if I have a detailed outline to work from. You may find it just as easy to drop images onto the page and add text in the available space as you work.

The following is an example of a detailed outline using one of the topical sections above:

Image—Betty and 3 small children
    Caption, Betty, Don, Lizzie and Hope, 1180 Main St
Image—Ration coupon
    Citation: (endnote) War Ration Book Two, Office of Price Administration, accessed 2 June 2014, http://www.memorialhall.mass.edu/collection/itempage.jsp?itemid=18231. Used with permission from Pocumtuck Valley Memorial Association, Deerfield MA.
    Explanation: see quote [rationbook.txt].
Image—Grandma's Wartime Kitchen (cookbook for rationed food)

❧❧

Use whatever method helps you organize the material best. In the next section, you will determine how much text should accompany each image, if any.

SECTION 3

The goal in this section on writing is for you to explain the images by identifying who or what is depicted, create a first draft, and then edit and polish the captions or manuscript.

Everyone should:

- Caption, explain or identify their photographs.
- Edit. Every book—even one that has only page titles or caption on photographs—deserves a good once over before printing.

Baby Steps

If you are planning to use a drag-and-drop photo book printer, you will still save time by organizing your images and writing the captions before you go to the website to create the book.

Next Steps

If your book consists primarily of photographs and captions, it pays to develop a style guide so that your captions are stylistically consistent.

Once you have a draft, content edit the complete manuscript looking for too many images of one subject, or too few of others, proofread the captions for typos, and fact check. The content editing is an additional step, but your manuscript will be better for it.

Giant Leaps

For longer narratives, once you have a draft, conduct a full edit. Your hard work deserves nothing less.

Chapter 12

Explaining the Images

It would seem that some images in photo books need no explanation. If you are creating a book where every image is familiar to your family—the intended audience—then no explanation or captions may be needed. At least *not right now*. If you are creating a photo book showing images from a 50th wedding anniversary, for example, everyone who is in the book may recognize everyone else. But how about the next generation when they see the book twenty years from now? Will they recognize everyone? Chances are good that they will not. I find it tragic that there are so many photographs of people from days gone by that will never be identified because there is no one left who can recognize the people in the photo.

Most images, therefore, deserve a bit of explanation, to identify the people, the event, date (or approximate date), or the location. There are any number of ways to explain the image on the page including page titles, chapter titles if a much longer explanation will follow, captions and endnotes.

Page Titles

One way to avoid having to caption each and every photograph, especially if they are of the same subject on the same page, is to use a page title. See the example on the next page.

Chapter Titles

If you have a much longer explanation of an image, you may want to title the chapter in a way that describes the image. See the example on the next page.

Emily Anne's

School Days

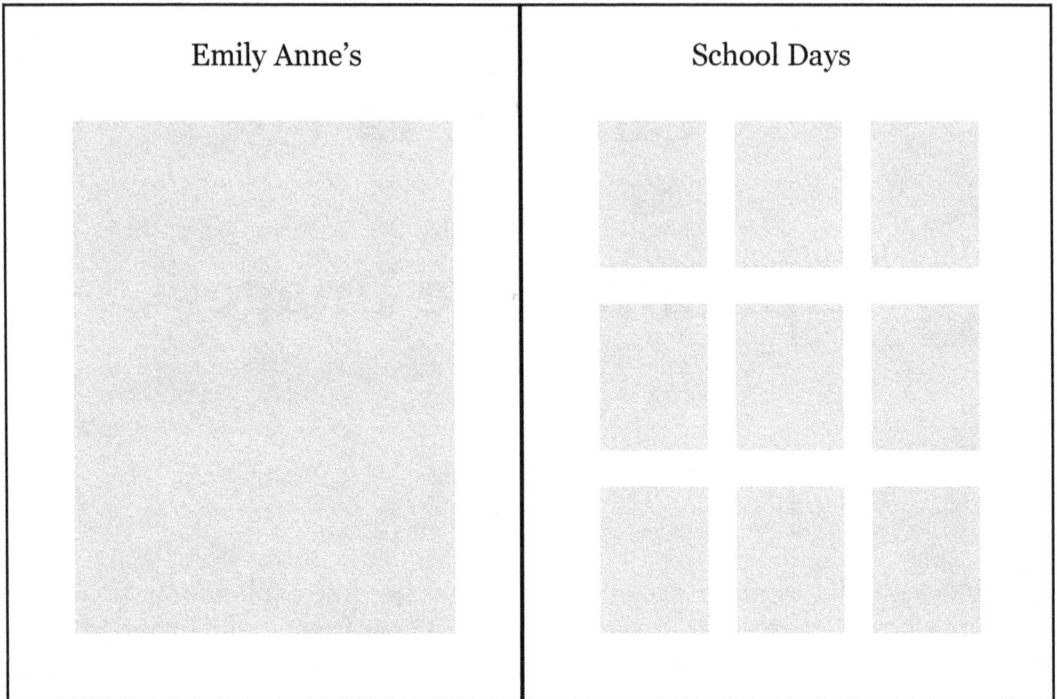

Page title describing the images on the page.

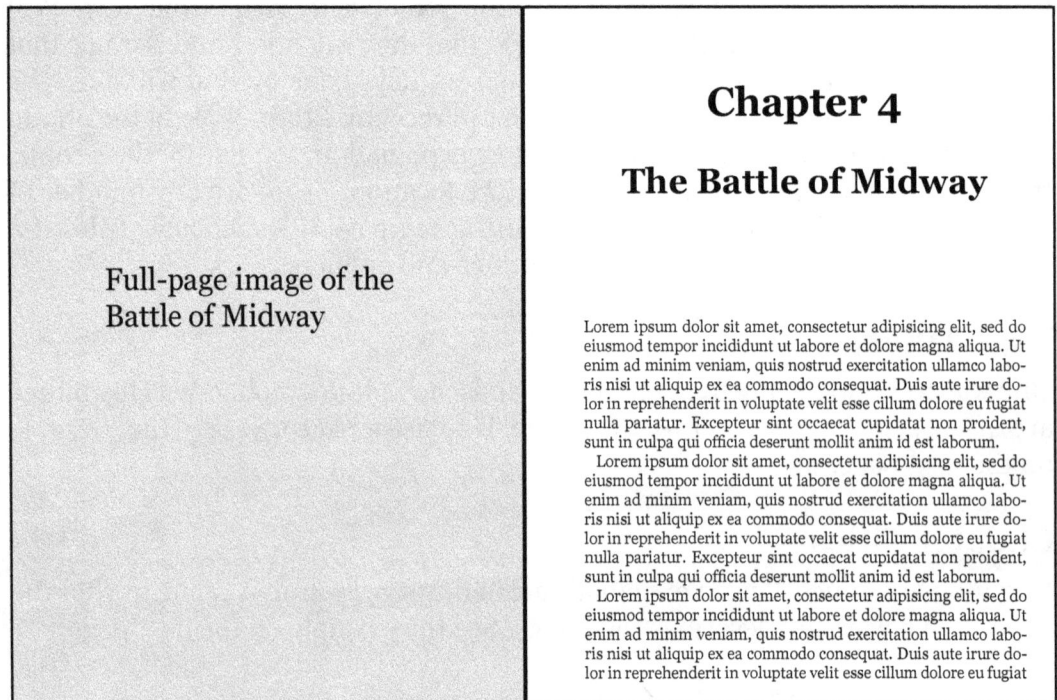

Chapter 4

The Battle of Midway

Full-page image of the Battle of Midway

Lorem ipsum dolor sit amet, consectetur adipisicing elit, sed do eiusmod tempor incididunt ut labore et dolore magna aliqua. Ut enim ad minim veniam, quis nostrud exercitation ullamco laboris nisi ut aliquip ex ea commodo consequat. Duis aute irure dolor in reprehenderit in voluptate velit esse cillum dolore eu fugiat nulla pariatur. Excepteur sint occaecat cupidatat non proident, sunt in culpa qui officia deserunt mollit anim id est laborum.

Lorem ipsum dolor sit amet, consectetur adipisicing elit, sed do eiusmod tempor incididunt ut labore et dolore magna aliqua. Ut enim ad minim veniam, quis nostrud exercitation ullamco laboris nisi ut aliquip ex ea commodo consequat. Duis aute irure dolor in reprehenderit in voluptate velit esse cillum dolore eu fugiat nulla pariatur. Excepteur sint occaecat cupidatat non proident, sunt in culpa qui officia deserunt mollit anim id est laborum.

Lorem ipsum dolor sit amet, consectetur adipisicing elit, sed do eiusmod tempor incididunt ut labore et dolore magna aliqua. Ut enim ad minim veniam, quis nostrud exercitation ullamco laboris nisi ut aliquip ex ea commodo consequat. Duis aute irure dolor in reprehenderit in voluptate velit esse cillum dolore eu fugiat

Chapter name describing the image on the left-hand page.

6   Book Title

Chapter Title   7

Lorem ipsum dolor sit amet, consectetur adipisicing elit, sed do eiusmod tempor incididunt ut labore et dolore magna aliqua. Ut enim ad minim veniam, quis nostrud exercitation ullamco laboris

Lorem ipsum dolor sit amet, consectetur adipisicing elit, sed do eiusmod tempor incididunt ut labore et dolore magna aliqua. Ut enim ad minim veniam, quis nostrud exercitation ullamco laboris nisi ut aliquip ex ea commodo consequat. Duis aute irure dolor in reprehenderit in voluptate velit esse cillum dolore eu fugiat nulla pariatur. Excepteur sint occaecat cupidatat non proident, sunt in culpa qui officia deserunt mollit anim id est laborum.

Lorem ipsum dolor sit amet, consectetur adipisicing elit, sed do eiusmod tempor incididunt ut labore et dolore magna aliqua. Ut enim ad minim veniam, quis nostrud exercitation ullamco laboris nisi ut aliquip ex ea commodo consequat. Duis aute irure dolor in reprehenderit in voluptate velit esse cillum dolore eu fugiat nulla pariatur. Excepteur sint occaecat cupidatat non proident, sunt in culpa qui officia deserunt mollit anim id est laborum.

Lorem ipsum dolor sit amet, consectetur adipisicing elit, sed do eiusmod tempor incididunt ut labore et dolore magna aliqua. Ut enim ad minim veniam, quis nostrud exercitation ullamco laboris

Lorem ipsum dolor sit amet, consectetur adipisicing elit, sed do eiusmod tempor incididunt ut labore et dolore magna aliqua. Ut enim ad minim veniam, quis nostrud exercitation ullamco laboris nisi ut aliquip ex ea commodo consequat. Duis aute irure dolor in reprehenderit in voluptate velit esse cillum dolore eu fugiat nulla pariatur. Excepteur sint occaecat cupidatat non proident, sunt in culpa qui officia deserunt mollit anim id est laborum.

Lorem ipsum dolor sit amet, consectetur adipisicing elit, sed do eiusmod tempor incididunt ut labore et dolore magna aliqua. Ut enim ad minim veniam, quis nostrud exercitation ullamco

Images with captions in a standard book layout using a page layout program.

Lorem ipsum dolor sit amet, consectetur adipisicing elit, sed do eiusmod tempor incididunt ut labore et dolore magna aliqua. Ut enim ad minim veniam, quis nostrud exercitation ullamco laboris nisi ut aliquip ex ea commodo consequat. Duis aute irure dolor in reprehenderit in voluptate velit esse cillum dolore eu fugiat nulla pariatur. Excepteur sint occaecat cupidatat non proident, sunt in culpa qui officia deserunt mollit anim id est laborum.

Exit Glacier, Alaska.

Sed ut perspiciatis unde omnis iste natus error sit voluptatem accusantium doloremque laudantium, totam rem aperiam, eaque ipsa quae ab illo inventore veritatis et quasi architecto beatae vitae dicta sunt explicabo. Nemo enim ipsam voluptatem quia voluptas sit aspernatur aut odit aut fugit, sed quia consequuntur magni dolores eos qui ratione voluptatem sequi nesciunt. Neque porro quisquam est, qui dolorem ipsum quia dolor sit amet, consectetur, adipisci velit, sed quia non numquam eius modi tempora incidunt ut labore et dolore magnam aliquam quaerat voluptatem. Ut enim ad minima veniam, quis nostrum exercitationem ullam corporis suscipit laboriosam, nisi ut aliquid ex ea commodi consequatur? Quis autem vel eum iure reprehenderit qui in ea voluptate velit esse quam nihil molestiae consequatur, vel illum qui dolorem eum fugiat quo voluptas nulla pariatur?

Image with a caption using a text box in word processor.

Captions

Captions are an easy way to include a brief explanation with the image. Typically, the caption is placed below the image, but there may be instances where you may want to place the caption alongside it instead.

There are two easy ways to caption a photograph. The first is to place text with the image. It is easier to do this in a page layout program than in a word processor because the image and the caption will hold their places on the page regardless of what the other text is doing around it. In most word processors, you can add a text box that will hold an image and its caption together as one piece, while the other text flows around (or above and below) the text box. See the examples on the previous page.

Another way to caption images is to add the captions in an image editing program such as Photoshop or Photoshop Elements. This way, the captions will always remain with the image. One caution about doing this, however, is that unless you size the images for the page layout first, you may find the text displayed in many different sizes which will not look as good as when the font size and style are uniform on the page.

Endnotes

Another way to explain your images is to push all of the captions into endnotes. This is one way to maintain the design or look of the pages, showing only the images. The disadvantage is that readers must turn to the back to figure out who or what is on the page.

Credits

One last word about text to accompany your images—some photographs should include credits, mentioning either the photographer who took the picture or the person or institution that owns or holds the image. If you have used historical images from an archive, for example, they may require that you credit the image in a particular way.

If possible, credit the photographer. In some instances, you may have no idea who took the image, but when you can, give credit. Credits can be placed just after the caption or could go into endnotes at the end of a chapter or the end of the book.

❧⌘

Even though it is tempting to forgo the captions or explanation of your images, please do not. At some point in the future, someone will look at those images and be thankful that you identified them.

Chapter 13

Creating Your Own Style Guide

Even if you will only title the page or caption the photographs, maintaining a consistent style is useful. For more lengthy explanations, a consistent style is necessary. Styles vary from newspaper to newspaper, magazine to magazine, and publisher to publisher. There is no one, all-encompassing style guide. There are a few stylistic conventions you may want to conform to because they are what readers will expect, and, usually, because the style helps reading comprehension. The final decisions, however, are up to you.

The purpose of creating your own style guide is to save time while you are compiling or writing the first draft and later when you edit. Create a file or a hand-written list that you can keep handy as you work to record each style decision you make as you make it. That way, you can adhere to your style guide as the book progresses.

Industry Style Guides

The two most used style guides are William Strunk & E.B. White's, *The Elements of Style* (or William Strunk Jr.'s *The Elements of Style, 2014*) and *The Chicago Manual of Style, 16th Edition*. There are dozens of other style guides available, most of which are designed for students, business writing, technical writing or other specific purposes.

Evidence Explained by Elizabeth Shown Mills is a source citation guide not a style guide for the body of the manuscript. You may choose to use her style guide for your footnotes or endnotes, or not.

If you are planning explanations longer than captions and have no experience with formatting a manuscript, you may want to jump ahead and read the four chapters on typesetting to get an idea of what conventions to follow during the production stage before you create styles that conflict with what will make the book look its best and read easiest.

Abbreviations and Acronyms

Use abbreviations to avoid incessant repetition of long expressions. If you abbreviate, be consistent and provide the reader with a key to the abbreviations in the front matter.

Common abbreviations in a genealogy are: born (b.), christened (chr.), married (m.), divorced (div.), died (d.) and buried (bd.). These abbreviations are fine where you are giving the details of a person's life in a short paragraph. In a family photo book, you may wish to confine full details to an appendix or include them as a part of a genealogical chart (see below) rather than trying to include them in a photo caption.

Acronyms, on the other hand, are expected. NASA is a good example. Few people will misidentify NASA as something other than the National Aeronautic and Space Administration. For most acronyms there is no need for punctuation between the letters—so NASA, not N.A.S.A. As with abbreviations, if you create acronyms that are not familiar to the reader, use the full name in the text first, followed by the acronym in parentheses. In some cases, you may want to use the full name a few times so that the reader becomes familiar with the name before switching to an acronym. For example: Rocky Mountain & Overland Stagecoach Company (RM&OS Co.) Include the acronym in your list of abbreviations and acronyms in the front matter.

Genealogical Charts

For the most part, I consider genealogical charts as images rather than text, but I include them here because they can help readers become familiar with the relationships between people at a glance.

Genealogical charts do not have to be uniform throughout the book, but should be consistent enough in appearance and content that the reader can find roughly the same information in each. In other words, do not use a four-generation pedigree chart on one page, and a ten-generation linear chart on the next. If you want to show a large or complex chart, you may want to spread it out across a number of pages rather than trying to make it fit into a single page or spread.

Numbering Systems

Numbering systems are necessary for a *genealogy* to help readers understand relationships. In a family photo book, numbering systems within the captions are probably not necessary because you can use the organization of the photographs or other genealogical charts to establish relationships between people.

If you wish to include a multi-generational descendants list or an ancestors list in an appendix, however, use the Ahnentafel numbering system to go backward in time (ancestors) and the register-style numbering system to come forward in time (descendants). The modified register-style used by the National Genealogical Society Quarterly is also acceptable.

Most genealogical software will generate descendants or ancestors lists for you. If you are not using genealogical software, consult *Genealogical Writing in the 21st Century: A Guide to Register Style and More* by Henry B. Hoff, or *Dollarhide Numbering for Genealogists—An Authorized Guide for the Serious User* by Brian R. Smith.

Place Names

Place names can be tricky in a family photo book because they are not as easy to spell out in their entirety within a caption as they are in a genealogy. In a genealogy, for example, readers would expect to see: Stanley Township, Lyon County, Minnesota, United States. Spelling a place name out that way in a caption may seem odd.

For clarity, however, include full details of each place in footnotes or endnotes, or in an appendix in the back matter. Include city (or township), county, state and country *as they existed* at the time the image was created.

If all locations are within the same country, however, you may indicate that fact somewhere at the beginning of the appendix or place names list, so that you do not have to repeat United States (or other country names) in each listing.

Spell checking place names can be challenging, but necessary. If in doubt, keep a geographical atlas handy while you are writing or get the place name from a good online map site, such as Google Maps or Bing Maps.

Most publishers use the Anglicized names of non-U.S. places when books are written in English because Anglicized names may be more familiar to the reader. How you wish to handle place names, both in the captions and a place names list, is up to you. However, if a place name would be difficult for an English-speaker to recognize in the native language, give reference to both the local version and the Anglicized version. There are some locations (many in Eastern Europe) that have changed hands and languages a number of times for which you may want to give the reader an idea of the time period a place held one name, and when the name changed.

People's Names

In a narrative, use names in the context of the larger explanation of the image. Use people's names as they would have been called at the time the image was created. In a caption, you may not need people's full names to make clear who they are or why they are in the photograph. Take a formal family portrait, for example. The caption could read: "Miller Family 1990. (Back row, l to r) Alan, Chester, William and Thomas. (Front row, l to r) Gina, Belle, and Jenny. In this case, there would be no need to use each individual's full name.

Decide how you will use names and be consistent. If you prefer to use informal names along with the images (e.g. Gina at prom), then make sure full names (e.g. Gina Allison King) appear in a list of family members, ancestors or descendants elsewhere in the book.

The following are a few considerations for people's names:

Spellings

Surnames, in particular, have been known to change over time, or even within close families depending upon individual preference. Sometimes, a name change requires explanation either within the narrative or in a footnote or endnote. If you use a common or single spelling, even though documentary evidence suggests alternatives, explain that somewhere.

Name Changes

When people changed their names entirely, more often than not, an explanation will be necessary. A cross reference in the index and any other list of names would be helpful, as well.

Nicknames

It is fine to use a person's nickname in the narrative or a caption as long as you make it clear somewhere so that the images are not mis-identified by later viewers. For example, you could label an image, "Buddy at age 3," without using his full name, but you would want to include the nickname along with his full name (i.e. Nicholas 'Buddy' Sparks) in the index and any other lists of names, as well.

Women's Names

Women's names can be tricky. In a narrative or caption, a woman should be referred to by the name she would have used at the time she appears in the image. In the index and other lists of names, include both maiden and married names. If a maiden name is unknown, you may want to use a symbol such as "(—)" to inform the reader. The following are examples of ways to list women's names:

Mary Jane Robertson (nee Smith)
Mary Jane (Smith) Robertson
Mary Jane Smith Robertson

Prefixes or Titles

There may be occasions when you want to use Mr., Mrs., or Miss; or a title such as Reverend (Rev.) or Doctor (Dr.) as a prefix to a person's name. Prefixes are helpful to the reader when gender is not obvious from the name or in the image.

Miss Leslie Gore would have a clearer meaning than simply Leslie Gore without other context. Use titles only after the individual earned the title, thus a high-school aged Martin Luther King would not hold the title of Reverend.

If you abbreviate, be consistent. The abbreviations for mister and missus are well-enough known that they need not be included in your list of abbreviations. Reverend (Rev.) and Doctor (Dr.) are well understood, as are most military ranks. If you have any doubts, include the abbreviation in your list.

Suffixes

Suffixes within the narrative can help distinguish one person from the other. Common suffixes are Sr., Jr., a roman numeral (such as III or IV), Esq., MD or M.D. (doctor), PhD or Ph.D. and DDS or D.D.S. (dentist). Some style guides use punctuation in suffixes, others do not.

Business Names

Business names, in general, should be listed however the business uses its own name. So, if the firm of Blanding & Fell, Inc., uses the abbreviation for incorporation after its name, so should you. If, at some point, you choose to abbreviate an unfamiliar business name, use the full name enough times in the narrative for readers to become familiar with it. In academic writing, it is acceptable to use the name once followed by the abbreviation in parentheses and never use the formal name again throughout the work. Readers may be frustrated, however, at having to remember an unfamiliar business name by its abbreviation.

Dates

If you are using captions, keep dates short and sweet according to the genealogical convention below. If you are writing a narrative, keeping dates straight can be a challenge for readers if you do not mention complete dates often. One way to help the reader is to make a change in years clear or to give a complete date often enough to let the reader know how much time has passed during the story.

If you are not sure of the date of an image, it is acceptable to approximate, such as "Grandma Jenny Henderson, about 1940."

The genealogical convention for dates is to use the day (expressed in numbers) followed by the month (spelled out or abbreviated) followed by a four-digit year, such as 24 March 1900 or 24 Mar 1900. The reason for this is clarity. There is no mistaking whether someone is using the American-style Month/Day/Year or the European-style Day/Month/Year. Looking at 9/3/26 leaves readers wondering whether that date is the 9th of March or the 3rd of September? The image should help the reader determine what century, but it is better to be precise.

In narratives, the most common date style is month (spelled out or abbreviated), day (expressed in numbers), followed by a comma, and a four-digit year, such as March 24, 1900, or Mar 24, 1900. Written dates may read better if they are given the way they would be spoken, such as March 24th, 1900.

Numbers

There are long-established rules for numbers that do not occur within dates. Spell out numbers one through ten. Use roman numerals for numbers 11 and greater. These rules are not hard and fast, although most publishers stick to the rules.

Permissions and Credits

If you have historical images and they all come from a single collection, you may want to explain that in the front matter and not include credits or permissions in every caption. Another option is to create a list of permissions or credits and place those in the back matter.

In Quotes or Italics?

Conventional style guides put the titles of articles, short stories and poems in quotes, but the titles of books, plays, magazines, newspapers, films, television programs, major musical compositions, and epic poems in italics. Use italics for foreign words or phrases, and if unfamiliar to your readers, explain them in a glossary. Use italics for the names of ships, aircraft, and space vehicles, as well.

Footnotes or Endnotes

If you are writing a narrative, decide how you will handle the placement of source citations, in footnotes or endnotes, before you begin writing. Most word processing software makes it easy to create either. The important consideration is what you feel will be easiest for your readers.

A suggestion: although footnotes provide instant access to a citation or supplemental information, if your footnotes could squeeze the main text down to less than half the real estate on the page, use endnotes. Most readers are more interested in what happens next than background information or explanation, and will ignore the footnotes anyway.

❧☙

Style guides have evolved over time, but their purpose is to help readers understand the text or the caption. For the most part, following established style guides is in your book's best interest, although there is room for your personal preferences. Consistency is the key.

Chapter 14

Creating the First Draft

The process of creating a first draft is different for each style of photo book. If you will create page titles or captions without any longer narrative, the first draft is more about fitting the images into the layout than writing the captions or text.

If you are writing a longer narrative, you may prefer to get the entire book down on paper before going back to edit. Or, you could tackle one section at a time until the full book shapes up.

Proceed in whatever way makes the most sense to you. However, avoid fiddling and fussing with a single section so much that the thought of finishing the book becomes overwhelming.

Set Up

The set up is different depending on whether you plan to use a drag-and-drop photo book printer or a print-on-demand printer or offset printer.

Images for a Drag-and-Drop Photo Book Printer

For the drag-and-drop printer, you may only need to organize your images and accompanying text because you will not create a master book file to upload all at once. You will upload images as you need them, write or copy and paste the accompanying captions or text, and move on to the next page or page spread (the online tools may show you two pages lying side-by-side as if the book were open, which is a page spread).

If you have your images and text files (.txt) organized into folders for each planned page (or page spread), the process should go quickly. Most drag-and-drop photo book printers allow you to save a project as you go so that you can return to the place you left off if you are unable to finish the entire book at once.

If you plan to add any of the traditional front or back matter to the book such as a copyrights page, an appendix with a complete list of descendants or an index, those pages require a bit more planning depending upon the text tools available online. Section 4: Production has a longer discussion of what constitutes front and back matter. If your project includes front and back matter, you may want to use a print-on-demand or offset printer (see below) rather than a drag-and-drop photo book printer.

Images for a Print-on-Demand or Offset Printer

Print-on-demand or offset printers give you more flexibility in the design of each page. You will design each page (or page spread) in its entirety and save it as a PDF. The PDFs, together in the correct order, will make up the final file the printer will use to create the book.

The simplest route is to create separate files for each page (or page spread) and number them in the order they will appear in the book, front to back. Another method is the one described below for a longer narrative.

Manuscript Files for a Longer Narrative

If you are writing a longer narrative, before you do anything else, set up your book in chapters so that your entire manuscript is not in one enormous file. It will be easier to work with smaller files. If you want feedback from others, you can send a small file at a time, and when you get ready to lay the book out in its final form, you will have all of the parts assembled in a way that makes creating the book easy.

To set up my manuscript files, I use a file-naming convention that lets the computer organize the files for me. I divide the book into front matter (FM), parts (P), chapters (CH) and back matter (BM).

The numbers preceding the file names are split up into front matter, body, and back matter. The front matter files all begin with 00_. Because there are parts in addition to chapters, Part 1 and the chapters within that part are given a file starting number of 10_. Part 2 starts with 20_, and so on. The back matter files start with 60_ because there are only five parts preceding the back matter.

An abbreviated file names list for this book would look like:

001FM_Title Page/Copyrights
002FM_Dedication
...
101P01_Getting Started
102CH1_Who Needs This Book?
...
201P02_Before You Write
202CH6_Identifying Your Target Market

...
301P03_Writing
302CH12_Explaining the Images

...
401P04_Production
402CH16_Creating a Page Layout

...
501P05_Marketing
502CH23_Creating a Marketing Plan

...
601BM_Conclusion
602BM_About the Author

...

Time Savers for Longer Narratives

If you are writing a longer narrative, the following tips are time savers.

Wait to Add Images

If you are writing a longer narrative, wait to add images to the manuscript files. A chapter full of text and images can become quite large, especially if you are adding the images in the correct size and resolution for printing. To save time, wait to add images until you are finished editing. If you need to give yourself a reminder of what image goes where, put the image name in brackets next to the appropriate text (e.g. [grandpa_ca1903.jpg]).

Learn a Few Word Processing Features

A few features in word processing programs can make your writing life easier if you take the time to learn them. Most word processing software has customizable features. Use the help guide in your word processing software to determine how to enable the following functions.

Track Changes. Enabling the Track Changes feature will allow you to show your manuscript to an editor, who can type their suggested changes directly into the document. You then have the option of accepting the changes you want and ignoring the ones you do not without any re-typing.

Customize AutoCorrect. If you find it annoying to type the same location repeatedly, you can set up a command that will automatically fill in the blank as you start typing. For example, if you must repeat the expression, "Clifton Forge, Alleghany County, Virginia," you could set up an AutoCorrect command to replace "Clift" with the full name of the city, county and state.

Customize AutoText. Most word processing programs allow you to build a gallery of frequently typed text or frequently inserted images (such as a logo or an icon), so that a simple combination of a function key and a letter will automatically add the text or image to your document.

Build a Custom Dictionary. If you use foreign words or have names that incorrectly trigger AutoCorrect or the squiggly red line of Spell Check, add them to the dictionary as you use them to save time spell checking later. I have managed to teach Microsoft Word to respect the iTunes company name even when the little "i" begins a sentence.

Use the Synonym Finder. If you are searching for a word and cannot come up with the perfect expression to convey your meaning, type a word with a similar meaning, right-click on the word to activate the synonym finder for suggestions.

Find/Replace. Inevitably, I find mistakes in my manuscripts that could use a good, global Find and Replace, such as double spaces where only one was needed, the persistent misspelling of a name, or an incorrect use of a font or a feature. Each of these can be found and replaced using the Find/Replace feature in your software. In fact, you can replace text with other text, an icon or an image by using the characters "^c" in the replace field. This function grabs whatever you copied into the clipboard and places it into the manuscript.

If You Get Stuck, Get Help

Undertaking a photo book is an incredible task, even for experienced or professional photographers or writers who have an abundance of people with similar experience to ask for help if the project bogs down. For those with less experience, it may take someone with more experience working with photographs or writing books to help you. If you become stuck or frustrated, banish any thoughts of abandoning the project and get help.

Attend a Class on Image Editing

Many local adult-education programs offer courses in using Photoshop or other image editors. Another option is to take a course online at a service such as Lynda.com (www.lynda.com) or Adobe (www.adobe.com). There are also thousands, if not hundreds of thousands of image editing tutorials on YouTube (www.youtube.com).

Use a Professional Scanning Company to Digitize Your Images

If obtaining usable scans is the obstacle, pay a professional scanning company to digitize your images or look for one of FamilySearch's "Photopalooza" days in your area.

Use a Photo Restoration Service

If one or two faded, ripped, stained or torn photographs are stopping you from finishing the book, hire a photo restoration company to fix those images for you.

Attend a Writing Class

Most communities have extension learning courses where adults can take classes. Many local governments, senior services, universities, colleges and community colleges offer extension classes. If you can find a class on creative non-fiction, fantastic. There are some online options for non-fiction writing courses as well, including the Writer's Digest University (www.writersonlineworkshops.com).

Hire a Writing Coach

While you are searching through the extension learning catalogs for your area, look at who are teaching the courses. You may be able to find a writing coach by contacting an instructor. Look at the faculty of your local schools, as well. You may find an excellent writing coach in the local high school English department.

Join a Writer's Group

You can learn good techniques from fiction as well as non-fiction, but be sure to explain to members of the group that there are some lines you cannot cross with a family history—even one in pictures—and remain true to the facts.

Most writer's groups will allow prospective members to attend a few meetings without contributing any writing to observe how the group works. Do so. A meeting or two will give you a feel for how constructive the criticism is and whether the group will be able to give you good advice.

I have a Facebook group called Genealogical Writers and Publishers (www.facebook.com/groups/187826861370278/). Come on in. Ask your questions. Perhaps someone in the group will have a great idea for you.

I have mentioned previously that showing your work to friends or family has potential pitfalls, and I will reiterate that sentiment here. Friends and family members who are not writers tend to fall into two groups—those who do not want to hurt your feelings, and those who do. I must warn you that some people who attend writing classes, coach writers and join writer's groups fall into the same categories.

You need neither obsequious nor domineering critics. If you encounter them, find another way to get help. What you need are honest critics with good intentions, and enough humility to let the good critics guide your writing without diminishing your enthusiasm for the project. Frankly, if you can listen to good criticism of your work and boldly return to the computer the next day to make necessary changes, I have no doubt you will finish your book.

❦

The only thing left to do is to start writing if your book is a longer narrative, and start designing the page layouts if it is not.

Chapter 15

Editing Your Manuscript

Professional editing benefits most books. Unfortunately, professional editing is expensive. If you are going to invest in editing—even if you trade editing projects with another writer—edit the manuscript yourself first, to catch any obvious errors and to make the manuscript the best it can be before you turn it over.

Professional editing addresses a manuscript first from the big, broad strokes (the themes, context, and organization) before looking at the finer details (spelling, punctuation, fact checking and typographical errors). If you are editing a longer narrative, you should do the same—begin with a big-picture look at the book then hone in on the smaller details.

Even while editing the captions on photographs, your priority may be on making sure the correct caption (along with credits and permissions, if appropriate) go with each photograph, and that there are no factual errors within each caption, but also that the captions are consistent in style and tone throughout the book.

What follows are the major steps a professional editor would take on a book-length manuscript. Take from each of these steps whatever is most appropriate to your project.

Context Editing

When a professional editor takes on a manuscript for the first time, the initial read through should reveal whether the book feels like a single entity or whether there are loose ends that need to be clipped or re-worked.

Does the manuscript reflect your focus for the project? Have you maintained the focus you intended or have you strayed into tangents? Straying is easy, especially if the additional information or stories are delicious. Bringing the focus back to your original intent, however, may tighten up the book and make it feel more coherent overall.

Did you focus too narrowly? If your focus changed while writing and the book feels complete as is, fine.

Is your meaning clear? Is the book organized logically? Is there anything about the way the images are organized or how the explanations are given that will confuse readers?

To edit a book with mostly images and captions, use the screen version. (This goes for each of the following editing steps as well. Printing a full-color version to make multiple round of edits will become expensive, and is mostly unnecessary if you are editing mostly captions.) Before you begin editing on the screen, set the book aside for a few days or a week so that when you look at it again, it is with fresh eyes. Then move through the manuscript page by page checking for flow and consistency.

When context editing a longer narrative, make a copy so that you can eliminate the images. Set the font to a comfortable size to read, and use margins of an inch or more so that you have room to write notes while you edit. Take your manuscript file to the local copy shop and have it printed on both sides of each page, and spiral bound. Even though the book will not be formatted or bound as it will be for final production, it will give you a sense of how the book reads.

If the manuscript requires changes, make them before you move to the next stage of editing.

Content Editing

Content editing is about making certain you wrote what you meant. Author and editor William Zinsser describes it as, "stripping down every sentence to its cleanest components." I like to describe it as making sure every sentence conveys your meaning and sounds like you wrote it.

I do not think a photo book or family photo history must be written with such strict adherence to literary and grammatical rules that it comes out sounding like Leo Tolstoy wrote it. However, deleting the clutter, making meaning clear, assuring subjects and verbs agree, keeping to the active not passive voice when appropriate, and using smooth transitions between explanatory elements will make your book better.

The content editing stage is also where you evaluate whether you have given some subjects too much attention (overkill). If you have explained what should be common knowledge or common sense, eliminate it. Admittedly, cutting good writing is difficult. Deleting words or phrases you have struggled to put down on the page can be painful. However, if a slimmer, sleeker version explains the images better, cut away.

When you are ready to edit for content, print your manuscript. Errors and contradictions are more obvious on paper than on the computer screen. Double space anything longer than a caption so that it will be easy to make corrections between the lines. Print it single-sided on three-hole-punch paper, so you can remove a small section at a time from a binder, to edit. Make any changes necessary before moving on to copy editing.

Copy Editing

I promised no death by grammar, but the copy editing stage is when you *should* closely examine your words.

Have you mixed your metaphors, or used the active voice when a passive construction would be clearer? Have you let commas or exclamation points run amok? Have you used parallel construction in compound sentences and bulleted lists? Have any malapropisms slipped in? Do subjects and verbs agree, and have you used pronouns properly without muddling the meaning?

Have you followed your style sheet? Do dates conform? Are names spelled the way you intended throughout the book? Are abbreviations and acronyms consistent? Are sources cited appropriately?

Copy editing is what author Guy Kawasaki, in his book *APE: Author, Publisher, Entrepreneur—How to Publish a Book,* describes as "turning an amateurish book into a polished, professional one."

One of my favorite resources is *The Copyeditor's Handbook: A Guide for Book Publishing and Corporate Communications* by Amy Einsohn. She gives easy-to-read explanations for the most common grammatical errors and problems. Before you begin copy editing, you may want to consult this book.

The following software will check grammar, word use and suggest changes:

- Grammerly (www.grammerly.com)
- Hemmingway App (www.hemingwayapp.com)
- StyleWriter (www.stylewriter-usa.com)

While context and content editing take time, for me, copy editing is a chore. In fact, my house is never cleaner than during the copy editing stage because even cleaning out the garage can look like a lark, by comparison.

Steel yourself. Print out anything longer than a caption double spaced, single sided on three-hole-punched paper so you can pull out a small section at a time from a binder. Set up a comfortable chair and table on which to spread out your style guide, a good dictionary, and a copy editing reference, or your laptop if you prefer Internet-based guides. I give you permission to stay in your jammies, drink as much coffee as you require, and consume an entire box of chocolates if need be.

Fact Checking

If you misstate facts, someone will notice and take issue with it. Errors not only cast doubt on other facts within the book, they diminish your relationship with your readers. Not every reader will notice every error, mind you, but if you can catch the errors before readers have a chance to, why not?

Some writers will fact check while copy editing. I cannot. I prefer to have the language in tip top shape before I crawl through every date, place and event in the book for accuracy. I will correct errors as I catch them, however, in whatever stage of editing it happens.

The most common errors that sneak into family photo books and historical photo histories are:

Wrong Dates

In particular, look for places where the century was mis-typed. A person cannot die in 1919 and be born in 1956. Not many people live past one hundred, let alone more than one hundred and ten. Watch for dates that make a lifespan highly improbable.

Wrong Places

Arkansas is not abbreviated as AK. Abbreviations tend to be misused much more often than actual place names. However, look for places where the same city is listed in different counties, or the same counties are listed in different states. A change of boundaries can lead to the circumstance above, but make sure there is an explanation so that the reader does not assume you made an error.

Improbable Events

Look for events that were unlikely to have happened. Not many soldiers enlisted at the age of nine. If it happened and you have documentary evidence of it, fantastic. Look for women having children before or after their child-bearing years, and children attributed to women who have already died or not yet married their husbands. These children are most probably the result of a different marriage.

John Colletta tells the story of the letter he received from an ornithologist who read Colletta's book, *Only a Few Bones: A True Account of the Rolling Fork Tragedy and Its Aftermath*. The ornithologist took issue with the description of starlings in the book, explaining that starlings were not introduced into the area until later. An incorrect fact about something as easy to gloss over as the presence of a specific species of bird, damaged the credibility of the book for that reader.

Graphic Elements

For longer narratives, I usually wait until I have a manuscript in its best shape before I add images. Some writers prefer to see the images with the text as they write, and I appreciate that. If you have done so, great. If you have not, whether you add them now before a final proofread or as a part of your final draft, is up to you.

During the discussion of scanning in Chapter 8: Scanning and Optical Character Recognition, I made a suggestion that you scan each image at a size and resolution big enough for print production. One thing that is hard to determine at this stage, however, is the exact size you will need based upon the layout you will choose for the final book. Chapter 16: Creating a Page Layout will cover this.

Another consideration is whether you will create an eBook version because the size and resolution, as well as where the images are placed within an eBook, are different than for a print edition.

The best time-saving advice I can give you is to leave the images out until the manuscript is as close to perfect as it is ever going to be. That way, you can make a copy of the manuscript to be used for an eBook version and another for the print edition because the images will be placed into the manuscript in different ways. In addition, I usually leave one copy of the completed manuscript alone as a backup, and work from copies to create final eBook and print editions.

Once images are added in their appropriate size, resolution and placement for as many editions are you are planning, you can proofread the captions, copyrights and permissions that go along with the images.

Proofreading

I am sure you must be thinking, "I have just edited a half a dozen times, and now I have to proofread?" Well, yes. Every time you make changes to the manuscript, you introduce the possibility that an error crept in.

While spell check and grammar editors are helpful tools, there is nothing like a fresh set of eyes to catch the errors that software-based tools cannot. Your word processor will not alert you if you typed lack, when you meant lake.

Proofreading is a task that you could hand over to a paid professional or someone who is well-read. Make your instructions clear, however, that you are asking for proofreading, not editorial advice.

Many proofreaders read each page starting at the bottom so that they are looking at snippets of sentences rather than whole passages. Misspellings are easier to spot this way. The misuse of words is easier to spot, however when reading in context.

If you hand over a printed copy to proof, ask your proofreader to use a red pen, common proofreader's marks, and to place a small "x" in the margin wherever a change has been made. You will find a nice chart of proofreader's marks on the Merriam-Webster website (www.merriam-webster.com/mw/table/proof-rea.htm). A more efficient method, however, is to use the review features of your word processor (e.g. Track Changes in Word) so that your proofreader can type directly into a copy of the manuscript file, and so you can accept or reject any changes with the click of a mouse.

Typescript Editing

The next stage in the publishing process is production, where you will typeset (format) the manuscript. It is not unusual for errors to creep in during the type-setting process. Typescript editing is one final chance to make changes. It occurs after the manuscript has been typeset or laid out as an eBook, and is described more fully in Chapter 22: Preparing the Final Files.

Making changes to the typescript can be problematic. It is frustrating to have to re-work perfect-looking pages to correct a misused word or phrase, and if a professional typesets your manuscript, changes can be expensive.

⌘⌘

Every manuscript can use a good edit. There are many people who can catch typos for you, fewer who can fact check, and even fewer who can conduct a professional edit while giving constructive advice. Professional editors are good at what they do, and charge accordingly. If your book is likely to appeal to the general public and therefore generate thousands of sales, you may wish to invest in professional editing before you release the book.

Working with an Editor

Editors help authors express what they mean. Editors know when to stick to the rules and when to break them. They look for consistency and fix muddled meaning. Most books benefit from professional editing, but a good editor can be expensive. Editors offer a range of services similar to the styles of editing described above. The more comprehensive the edit, the greater the cost.

Cost

Most editors charge either by the page or by the hour. The more experienced the editor, the more the hourly rate makes sense. Ask for an estimate based upon the number of pages in the final manuscript on standard paper with normal margins, double-spaced. An editor usually will want to see the table of contents and at least a chapter or two prior to giving you an estimate.

Portfolio

Most editors will be able to point you to commercially available work they have edited, and will have chapters or article-length pieces ready to show you.

Expectations

It is important for both you and the editor to make expectations clear in the beginning. Ask for what the book needs. The job and the cost of proofreading are different than content or context editing. Some editors do not proofread. They specialize in the bigger picture and will leave the proofreading or fact checking to others.

If you are asking for a more comprehensive edit, most editors will offer to edit a chapter to give you an idea of the editor's style before you give the go-ahead.

Personal Style

Good editors will tell you what you *need* to hear rather than what you *want* to hear about your work. That part of the job is not easy. Your editor should offer criticism in a way that will inspire you to make changes for the good of the book. He or she will never belittle or undermine your confidence. If you run into an editor who consistently rubs you the wrong way, find another editor.

Professional Style

The most common conflict between authors and editors is stylistic. No editor and author will write exactly the same way. Editors do not have the final say in what stays or goes in your manuscript, you do. Most editors will not suggest changes that alter your writing style without good reason. A good editor, when confronting stylistic problems, will stop the editing process and consult you before proceeding. There may be instances where your style conflicts enough with the editor's that choosing a different editor is best. A good editor will recognize this and tell you.

Be open to suggestion, however. Editors edit. They are going to make changes. Read the changes with an open mind, and if need be, leave it alone for a few days, and come back for a fresh look. A good editor wants you to be successful. He or she is making suggestions in the best interest of the manuscript.

Give the editor your best work. Run the spelling and grammar check. Use proper capitalization and punctuation. Give the book a good once-over before you give it to your editor.

Communication

Communication is a two-way street. If you hear feedback that does not make sense or hurts your feelings, say so. Misunderstandings have ruined many an author-editor relationship. If you have a question, ask. If you do not like the direction things are going, say so. Keep frustration between you and your editor private. Leave it out of your Twitter feed and off of your Facebook page. Spouting off in public will not end well.

Follow the Instructions

Most editors have a process. Give the manuscript to your editor in the form they prefer and follow the instructions for accepting or rejecting changes. The goal is to get the manuscript back to you in the fewest number of complete edits to keep costs down. If you make changes during the initial edit, for example, each section you change must be re-edited as a part of the whole. Anything that slows down the process, raises the cost.

Deadlines

Both you and your editor have schedules and deadlines to meet. Be realistic when setting deadlines to make certain you can both meet them. Giving an editor a month with your manuscript is a starting point. And, your book may be competing with others for time in the editor's schedule.

Write a Formal Proposal or Contract

Once you have a cost estimate from the editor, write an additional proposal making your expectations clear about the work to be done as well as deadlines for submissions, returns, and payment. Expect to pay half down, and half upon completion. Include how you will send the manuscript, receive changes, and communicate with the editor. Include all charges and fees, as well as a do-not-exceed clause if you want the editor to stick within a defined budget.

A Less-Costly Alternative

Some authors crowdsource the editing. They put the manuscript up online, ask readers for feedback and require that no one distribute the book. I like this idea for a non-fiction or a how-to book, but it is probably not the best idea for a family history unless the people you are asking for opinions are other genealogists or family historians. Crowdsourcing may work best in the early stages of planning while you are still gathering ideas. Beware, also, the potential pitfalls. You may get stellar advice, or you may get drivel—and the drivel is often mean-spirited.

꧁꧂

I often feel triumphant when finishing a manuscript. Unfortunately, triumph fades when the shadow of editing looms. Be kind to yourself in the first round of editing. Read the book through and put it away for a few days. Post pictures of family nearby to remind you who your readers will be. Then, return to editing with a critical eye and a red pen to benefit the book.

SECTION 4

The goal in this section is for you to learn how to produce a book that looks as good and reads as easily as any book produced by a traditional publisher.

There is not enough space in this book to give instructions for formatting using each of the major word processing or page layout programs. The terminology used in this section, however, should give you what you need to use the help features in your software to accomplish each task.

Most of this Section is devoted to print production because most family histories are printed. If you are interested in producing an electronic or online version of your book, there is information about those formats in Chapter 22: Preparing the Final Files, or a more comprehensive look at the process is available in *Set Yourself Up to Self-Publish: A Genealogist's Guide*.

Everyone should:

- Read Chapter 16 about page layouts.
- Read the section in Chapter 17 about the elements that affect readability.
- Read Chapter 21 regarding designing a good cover.

Baby Steps

If you going to use a drag-and-drop photo book printer, you will have to use the page templates available through the printer's online tools, but you may get a few ideas for customizing the printer's layouts. Most of the other typesetting and final file information will not apply.

Next Steps

If you are planning a book with mostly photographs and captions, skim Chapters 18 and 20 on typesetting the front and back matter because you may wish to include some of these elements in your book. Read Chapter 22 on preparing final files for the printer.

Giant Leaps

If your book features photographs but contains a longer narrative, read each chapter in this section. Learning how to properly typeset your book will make it look as good as any publisher could.

Note: In this section you will see examples that are filled with text beginning, "Lorem ipsum." Latin text is used as filler so that you can see how different layouts would look.

Chapter 16

Creating a Page Layout

The most important element in a photo book is laying out the pages to feature the photographs and, if there is additional text, to make the pages easy to read. Too much work goes into choosing photographs and creating a book to have that effort spoiled by poor design, when good design is so easy to accomplish.

The best way to create a good page layout design is to follow the long-established rules of readability. Desktop publishing offers many options for innovative ways to create columns, employ fonts, and place illustrations—too many perhaps. Leave the wild innovating to the graphic designers on magazine staffs. The tried and true rules for book design are still the best.

Page Size

How much real estate you have to work with depends upon the trim size of the page. The trim size is the finished size of the book. Choosing a trim size pits look against cost, and usability. A 12" x 12" coffee table book is fabulous to look at, but a 6" x 9" book is much easier to sit and read. Here is where the type of photo book is of great importance. If you are showcasing a few historical images with a lot of narrative to back up your research about each image, a smaller, easy-to-read page size may be better than a larger format. You could still use an entire 6" x 9" page to show a single image, followed by multiple pages of text. A book of photographs with captions, on the other hand, may look and read better in a larger 12" x 12" format.

Your choice of printer also makes a difference. An offset printer can create books in just about any size, but you must order a minimum number of books to make the price per book worth it. If the cost of setup for a run of specially sized books is $500 and the print-per-book charge is $20, if you only order 10 books, the cost per book would be $70 ($50 + $20).

PUBLISH A PHOTO BOOK

You will save money if you choose one of the common page sizes offered by print-on-demand printers. Most print-on-demand printers do not charge a fee for setup, they only charge to produce each book—and they can produce books one at a time. The most common page sizes for print-on-demand printers are (in inches) 6 x 9, 7 x 10, 8 x 10 and 8.5 x 11 for books with lots of text, or 8.5 x 8.5, 9 x 7, 10 x 8, 12 x 12 or 13 x 11 in full-color photo-quality books.

No matter what page size you choose, the rules for good layout are essentially the same. The one small exception is that the larger the page, the larger proportionally the elements such as fonts, white space and images should be.

Page Count

Book interiors must be multiples of two (front and back of a single sheet). If you use an offset printer, they may require page counts in signatures (multiples) of 4, 8, 16, 32, 48, 64 or even 80. Offset printers print use paper on rolls many feet wide, and when the paper is folded and cut, it will form a signature of one of the multiples of four (4).

Signatures can be an issue if, for example, you have written a one hundred-page book, but the printer's signature requirement is eighty pages. In that case, you would have to reduce your book by twenty pages, or increase it by sixty pages in order to meet the signature requirement. Otherwise, you would have sixty blank pages at the end of your one hundred-page book.

Luckily, print-on-demand printers use simple two-page signatures—front and back.

Blank Pages

By publishing tradition, chapters and most front matter and back matter elements, should begin on a right-hand page. You may have blank pages if a chapter runs an odd number of pages because the last page will be blank so that the next element will begin on a right-hand page.

If you have blank pages, they should be completely blank—no headers and no page numbers.

White Space

The biggest misconception about laying out a book is that you must economize the space by cramming as much as you can onto a single page. Please do not. The reader needs a break from solid text either from the margins around the edges, the space between columns, paragraphs, words, and letters, or all of the above.

Images need a bit of breathing room around them as well. Too many images on a page crammed together with little space in between makes it difficult to distinguish when one image ends and another begins.

Altering the spacing between the letters (tracking) and the space between the lines of text (leading) can make the page look more or less dense. If you want to

---

Lorem ipsum dolor sit amet, consectetur adipisicing elit, sed do eiusmod tempor incididunt ut labore et dolore magna aliqua. Ut enim ad minim veniam, quis nostrud exercitation ullamco laboris nisi ut aliquip ex ea commodo consequat. Duis aute irure dolor in reprehenderit in voluptate velit esse cillum dolore eu fugiat nulla pariatur. Excepteur sint occaecat cupidatat non proident, sunt in culpa qui officia deserunt mollit anim id est laborum.

Lorem ipsum dolor sit amet, consectetur adipisicing elit, sed do eiusmod tempor incididunt ut labore et dolore magna aliqua. Ut enim ad minim veniam, quis nostrud exercitation ullamco laboris nisi ut aliquip ex ea commodo consequat. Duis aute irure dolor in reprehenderit in voluptate velit esse cillum dolore eu fugiat nulla pariatur. Excepteur sint occaecat cupidatat non proident, sunt in culpa qui officia deserunt mollit anim id est laborum.

Lorem ipsum dolor sit amet, consectetur adipisicing elit, sed do eiusmod tempor incididunt ut labore et dolore magna aliqua. Ut enim ad minim veniam, quis nostrud exercitation ullamco laboris nisi ut aliquip ex ea commodo consequat. Duis aute irure dolor in reprehenderit in voluptate velit esse cillum dolore eu fugiat nulla pariatur. Excepteur sint occaecat cupidatat non proident, sunt in culpa qui officia deserunt mollit anim id est laborum.

Lorem ipsum dolor sit amet, consectetur adipisicing elit, sed do eiusmod tempor incididunt ut labore et dolore magna aliqua. Ut enim ad minim veniam, quis nostrud exercitation ullamco laboris nisi ut aliquip ex ea commodo consequat. Duis aute irure dolor in reprehenderit in voluptate velit esse cillum dolore eu fugiat nulla pariatur. Excepteur sint occaecat cupidatat non proident, sunt in culpa qui officia deserunt mollit anim id est laborum.

Lorem ipsum dolor sit amet, consectetur adipisicing elit, sed do eiusmod tempor incididunt ut labore et dolore magna aliqua. Ut

Lorem ipsum dolor sit amet, consectetur adipisicing elit, sed do eiusmod tempor incididunt ut labore et dolore magna aliqua. Ut enim ad minim veniam, quis nostrud exercitation ullamco laboris nisi ut aliquip ex ea commodo consequat. Duis aute irure dolor in reprehenderit in voluptate velit esse cillum dolore eu fugiat nulla pariatur. Excepteur sint occaecat cupidatat non proident, sunt in culpa qui officia deserunt mollit anim id est laborum.

Lorem ipsum dolor sit amet, consectetur adipisicing elit, sed do eiusmod tempor incididunt ut labore et dolore magna aliqua. Ut enim ad minim veniam, quis nostrud exercitation ullamco laboris nisi ut aliquip ex ea commodo consequat. Duis aute irure dolor in reprehenderit in voluptate velit esse cillum dolore eu fugiat nulla pariatur. Excepteur sint occaecat cupidatat non proident, sunt in culpa qui officia deserunt mollit anim id est laborum.

Lorem ipsum dolor sit amet, consectetur adipisicing elit, sed do eiusmod tempor incididunt ut labore et dolore magna aliqua. Ut enim ad minim veniam, quis nostrud exercitation ullamco laboris nisi ut aliquip ex ea commodo consequat. Duis aute irure dolor in reprehenderit in voluptate velit esse cillum dolore eu fugiat nulla pariatur. Excepteur sint occaecat cupidatat non proident, sunt in culpa qui officia deserunt mollit anim id est laborum.

Lorem ipsum dolor sit amet, consectetur adipisicing elit, sed do eiusmod tempor incididunt ut labore et dolore magna aliqua. Ut enim ad minim veniam, quis nostrud exercitation ullamco laboris nisi ut aliquip ex ea commodo consequat. Duis aute irure dolor in reprehenderit in voluptate velit esse cillum dolore eu fugiat nulla

Dense page (left); Less dense (right).

make the page look a little less dense or dark, use a book font such as Bookman because it is wider and more open, rather than a newspaper font such as Times which is thin and meant to be read in narrow newspaper columns. By increasing the space between the lines of text (leading) or between the paragraphs, the page will look less dense. In the example, the page on the left looks dense. The one on the right is much more open.

While giving the page white space, you must also follow the rules governing proximity. Proximity means that objects that belong together should be closer to each other. A caption for a photograph, for example, should be closer to the bottom of the photograph than the next line of text.

Even spacing, between paragraphs or between subheads and paragraphs, is a red flag that the person who designed the layout has little experience. It is easiest in a word processing program to use double returns to separate paragraphs, or to put extra space between a paragraph and the next headline or subhead. Easiest, yes. Most attractive, no. Use styles to create additional space either above or below paragraphs, headlines or subheads without using an extra return. A headline or a subhead should be closer to the text below it than the paragraph above it. In the example on the next page, the type on the left has even spacing. The type on the right has correct spacing.

Lorem ipsum dolor sit amet, consectetur adipisicing elit, sed do eiusmod tempor incididunt ut labore et dolore magna aliqua. Ut enim ad minim veniam, quis nostrud exercitation ullamco laboris nisi ut aliquip ex ea commodo consequat. Duis aute irure dolor in reprehenderit in voluptate velit esse cillum dolore eu fugiat nulla pariatur. Excepteur sint occaecat cupidatat non proident, sunt in culpa qui officia deserunt mollit anim id est laborum.

Headline Headline Headline

Lorem ipsum dolor sit amet, consectetur adipisicing elit, sed do eiusmod tempor incididunt ut labore et dolore magna aliqua. Ut enim ad minim veniam, quis nostrud exercitation ullamco laboris nisi ut aliquip ex ea commodo consequat. Duis aute irure dolor in reprehenderit in voluptate velit esse cillum dolore eu fugiat nulla pariatur. Excepteur sint occaecat cupidatat non proident, sunt in culpa qui officia deserunt mollit anim id est laborum.

Headline Headline Headline

Lorem ipsum dolor sit amet, consectetur adipisicing elit, sed do eiusmod tempor incididunt ut labore et dolore magna aliqua. Ut enim ad minim veniam, quis nostrud exercitation ullamco laboris nisi ut aliquip ex ea commodo consequat. Duis aute irure dolor in reprehenderit in voluptate velit esse cillum dolore eu fugiat nulla pariatur. Excepteur sint occaecat cupidatat non proident, sunt in culpa qui officia deserunt mollit anim id est laborum.
    Lorem ipsum dolor sit amet, consectetur adipisicing elit, sed do eiusmod tempor incididunt ut labore et dolore magna aliqua. Ut enim ad minim veniam, quis nostrud exercitation ullamco laboris

Lorem ipsum dolor sit amet, consectetur adipisicing elit, sed do eiusmod tempor incididunt ut labore et dolore magna aliqua. Ut enim ad minim veniam, quis nostrud exercitation ullamco laboris nisi ut aliquip ex ea commodo consequat. Duis aute irure dolor in reprehenderit in voluptate velit esse cillum dolore eu fugiat nulla pariatur. Excepteur sint occaecat cupidatat non proident, sunt in culpa qui officia deserunt mollit anim id est laborum.

Headline Headline Headline
Lorem ipsum dolor sit amet, consectetur adipisicing elit, sed do eiusmod tempor incididunt ut labore et dolore magna aliqua. Ut enim ad minim veniam, quis nostrud exercitation ullamco laboris nisi ut aliquip ex ea commodo consequat. Duis aute irure dolor in reprehenderit in voluptate velit esse cillum dolore eu fugiat nulla pariatur. Excepteur sint occaecat cupidatat non proident, sunt in culpa qui officia deserunt mollit anim id est laborum.

Headline Headline Headline
Lorem ipsum dolor sit amet, consectetur adipisicing elit, sed do eiusmod tempor incididunt ut labore et dolore magna aliqua. Ut enim ad minim veniam, quis nostrud exercitation ullamco laboris nisi ut aliquip ex ea commodo consequat. Duis aute irure dolor in reprehenderit in voluptate velit esse cillum dolore eu fugiat nulla pariatur. Excepteur sint occaecat cupidatat non proident, sunt in culpa qui officia deserunt mollit anim id est laborum.
    Lorem ipsum dolor sit amet, consectetur adipisicing elit, sed do eiusmod tempor incididunt ut labore et dolore magna aliqua. Ut enim ad minim veniam, quis nostrud exercitation ullamco laboris nisi ut aliquip ex ea commodo consequat. Duis aute irure dolor in reprehenderit in voluptate velit esse cillum dolore eu fugiat nulla

Even spacing (left); Correct proximity (right).

Page Spreads

Books are laid out in spreads (pages side by side), not individual pages. When a reader opens a book, they see page spreads as a single visual unit. Because of the binding in the center, right and left pages are laid out differently. The rules for what goes on each side of the page spread follows shortly. The rules are slightly different for books with traditional chapters that have headers and page numbers, and books with photographs and captions only. Let us look at the rules for more traditional books in this section. Less traditional layout suggestions for photo books will follow.

Grids

A basic grid pattern imposes order on the layout. Grids align objects and space them properly which is pleasing to the eye. Used throughout, grids employ repetition to help the reader move through the book easily. This is true of photo books and more traditional books with chapters.

Grids help with consistency. For the most part, columns should be the same width and used to help the text fit within the grid. Images should be sized to fit the grid and maintain uniform distance from the text. Grids are determined by margins, columns, and the size of the page. The smaller the page, the fewer col-

6   Book Title

Chapter Title   7

3x4 grid (left); 3x3 grid (right).

6   Book Title

Chapter Title   7

2x2 grid (left); 2x3 grid (right).

Lorem ipsum dolor sit amet, consectetur adipisicing elit, sed do eiusmod tempor incididunt ut labore
et dolore magna aliqua. Ut enim ad minim veniam,
quis nostrud exercitation ullamco laboris nisi ut
aliquip ex ea commodo consequat. Duis aute irure
dolor in reprehenderit in voluptate velit esse cillum
dolore eu fugiat nulla pariatur. Excepteur sint occaecat cupidatat non proident, sunt in culpa qui officia
deserunt mollit anim id est laborum.

Lorem ipsum dolor sit amet, consectetur adipisicing elit, sed do eiusmod tempor incididunt ut labore
et dolore magna aliqua. Ut enim ad minim veniam,
quis nostrud exercitation ullamco laboris nisi ut
aliquip ex ea commodo consequat. Duis aute irure
dolor in reprehenderit in voluptate velit esse cillum
dolore eu fugiat nulla pariatur. Excepteur sint occaecat cupidatat non proident, sunt in culpa qui officia
deserunt mollit anim id est laborum.

Lorem ipsum dolor sit amet, consectetur adipisicing elit, sed do eiusmod tempor incididunt ut labore
et dolore magna aliqua. Ut enim ad minim veniam,
quis nostrud exercitation ullamco laboris nisi ut
aliquip ex ea commodo consequat. Duis aute irure
dolor in reprehenderit in voluptate velit esse cillum
dolore eu fugiat nulla pariatur. Excepteur sint occaecat cupidatat non proident, sunt in culpa qui officia

Lorem ipsum dolor sit amet,
consectetur adipisicing elit,
sed do eiusmod tempor in-
cididunt ut labore et dolore
magna aliqua. Ut enim ad
minim veniam, quis nostrud
exercitation ullamco laboris
nisi ut aliquip ex ea commodo consequat. Duis aute
irure dolor in reprehenderit
in voluptate velit esse cillum

Lorem ipsum dolor sit amet,
consectetur adipisicing elit,
sed do eiusmod tempor in-
cididunt ut labore et dolore
magna aliqua. Ut enim ad
minim veniam, quis nostrud

Lorem ipsum dolor
sit amet, consectetur
adipisicing elit, sed do
eiusmod tempor incidi-
dunt ut labore et dolore
magna aliqua. Ut enim
ad minim veniam, quis
nostrud exercitation
ullamco laboris nisi ut
aliquip ex ea commodo
consequat. Duis aute
irure dolor in repre-
henderit in voluptate
velit esse cillum dolore
eu fugiat nulla pariatur.
Excepteur sint occaecat
cupidatat non proident,
sunt in culpa qui officia
deserunt mollit anim id
est laborum.

Lorem ipsum dolor
sit amet, consectetur
adipisicing elit, sed do
eiusmod tempor incidi-
dunt ut labore et dolore
magna aliqua. Ut enim
ad minim veniam, quis
nostrud exercitation
ullamco laboris nisi ut
aliquip ex ea commodo
consequat. Duis aute
irure dolor in repre-
henderit in voluptate
velit esse cillum dolore
eu fugiat nulla pariatur.
Excepteur sint occaecat

cupidatat non proident,
sunt in culpa qui officia
deserunt mollit anim id
est laborum.

Lorem ipsum dolor sit
amet, consectetur adip-
isicing elit, sed do eiusmod tempor incididunt
ut labore et dolore magna
aliqua. Ut enim ad min-
im veniam, quis nostrud

exercitation   ullamco
laboris nisi ut aliquip ex
ea commodo consequat.
Duis aute irure dolor
in reprehenderit in vo-
luptate velit esse cillum
dolore eu fugiat nulla
pariatur. Excepteur sint
occaecat cupidatat non
proident, sunt in culpa
qui officia deserunt mol-

Lorem ipsum dolor sit amet, consectetur adipisicing elit, sed do
eiusmod tempor incididunt ut labore et dolore magna aliqua. Ut

Filled-in grid.

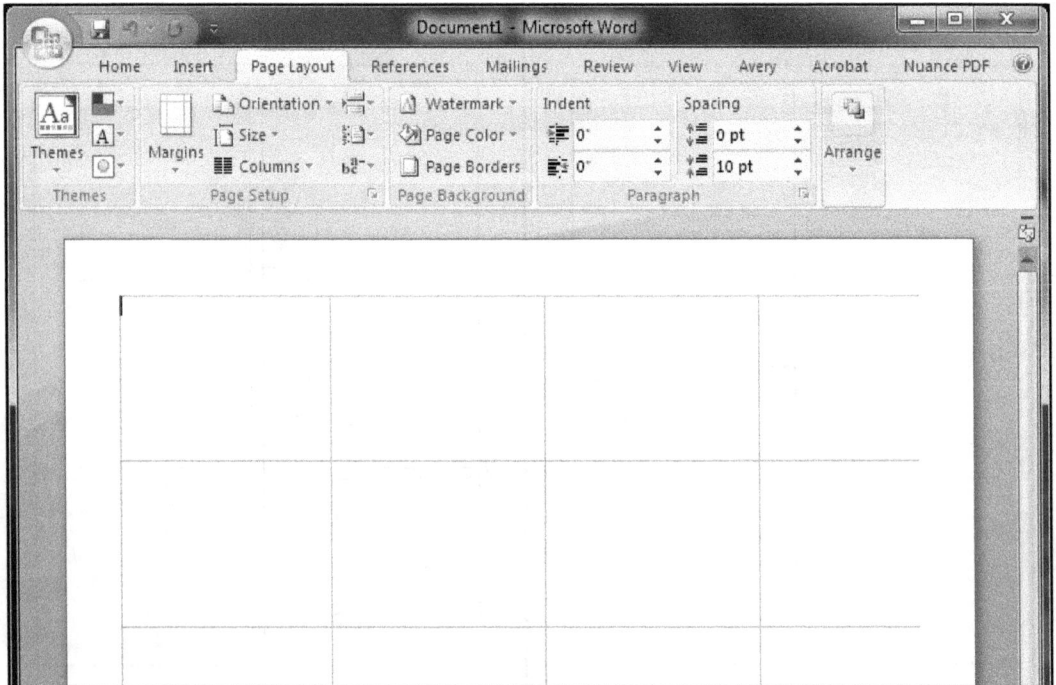

Four column grid in Word.

umns you can use comfortably before they become too narrow. The larger the page, the more columns you need to keep line lengths short enough to read easily.

In the example, you can see a 3x4 grid on the left-hand page, and a 3x3 grid on the right. Another possibility for smaller pages is a 2x2 grid.

Text can flow across two grid columns as seen on the left-hand page in the example labeled "Filled-in grid," or, an image could fill two grid columns as seen on the right-hand page example. A grid should not limit flexibility, rather, it should bring predictability to the page.

Lines, also called rules or strokes, should be of the same weight whenever they are used, with rare exceptions for emphasis (see Pull Quotes below).

In a page layout program, you can set up margins and columns in master pages—different master pages for different uses, such as the first page in a chapter, main body pages, and a final blank page, if needed.

In a word processing program, you can establish the size of the grid squares and turn on the grid lines so that you can see them as you work. Word processing programs are not as flexible with layouts as page layout programs. You can design a good looking book using a word processing program, however, if you will learn the more advanced features of the software.

Margins

Set your margins to accommodate headers, footers, the text and images. In general, no element should violate the margins. All elements, headers, footers, page numbers, text and images must fit within the margins. Margins impose order and help create white space on the page.

When the Gutenberg bible was printed, margins were set so that facing pages were close together. That was the style of the times—to make a two-page spread look as if it were a single image.

With binding methods today, text set too close to the middle creates an optical illusion that the pages run together. Set a slightly larger margin toward the spine than on the outside. The smallest margin you should consider is a one-half inch (.5") margin, and the larger the page size, the larger the margins should be.

Typical margin settings for a 6" x 9" book are: top—1"; inside—.75"; outside—.625" and bottom—.625." On an 8.5" x 11" book, typical margins are: top—1.25" to 1.5"; inside—1"; outside—.75"; and bottom—.75." The most common error is creating margins that are too narrow and of equal size.

Most books have running headers with the book's title on the left-hand page, and the chapter title on the right-hand page. Headers may also include the page numbers. If the header includes the page number, do not repeat page numbers in the footer.

In a page layout program, set up your master pages so that the top margin allows the book title or chapter title to rest above the text. In a word processor,

Lorem ipsum dolor sit amet, consectetur adipisicing elit, sed do eiusmod tempor incididunt ut labore et dolore magna aliqua. Ut enim ad minim veniam, quis nostrud exercitation ullamco laboris nisi ut aliquip ex ea commodo consequat. Duis aute irure dolor in reprehenderit in voluptate velit esse cillum dolore eu fugiat nulla pariatur. Excepteur sint occaecat cupidatat non proident, sunt in culpa qui officia deserunt mollit anim id est laborum.

Lorem ipsum dolor sit amet, consectetur adipisicing elit, sed do eiusmod tempor incididunt ut labore et dolore magna aliqua. Ut enim ad minim veniam, quis nostrud exercitation ullamco laboris nisi ut aliquip ex ea commodo consequat. Duis aute irure dolor in reprehenderit in voluptate velit esse cillum dolore eu fugiat nulla pariatur. Excepteur sint occaecat cupidatat non proident, sunt in culpa qui officia deserunt mollit anim id est laborum.

Lorem ipsum dolor sit amet, consectetur adipisicing elit, sed do eiusmod tempor incididunt ut labore et dolore magna aliqua. Ut enim ad minim veniam, quis nostrud exercitation ullamco laboris nisi ut aliquip ex ea commodo consequat. Duis aute irure dolor in reprehenderit in voluptate velit esse cillum dolore eu fugiat nulla pariatur. Excepteur sint occaecat cupidatat non

aliquip ex ea commodo consequat. Duis aute irure dolor in reprehenderit in voluptate velit esse cillum dolore eu fugiat nulla pariatur. Excepteur sint occaecat cupidatat non proident, sunt in culpa qui officia deserunt mollit anim id est laborum.

Lorem ipsum dolor sit amet, consectetur adipisicing elit, sed do eiusmod tempor incididunt ut labore et dolore magna aliqua. Ut enim ad minim veniam, quis nostrud exercitation ullamco laboris nisi ut aliquip ex ea commodo consequat. Duis aute irure dolor in reprehenderit in voluptate velit esse cillum dolore eu fugiat nulla pariatur. Excepteur sint occaecat cupidatat non proident, sunt in culpa qui officia deserunt mollit anim id est laborum.

Lorem ipsum dolor sit amet, consectetur adipisicing elit, sed do eiusmod tempor incididunt ut labore et dolore magna aliqua. Ut enim ad minim veniam, quis nostrud exercitation ullamco laboris nisi ut aliquip ex ea commodo consequat. Duis aute irure dolor in reprehenderit in voluptate velit esse cillum dolore eu fugiat nulla pariatur. Excepteur sint occaecat cupidatat non proident, sunt in culpa qui officia deserunt mollit anim id est laborum.

Lorem ipsum dolor sit amet, consectetur adipisicing elit, sed do eiusmod tempor incididunt ut labore et

Margins in the Gutenberg bible.

Lorem ipsum dolor sit amet, consectetur adipisicing elit, sed do eiusmod tempor incididunt ut labore et dolore magna aliqua. Ut enim ad minim veniam, quis nostrud exercitation ullamco laboris nisi ut aliquip ex ea commodo consequat. Duis aute irure dolor in reprehenderit in voluptate velit esse cillum dolore eu fugiat nulla pariatur. Excepteur sint occaecat cupidatat non proident, sunt in culpa qui officia deserunt mollit anim id est laborum.

Lorem ipsum dolor sit amet, consectetur adipisicing elit, sed do eiusmod tempor incididunt ut labore et dolore magna aliqua. Ut enim ad minim veniam, quis nostrud exercitation ullamco laboris nisi ut aliquip ex ea commodo consequat. Duis aute irure dolor in reprehenderit in voluptate velit esse cillum dolore eu fugiat nulla pariatur. Excepteur sint occaecat cupidatat non proident, sunt in culpa qui officia deserunt mollit anim id est laborum.

Lorem ipsum dolor sit amet, consectetur adipisicing elit, sed do eiusmod tempor incididunt ut labore et dolore magna aliqua. Ut enim ad minim veniam, quis nostrud exercitation ullamco laboris nisi ut aliquip ex ea commodo consequat. Duis aute irure dolor in reprehenderit in voluptate velit esse cillum dolore eu fugiat nulla pariatur. Excepteur sint occaecat cupidatat non proident, sunt in culpa qui officia

Lorem ipsum dolor sit amet, consectetur adipisicing elit, sed do eiusmod tempor incididunt ut labore et dolore magna aliqua. Ut enim ad minim veniam, quis nostrud exercitation ullamco laboris nisi ut aliquip ex ea commodo consequat. Duis aute irure dolor in reprehenderit in voluptate velit esse cillum dolore eu fugiat nulla pariatur. Excepteur sint occaecat cupidatat non proident, sunt in culpa qui officia deserunt mollit anim id est laborum.

Lorem ipsum dolor sit amet, consectetur adipisicing elit, sed do eiusmod tempor incididunt ut labore et dolore magna aliqua. Ut enim ad minim veniam, quis nostrud exercitation ullamco laboris nisi ut aliquip ex ea commodo consequat. Duis aute irure dolor in reprehenderit in voluptate velit esse cillum dolore eu fugiat nulla pariatur. Excepteur sint occaecat cupidatat non proident, sunt in culpa qui officia

Top margin allowing for the book title, chapter title and page number.

choose one of the pre-installed headers for left and right pages and enter the appropriate text.

Page Numbers

Place page numbers in either the header or footer. Typically they are placed at the outside edge or in the center of the page, but not at the spine edge. It is difficult to locate page numbers while flipping through the book if they are near the spine.

Page numbers in the front matter (title page, table of contents, and so on) are given in lowercase Roman numerals, so the first half-title page would be page i. Page numbers beginning with the introduction are given in Arabic numerals, so the first page of the introduction would be page 1, although some publishers continue page numbering from the front matter.

Columns

Columns are the easiest way to control line length. Text stretching too far across the page is difficult for the reader to follow. Pages six inches wide or narrower can be set in a single column, but larger books need two or more columns.

Columns have two components—distance between (gutter) and width (line length). Try to keep line lengths from 60 to 70 characters. Columns do not have to be equal in width, but most often they look best when they are. In both page layout programs and word processors, you can adjust the number of columns,

---

6   Book Title

Lorem ipsum dolor sit amet, consectetur adipisicing elit, sed do eiusmod tempor incididunt ut labore et dolore magna aliqua. Ut enim ad minim veniam, quis nostrud exercitation ullamco laboris nisi ut aliquip ex ea commodo consequat. Duis aute irure dolor in reprehenderit in voluptate velit esse cillum dolore eu fugiat nulla pariatur. Excepteur sint occaecat cupidatat non proident, sunt in culpa qui officia deserunt mollit anim id est laborum.

Lorem ipsum dolor sit amet, consectetur adipisicing elit, sed do eiusmod tempor incididunt ut labore et dolore magna aliqua. Ut enim ad minim veniam, quis nostrud exercitation ullamco laboris nisi ut aliquip ex ea commodo consequat. Duis aute irure dolor in reprehenderit in voluptate velit esse cillum dolore eu fugiat nulla pariatur. Excepteur sint occaecat cupidatat non proident, sunt in culpa qui officia

deserunt mollit anim id est laborum.

Lorem ipsum dolor sit amet, consectetur adipisicing elit, sed do eiusmod tempor incididunt ut labore et dolore magna aliqua. Ut enim ad minim veniam, quis nostrud exercitation ullamco laboris nisi ut aliquip ex ea commodo consequat. Duis aute irure dolor in reprehenderit in voluptate velit esse cillum dolore eu fugiat nulla pariatur. Excepteur sint occaecat cupidatat non proident, sunt in culpa qui officia deserunt mollit anim id est laborum.

Lorem ipsum dolor sit amet, consectetur adipisicing elit, sed do eiusmod tempor incididunt ut labore et dolore magna aliqua. Ut enim ad minim veniam, quis nostrud exercitation ullamco laboris nisi ut aliquip ex ea commodo consequat. Duis aute irure dolor in reprehenderit in voluptate velit

---

Chapter Title   7

Lorem ipsum dolor sit amet, consectetur adipisicing elit, sed do eiusmod tempor incididunt ut labore et dolore magna aliqua. Ut enim ad minim veniam, quis nostrud exercitation ullamco laboris nisi ut aliquip ex ea commodo consequat. Duis aute irure dolor in reprehenderit in voluptate velit esse cillum dolore eu fugiat nulla pariatur. Excepteur sint occaecat cupidatat non proident, sunt in culpa qui officia deserunt mollit anim id est laborum.

Lorem ipsum dolor sit amet, consectetur adipisicing elit, sed do eiusmod tempor incididunt ut labore et dolore magna aliqua. Ut enim ad minim veniam, quis nostrud exercitation ullamco laboris nisi ut aliquip ex ea commodo consequat. Duis aute irure dolor in reprehenderit in voluptate velit esse cillum dolore eu fugiat nulla pariatur. Excepteur sint occaecat cupidatat non proident, sunt in culpa qui officia deserunt mollit anim id est laborum.

Lorem ipsum dolor sit amet, consectetur adipisicing elit, sed do eiusmod tempor incididunt ut labore et dolore magna aliqua. Ut enim ad minim veniam, quis nostrud exercitation ullamco laboris nisi ut aliquip ex ea commodo consequat. Duis aute irure dolor in reprehenderit in voluptate velit esse cillum dolore eu fugiat nulla pariatur. Excepteur sint occaecat cupidatat non proident, sunt in culpa qui officia deserunt mollit anim id est laborum.

Columns incorrectly spaced; too far (left); too close (right).

Grid filled incorrectly.

6   Book Title

Chapter Title   7

Lorem ipsum dolor sit amet, consectetur adipisicing elit, sed do eiusmod tempor incididunt ut labore et dolore magna aliqua. Ut enim ad minim veniam, quis nostrud exercitation ullamco laboris nisi ut aliquip ex ea commodo consequat. Duis aute irure dolor in reprehenderit in voluptate velit esse cillum dolore eu fugiat nulla pariatur. Excepteur sint occaecat cupidatat non proident, sunt in culpa qui officia deserunt mollit anim id est laborum.

Lorem ipsum dolor sit amet, consectetur adipisicing elit, sed do eiusmod tempor incididunt ut labore et dolore magna aliqua. Ut enim ad minim veniam, quis nostrud exercitation ullamco laboris nisi ut aliquip ex ea commodo consequat. Duis aute irure dolor in reprehenderit in voluptate velit esse cillum dolore eu fugiat nulla pariatur. Excepteur sint occaecat cupidatat non proident, sunt in culpa qui officia deserunt mollit anim id est laborum.

Lorem ipsum dolor sit amet, consectetur adipisicing elit, sed do eiusmod tempor incididunt ut labore et dolore magna aliqua. Ut enim ad minim veniam,

Lorem ipsum dolor sit amet, consectetur adipisicing elit, sed do eiusmod tempor incididunt ut labore et dolore magna aliqua. Ut enim ad minim veniam, quis nostrud exercitation ullamco laboris nisi ut aliquip ex ea commodo consequat. Duis aute irure dolor in reprehenderit in voluptate velit esse cillum dolore eu fugiat nulla pariatur. Excepteur sint occaecat cupidatat non proident, sunt in culpa qui officia deserunt mollit anim id est laborum. Lorem ipsum dolor sit amet, consectetur adipisicing elit, sed do eiusmod tempor incididunt ut labore et dolore magna aliqua. Ut enim ad minim veniam, quis nostrud exercitation ullamco laboris nisi ut aliquip ex ea commodo consequat. Duis aute irure dolor in reprehenderit in voluptate velit esse cillum dolore eu fugiat nulla pariatur. Excepteur sint occaecat cupidatat non proident, sunt in culpa qui officia deserunt mollit anim id est laborum.

cupidatat non proident, sunt in culpa qui officia deserunt mollit anim id est laborum.

officia deserunt mollit anim id est laborum. Lorem ipsum dolor sit amet, consectetur adipisicing elit, sed do eiusmod tempor incididunt ut labore et dolore magna aliqua. Ut enim ad minim veniam, quis nostrud exercitation ullamco laboris nisi ut

Lorem ipsum dolor sit amet, consectetur adipisicing elit, sed do eiusmod tempor incididunt ut labore et dolore magna aliqua. Ut

Lorem ipsum dolor sit amet, consectetur adipisicing elit, sed do eiusmod tempor incididunt ut labore et dolore magna aliqua. Ut

---

Grid filled correctly.

6   Book Title

Chapter Title   7

Lorem ipsum dolor sit amet, consectetur adipisicing elit, sed do eiusmod tempor incididunt ut labore et dolore magna aliqua. Ut enim ad minim veniam, quis nostrud exercitation ullamco laboris nisi ut aliquip ex ea commodo consequat. Duis aute irure dolor in reprehenderit in voluptate velit esse cillum dolore eu fugiat nulla pariatur. Excepteur sint occaecat cupidatat non proident, sunt in culpa qui officia deserunt mollit anim id est laborum.

Lorem ipsum dolor sit amet, consectetur adipisicing elit, sed do eiusmod tempor incididunt ut labore et dolore magna aliqua. Ut enim ad minim veniam, quis nostrud exercitation ullamco laboris nisi ut aliquip ex ea commodo consequat. Duis aute irure dolor in reprehenderit in voluptate velit esse cillum dolore eu fugiat nulla pariatur. Excepteur sint occaecat cupidatat non proident, sunt in culpa qui officia

Lorem ipsum dolor sit amet, consectetur adipisicing elit, sed do eiusmod tempor incididunt ut labore et dolore magna aliqua. Ut enim ad minim veniam, quis nostrud exercitation ullamco laboris nisi ut aliquip ex ea commodo consequat. Duis aute irure dolor in reprehenderit in voluptate velit esse cillum

Lorem ipsum dolor sit amet, consectetur adipisicing elit, sed do eiusmod tempor incididunt ut labore et dolore magna aliqua. Ut enim ad minim veniam, quis nostrud

Lorem ipsum dolor sit amet, consectetur adipisicing elit, sed do eiusmod tempor incididunt ut labore et dolore magna aliqua. Ut enim ad minim veniam, quis nostrud exercitation ullamco laboris nisi ut aliquip ex ea commodo consequat. Duis aute irure dolor in reprehenderit in voluptate velit esse cillum dolore eu fugiat nulla pariatur. Excepteur sint occaecat cupidatat non proident, sunt in culpa qui officia deserunt mollit anim id est laborum.

Lorem ipsum dolor sit amet, consectetur adipisicing elit, sed do eiusmod tempor incididunt ut labore et dolore magna aliqua. Ut enim ad minim veniam, quis nostrud exercitation ullamco laboris nisi ut aliquip ex ea commodo consequat. Duis aute irure dolor in reprehenderit in voluptate velit esse cillum dolore eu fugiat nulla pariatur. Excepteur sint occaecat

Lorem ipsum dolor sit amet, consectetur adipisicing elit, sed do eiusmod tempor incididunt ut labore et dolore magna aliqua. Ut

the line length, and the distance between the columns. A distance of one-quarter of an inch (.25") is a good starting place. Too much distance between columns looks awkward, and too little distance between columns makes the text difficult to read, as you can see in the example.

Images

Adding images to a page can present layout challenges, especially if the image does not fit neatly into the grid. Your book will look best if they do, however, so you may need to re-scan at a larger size or crop images down to fit.

Avoid placing images so that their edges end in the middle of grid squares causing narrow columns of text to form beside the image. Neither should images and text fill grid columns incompletely leaving awkward white space as seen on the right-hand page in the example (previous page).

Most images can stand a bit of cropping. In fact, many images are stronger after they are cropped because the subject of the image takes center stage.

Size indicates relative importance. Try to keep this in mind when choosing images. The bigger the image, the more important the reader will think it is to the story.

Images need space around them. In most cases, the space between the columns serves as a good rule for the space to leave around your images. If the space

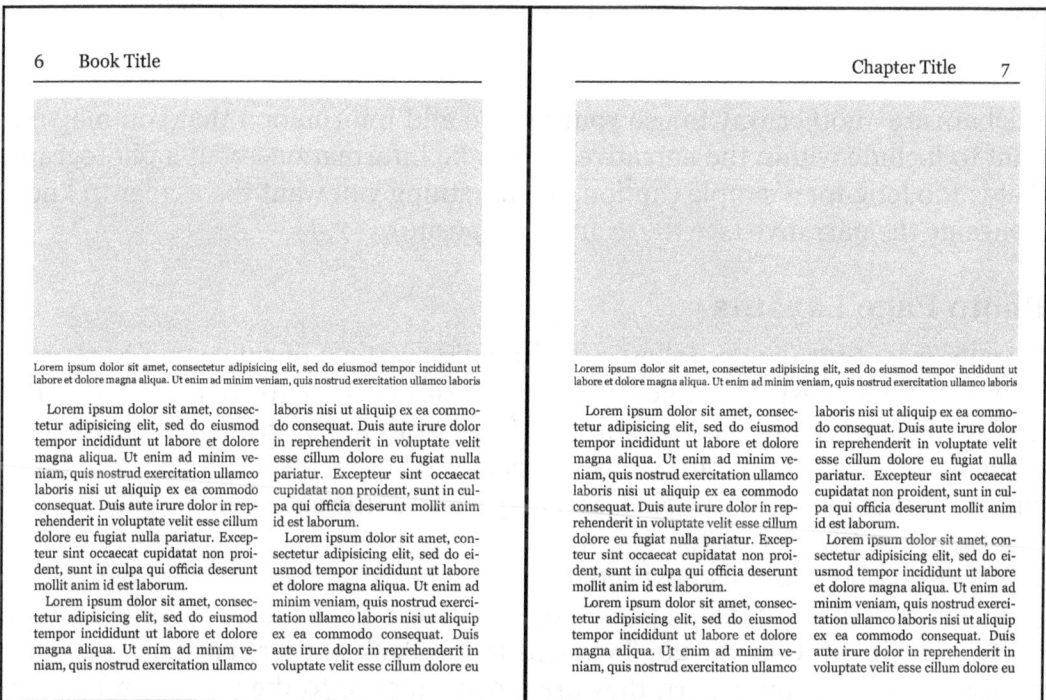

Images with captions.

between your columns is one-quarter of one inch (.25"), use the text wrap feature to give the image space on every side except the side where you want to place a caption. Captions, because they belong to the photo, should be closer (see below).

Note: Captions and credits are not the same. Captions explain who or what is in the image. Credits acknowledge who owns or has possession of the image. Captions should accompany the image on the page, aligned left beginning at the left edge of the photograph, not centered underneath. Centering captions creates visual obstacles for the reader. Credits can be given on the page with the image just after the caption, or in a list of credits at the end of the book or each chapter.

If you want to add fancy photo corners or edge effects to your images, do so in your image editing software after you have re-sized the image for its spot within the grid. Pick one or two fancy effects, and stick with them for consistency.

Advanced Page Layouts

What follows are advanced layout options often found in non-fiction books. Use them for visual interest, but only if they benefit the reader in some way.

Pull Quotes

Pull quotes are used by magazines to entice readers to stop flipping pages and start reading. They are an opportunity for a little creativity on the page. In a book, they can be used effectively, although they should be used sparingly.

Side Bars

Sidebars are another way to use your grid to add information that you may not want to include within the narrative. It may be information about a photograph that is too long for a simple caption, or something you want the reader to know alongside the narrative (see the example opposite).

Photo Page Layouts

Layouts meant for images follow a slightly different set of rules. In a book with chapters, readers expect to find the chapter heading at the top of the page so that they can easily find their place or scan ahead to the end of the chapter. In a book made up primarily of photographs, headers with the name of the book and the chapter title are entirely optional. You may wish to title each page or page spread instead or use titles every few pages.

Page numbers are also expected by readers using more traditional books. Page numbers are optional in photo books, but if you will include an index (more about indexing in Chapter 20: Typesetting the Back Matter) page numbers are necessary. For the most part, they are a convenience to the reader and can be included without much trouble or disrupting the design of the page.

Lorem ipsum dolor sit amet, consectetur adipisicing elit, sed do eiusmod tempor incididunt ut labore et dolore magna aliqua. Ut enim ad minim veniam, quis nostrud exercitation ullamco laboris nisi ut aliquip ex ea commodo consequat. Duis aute irure dolor in reprehenderit in voluptate velit esse cillum dolore eu fugiat nulla pariatur. Excepteur sint occaecat cupidatat non proident, sunt in culpa qui officia deserunt mollit anim id est laborum.

Lorem ipsum dolor sit amet, consectetur adipisicing elit, sed do eiusmod tempor incididunt ut labore et dolore magna aliqua. Ut enim ad minim veniam, quis nostrud exercitation ullamco laboris nisi ut aliquip ex ea commodo consequat. Duis aute irure dolor in reprehenderit in voluptate velit esse cillum dolore eu fugiat nulla pariatur. Excepteur sint occaecat cupidatat non proident, sunt in culpa qui officia deserunt mollit anim id est laborum.

Lorem ipsum dolor sit amet, consectetur adipisicing elit, sed do eiusmod tempor incididunt ut labore et dolore magna aliqua. Ut enim ad minim veniam, quis nostrud exercitation ullamco laboris nisi ut aliquip ex ea commodo consequat. Duis aute irure dolor in reprehenderit in voluptate velit esse cil-

lum dolore eu fugiat nulla pariatur. Excepteur sint occaecat cupidatat non proident, sunt in culpa qui officia deserunt mollit anim id est laborum.

Lorem ipsum dolor sit amet, consectetur adipisicing elit, sed do eiusmod tempor incididunt ut labore et dolore magna aliqua. Ut enim ad minim veniam, quis nostrud exercitation ullamco laboris nisi ut aliquip ex ea commodo consequat. Duis aute irure dolor in reprehenderit in voluptate velit esse cillum dolore eu fugiat nulla pariatur. Excepteur sint occaecat cupidatat non proident, sunt in culpa qui officia deserunt mollit anim id est laborum.

Lorem ipsum dolor sit amet, consectetur adipisicing elit, sed do eiusmod tempor incididunt ut labore et dolore magna aliqua. Ut enim ad minim veniam, quis nostrud exercitation ullamco laboris nisi ut aliquip ex ea commodo consequat. Duis aute irure dolor in reprehenderit in voluptate velit esse cillum dolore eu fugiat nulla pariatur. Excepteur sint occaecat cupidatat non proident, sunt in culpa qui officia deserunt mollit anim id est laborum. Ut

Lorem ipsum dolor sit amet

Lorem ipsum dolor sit amet, consectetur adipisicing elit, sed do eiusmod tempor incididunt ut labore et dolore magna aliqua. Ut enim ad minim veniam, quis nostrud exercitation ullamco laboris nisi ut aliquip ex ea commodo consequat. Duis aute irure dolor in reprehenderit in voluptate velit esse cillum dolore eu fugiat nulla pariatur. Excepteur sint occaecat cupidatat non proident, sunt in culpa qui officia deserunt mollit anim id est laborum.

Lorem ipsum dolor sit amet, consectetur adipisicing elit, sed do eiusmod tempor incididunt ut labore et dolore magna aliqua. Ut enim ad minim veniam, quis nostrud exercitation ullamco laboris nisi ut aliquip ex ea commodo consequat. Duis aute irure dolor in reprehenderit in voluptate velit esse cillum dolore eu fugiat nulla pariatur. Excep-

Lorem ipsum dolor sit amet

teur sint occaecat cupidatat non proident, sunt in culpa qui officia deserunt mollit anim id est laborum.

Lorem ipsum dolor sit amet, consectetur adipisicing elit, sed do eiusmod tempor incididunt ut labore et dolore magna aliqua. Ut enim ad minim ve-

niam, quis nostrud exercitation ullamco laboris nisi ut aliquip ex ea commodo consequat. Duis aute irure dolor in reprehenderit in voluptate velit esse cillum dolore eu fugiat nulla pariatur. Excepteur sint occaecat cupidatat non proident, sunt in culpa qui officia deserunt mollit anim id est laborum.

Lorem ipsum dolor sit amet, consectetur adipisicing elit, sed do eiusmod tempor incididunt ut labore et dolore magna aliqua. Ut enim ad minim veniam, quis nostrud exercitation ullamco laboris nisi ut aliquip ex ea commodo consequat. Duis aute irure dolor in reprehenderit in voluptate velit esse cillum dolore eu fugiat nulla pariatur. Excepteur sint occaecat cupidatat non proident, sunt in culpa qui officia deserunt mollit anim id est laborum.

Lorem ipsum dolor sit amet, consectetur adipisicing elit, sed do eiusmod tempor incididunt ut labore et dolore magna aliqua. Ut enim ad minim veniam, quis nostrud exercitation ullamco laboris nisi ut aliquip ex ea commodo consequat. Duis aute irure dolor in reprehenderit in voluptate velit esse cillum dolore eu fugiat nulla pariatur. Excepteur sint occaecat cupidatat non proident, sunt in culpa qui officia deserunt mollit anim id est laborum. Ut

Pull-quotes across columns (left); Pull-quotes within a column (right).

Lorem ipsum dolor sit amet, consectetur adipisicing elit, sed do eiusmod tempor incididunt ut labore et dolore magna aliqua. Ut enim ad minim veniam, quis nostrud exercitation ullamco laboris nisi ut aliquip ex ea commodo consequat. Duis aute irure dolor in reprehenderit in voluptate velit esse cillum dolore eu fugiat nulla pariatur. Excepteur sint occaecat cupidatat non proident, sunt in culpa qui officia deserunt mollit anim id est laborum.

Lorem ipsum dolor sit amet, consectetur adipisicing elit, sed do eiusmod tempor incididunt ut labore et dolore magna aliqua. Ut enim ad minim veniam, quis nostrud exercitation ullamco laboris nisi ut aliquip ex ea commodo consequat. Duis aute irure dolor in reprehenderit in voluptate velit esse cillum dolore eu fugiat nulla pariatur. Excepteur sint occaecat cupidatat non proident, sunt in culpa qui officia deserunt mollit anim id est laborum.

Lorem ipsum dolor sit amet, consectetur adipisicing elit, sed do eiusmod tempor incididunt ut labore et dolore magna aliqua. Ut enim ad minim veniam, quis nostrud exercitation ullamco laboris nisi ut aliquip ex ea commodo consequat. Duis aute irure dolor in reprehenderit in voluptate velit esse cillum dolore eu fugiat nulla pariatur. Excepteur sint occaecat cupidatat non proident, sunt in culpa qui officia deserunt mollit anim id est laborum.

Lorem ipsum dolor sit amet, consectetur adipisicing elit, sed do eiusmod tempor incididunt ut labore et dolore magna aliqua. Ut enim ad minim veniam, quis nostrud exercitation ullamco laboris nisi ut aliquip ex ea commodo consequat. Duis aute irure dolor in reprehenderit in voluptate velit esse cillum dolore eu fugiat nulla pariatur. Excepteur sint occaecat cupidatat non proident, sunt in culpa qui officia deserunt mollit anim id est laborum.

- Lorem ipsum dolor sit amet
- Consectetur adipisicing elit
- Sed do eiusmod tempor
- Incididunt ut labore
- Magna aliqua
- Ut enim ad minim veniam
- Quis nostrud exercitation

Lorem ipsum dolor cupidatat non proident, sit amet, sunt in culpa qui officia adipisicing elit, sed do deserunt mollit anim id eiusmod tempor incidi- est laborum. dunt ut labore et dolore   Lorem ipsum dolor magna aliqua. Ut enim sit amet, consectetur ad minim veniam, quis adipisicing elit, sed do nostrud exercitation eiusmod tempor incidi- ullamco laboris nisi ut dunt ut labore et dolore aliquip ex ea commodo magna aliqua. Ut enim consequat. Duis aute ad minim veniam, quis irure dolor in repre- nostrud exercitation henderit in voluptate laboris nisi ut aliquip ex velit esse cillum dolore ea commodo consequat. eu fugiat nulla pariatur. Duis aute irure dolor in Excepteur sint occaecat reprehenderit in voluptate cupidatat non proident, velit esse cillum dolore sunt in culpa qui officia eu fugiat nulla pariatur. deserunt mollit anim id Excepteur sint occaecat est laborum.   cupidatat non proident,

Lorem ipsum dolor sunt in culpa qui officia sit amet, consectetur deserunt mollit anim id adipisicing elit, sed do est laborum. Ut eiusmod tempor incidi-   Lorem ipsum dolor dunt ut labore et dolore sit amet, consectetur magna aliqua. Ut enim adipisicing elit, sed do ad minim veniam, quis eiusmod tempor incidi- nostrud exercitation dunt ut labore et dolore ullamco laboris nisi ut magna aliqua. Ut enim aliquip ex ea commodo ad minim veniam, quis consequat. Duis aute nostrud exercitation irure dolor in repre- ullamco laboris nisi ut henderit in voluptate aliquip ex ea commodo velit esse cillum dolore consequat. Duis aute eu fugiat nulla pariatur. irure dolor in repre- Excepteur sint occaecat henderit in voluptate

eu fugiat nulla pariatur. Excepteur sint occaecat cupidatat non proident, sunt in culpa qui officia deserunt mollit anim id est laborum.

Lorem ipsum dolor sit amet, consectetur adipisicing elit, sed do eiusmod tempor incididunt ut labore et dolore magna aliqua. Ut enim ad minim veniam, quis nostrud exercitation ullamco laboris nisi ut aliquip ex ea commodo consequat. Duis aute irure dolor in repre- henderit in voluptate velit esse cillum dolore eu fugiat nulla pariatur. Excepteur sint occaecat cupidatat non proident, sunt in culpa qui officia deserunt mollit anim id est laborum. Ut

Lorem ipsum dolor sit amet, consectetur adipisicing elit, sed do eiusmod tempor incidi- dunt ut labore et dolore magna aliqua. Ut enim ad minim veniam, quis nostrud exercitation ullamco laboris nisi ut aliquip ex ea commodo

Text spread across two columns with a side bar (left); Three columns (right).

Bleeds

Photo books often contain bleeds—images that reach to the edge of the page. What this means in design is that your book size may be 8.5" x 11" but the final trim size of the book will be 8.25" x 10.75" because the pages will be trimmed down so that the images reach the edges of the page. It is important to understand where the trimming will occur so that you do not place anything vital in the trim area such as a page number, part of a caption (or the top of someone's head).

Image with full bleed (left); Image within the margins (right).

Page Orientation

Photo books have three basic page orientation options—portrait (taller than they are wide), landscape (wider than they are tall) and square.

Portrait, although more traditional for books, can be a challenge with photographs because so many photos are taken in a landscape orientation. Landscape orientation can be easier with photos and captions only, but a challenge if you want a longer block of text on the page because it will end up in a narrow column beside the photographs. Square can present the same challenges with text, although is relatively easy to use for photographs and captions only.

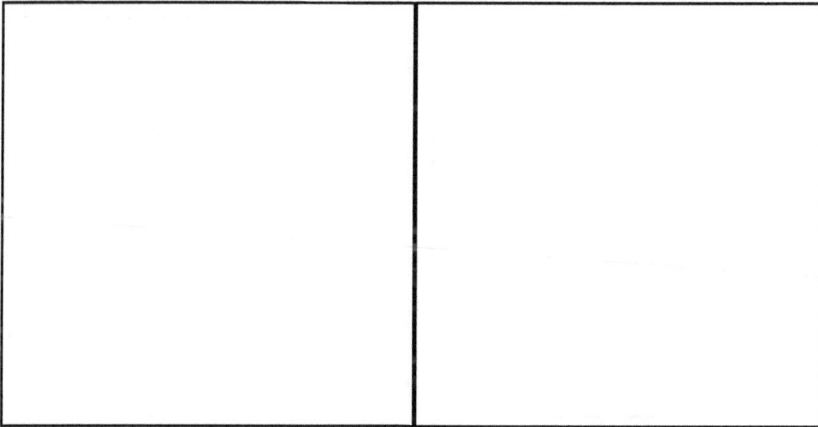

Portrait orientation (top); Landscape orientation (middle); Square orientation (bottom).

Portrait orientation (top); Landscape orientation (middle); Square orientation (bottom).

Grids

Grids help to impose order on the page, and books full of photographs look best when designed with grids. When I design a grid, I put in the bleed and spine lines first. The bleed lines are the lines around the outside of the pages. My images will go into these areas, but I use a grid line to remind me where the trimming will occur so that nothing vital ends up between these lines and edges of the pages.

The second set of lines on the grid are those surrounding the spine margin in the middle. These margins should be slightly larger than the bleed margins because the thickness of the book and whether the pages are designed to lay flat will determine what will be seen within this margin. The photographs (or background image or color) can extend all the way to the spine, but anything vital should stay outside the spine margin.

The next set of lines that go in will determine the regions on the page. The easiest grid contains only a single image shown on the left-hand pages of the examples. The others, beginning at the bottom are 2 x 2, a 3 x 2 and a 2 x 4 grids.

I have used double grid lines, but that does not mean that photographs can never touch. It is just one way to give the eye a way to easily distinguish one image from another.

When filling the grids, the images do not have to be uniform, either. They do not have to be the same size or the same orientation on the page.

They should, however, fill the edges of the bleed area so that when the book is trimmed there is no chance that a white (unprinted paper colored) border remains where the image stopped short. You will want the image to be trimmed off with a nice, clean edge.

Sizing and Cropping

One thing that can be tricky when laying out a photo book is making the image look its best while fitting into a grid. Sometimes that involves re-sizing or cropping the image so that some parts of the image are left out in order to fit better within the grid. It may also mean leaving or building a bit of extra image—sky, for example—so that there is enough image to fill the bleed space.

Genealogical Layouts

There are familiar genealogical charts that make good guides for page layouts for some photo books. For inspiration look at the multitudes of scrapbooking guides and kits available with "family tree" themes. What follows are a few ideas for using genealogical information to help plan the page layout. These are a few example of how each could work. There are many other options.

Portrait orientation.

Landscape orientation.

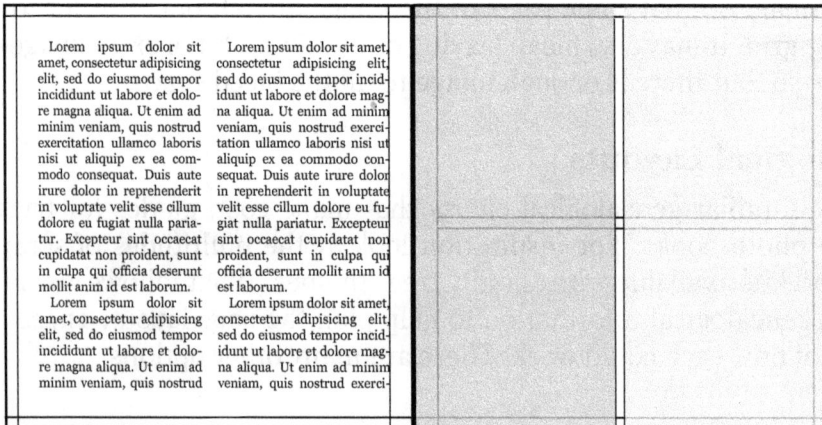

Lorem ipsum dolor sit amet, consectetur adipisicing elit, sed do eiusmod tempor incididunt ut labore et dolore magna aliqua. Ut enim ad minim veniam, quis nostrud exercitation ullamco laboris nisi ut aliquip ex ea commodo consequat. Duis aute irure dolor in reprehenderit in voluptate velit esse cillum dolore eu fugiat nulla pariatur. Excepteur sint occaecat cupidatat non proident, sunt in culpa qui officia

Lorem ipsum dolor sit amet, consectetur adipisicing elit, sed do eiusmod tempor incidi-dunt ut labore et dolore magna aliqua. Ut enim ad minim veniam, quis nostrud exercitation ullamco laboris nisi ut aliquip ex ea commodo consequat. Duis aute irure dolor in repre-henderit in voluptate velit esse cillum dolore eu fugiat nulla pariatur. Excepteur sint occaecat cupidatat non proident, sunt in culpa qui officia deserunt mollit anim id

Lorem ipsum dolor sit amet, consectetur adipisicing elit, sed do eiusmod tempor incididunt ut labore et dolo-re magna aliqua. Ut enim ad minim veniam, quis nostrud exercitation ullamco laboris nisi ut aliquip ex ea com-modo consequat. Duis aute irure dolor in reprehenderit in voluptate velit esse cillum dolore eu fugiat nulla paria-tur. Excepteur sint occaecat cupidatat non proident, sunt in culpa qui officia deserunt mollit anim id est laborum.
Lorem ipsum dolor sit amet, consectetur adipisicing elit, sed do eiusmod tempor incididunt ut labore et dolo-re magna aliqua. Ut enim ad minim veniam, quis nostrud

Lorem ipsum dolor sit amet, consectetur adipisicing elit, sed do eiusmod tempor incidi-dunt ut labore et dolore mag-na aliqua. Ut enim ad minim veniam, quis nostrud exerci-tation ullamco laboris nisi ut aliquip ex ea commodo con-sequat. Duis aute irure dolor in reprehenderit in voluptate velit esse cillum dolore eu fu-giat nulla pariatur. Excepteur sint occaecat cupidatat non proident, sunt in culpa qui officia deserunt mollit anim id est laborum.
Lorem ipsum dolor sit amet, consectetur adipisicing elit, sed do eiusmod tempor incid-idunt ut labore et dolore mag-na aliqua. Ut enim ad minim veniam, quis nostrud exerci-

Square orientation.

Pedigree Chart

A pedigree chart shows multiple generations in a way that makes clear how the individuals depicted are related. A pedigree chart works best on a square or portrait oriented page. In these examples, the size of each image is the same. In the square example, the fourth generation, the couple is side-by-side rather than above and below.

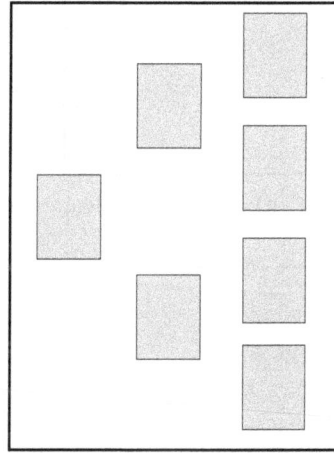

Square orientation (left); Portrait orientation (right).

Family Group Sheet

A family group sheet shows a nuclear family and could work in any orientation, portrait, landscape or square. In the examples below, the parents are represented by the larger image and the children by the smaller images.

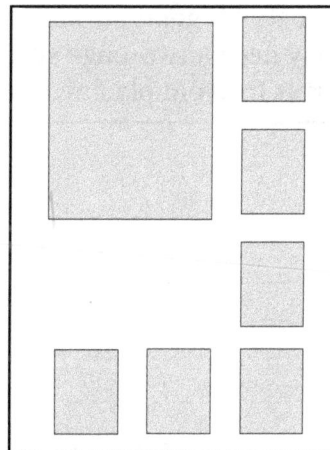

Portrait orientation (left and right).

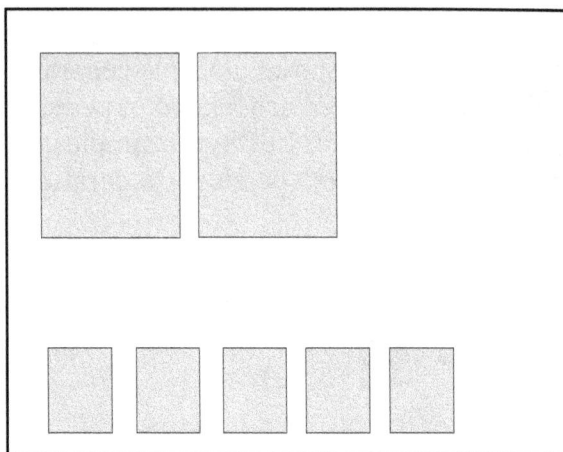

Square orientation (left); Landscape orientation (right).

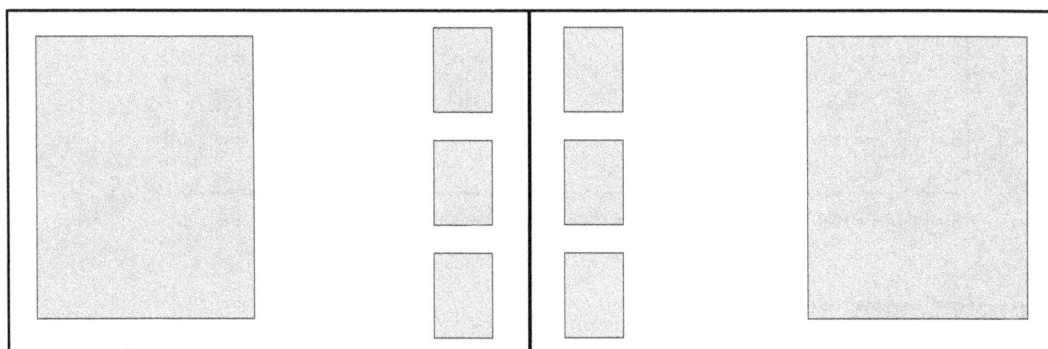

Landscape orientation (two-page spread).

Bow-Tie Chart

A bow-tie chart shows generations on both sides of the first generation person's family. You may need a two-page spread to make this work. The only trick about a bow-tie chart is to avoid placing images in the spine margin.

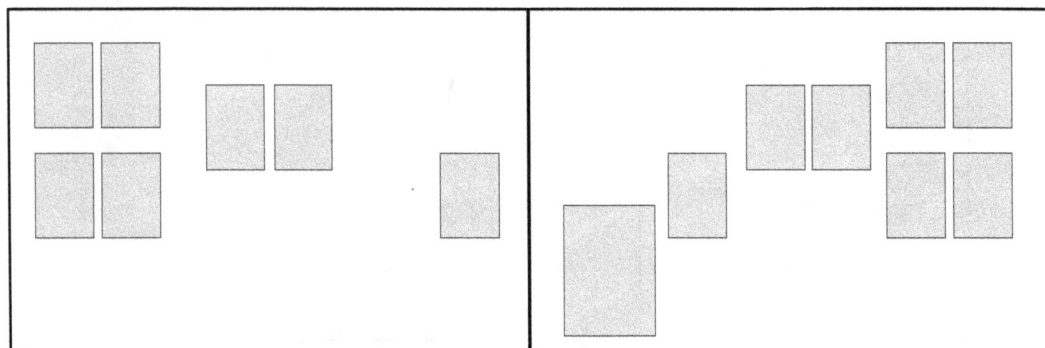

Landscape orientation (two-page spread).

Descendant Chart

A descendant chart starts with a couple at the top, and shows two or more generations below them. You may need a two-page spread if there are very many children in the second generation.

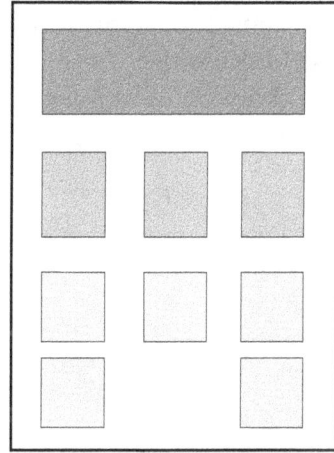

Square orientation (left); Portrait orientation (right).

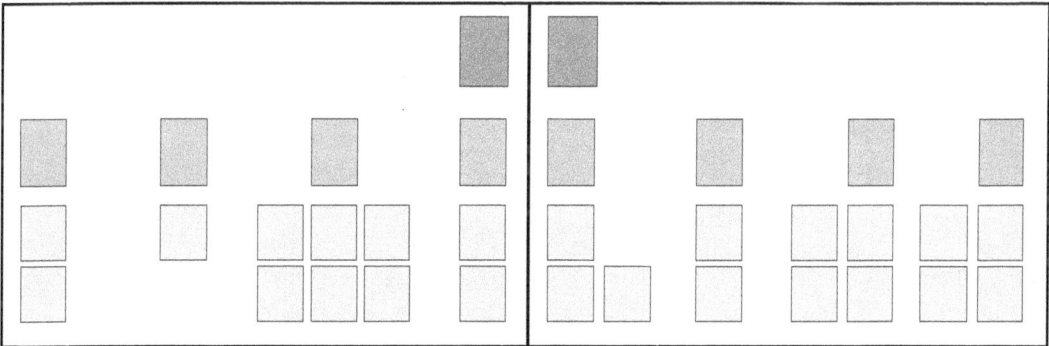

Landscape orientation (two-page spread).

Half-Fan Chart

A half-fan chart is one way to show many generations in a small space. In order to make a half-fan chart work in a book, however, your printer must offer lay-flat pages, and a layout that supports designing over a two-page spread.

❦

If you take the time to create a basic page layout that is easy to flow text and place images into, your book will look better than most. Look through scrapbooking guides that focus on genealogy or family history for ideas. Make a trip to the local library or check your personal collection for a simple layout that you like. Look at books of the same physical size—it can be hard to match layouts if you do not.

Now that you have a feel for the general layout of the page, the next chapter will explore the fundamentals of typesetting.

Chapter 17

Typesetting—The Basics

Typesetting conventions have developed over the last 400 years to make books both beautiful and easy to read. If you mess with the rules of readability, reading comprehension drops dramatically.

The rest of this chapter will help you avoid leaving little clues that the book is "self-published."

The Basics

Before you can start typesetting the different parts of your book, you need a good understanding of what affects reading comprehension.

The Rules of Readability

In addition to hundreds of years of publishing tradition, modern studies have determined what affects our ability to read and comprehend type. The rules that follow are based upon the results of tradition, observation and studies.

Use serif fonts, also called typefaces. Twice as many readers are able to understand words printed in serif typefaces. Serif fonts have small extenders between letters. Sans serif typefaces are easier to read on the screen, so these fonts are fine for websites and electronic communications, but stick to serif fonts for printed books.

High contrast is best. Black type on a white page is optimal. Even dark blues and browns are more difficult to read than black. Avoid placing type on a colored background unless the background is very light. Avoid reverse outs. It is difficult for readers to digest white type on a black background for more than a one- or two-word headline.

Avoid all capitals (all caps). Not only do readers feel as if you are shouting at them, they recognize words based upon the top half of the letters. Letters in all caps lack the characteristic upper extenders and rounded forms readers use to recognize whole words at a time, so text in all caps slows reading to a crawl.

Give the letters room to breathe. Squeezing type together makes text uncomfortable, if not impossible, to read.

Use bold sparingly. Headlines and subheads in bold help the reader skim through the material, but large blocks of type in bold looks dense and is difficult to read.

> A brilliant piece of graphic design which goes unread is a waste of paper, ink, money and effort, and perhaps above all, a lost opportunity to communicate something of value.
>
> **—Colin Wheildon and Mal Warwick**
> *Type & Layout: How Typography and Design*
> *Can Get Your Message Across or Get In the Way*

Fonts

Typography does not have to be sophisticated to look good and read easily. Typefaces often come in families that include Roman (plain), italics, bold and bold italics. A few font families will also have black (heavy) or light (narrow).

Choose a serif typeface for the main body of the book. These are common serif typefaces used in books: Adobe Caslon, Adobe Garamond, Baskerville Old Face, Bookman Old Style, Goudy Old Style, Palatino, and Utopia.

Common Body Text Fonts	Common Headline Fonts
Adobe Caslon	Franklin Gothic Book
Adobe Garamond	Gill Sans
Baskerville Old Face	Hypatia Sans Pro
Bookman Old Style	Myriad Pro
Goudy Oldstyle	Tahoma
Palatino	

Gill Sans Adobe Caslon	**Franklin Gothic Book** Goudy Old Style
Myriad Pro Baskerville	**Tahoma** Palatino
Hypatia Sans Bookman	

Common body and headline fonts (left); Font pairs (right).

You can keep the same font for headlines and subheads, but make them bolder and bigger, or you can use a sans serif typeface. If you prefer a sans serif font, choose one that creates a good contrast with your body text font. Weak contrasts do not look as good as strong contrasts.

These are common sans serif headline fonts: Franklin Gothic Book, Gill Sans, Hypathia Sans Pro, Myriad Pro, Nimbus Sans, Segoe and Tahoma.

Fonts to avoid: Times New Roman and Helvetica (both are newspaper fonts meant for narrow columns), Arial (overused), Copperplate (all caps), Courier (unless you want to look like you have used a typewriter), Papyrus (so overused it has become a cliché), Brush Script, Comic Sans, Curlz, anything that implies handwriting, and fonts supposed to make one think of the Dark Ages, the Middle Ages, the Renaissance, or the Book of Kells.

Avoid script fonts, even for something personal such as a transcription of a letter or a page from a diary. Loosely set script fonts may be fine for chapter titles but are difficult to read for more than a few words. Italics in one of the basic book fonts will distinguish itself enough to make a transcription stand out.

There are three major font file types: Open Type, TrueType and Postscript. Apple opened the world of scalable type design with its TrueType fonts. Adobe got into the game a bit later with its Type1 (Postscript) fonts. OpenType has been a collaboration of Microsoft and Adobe and looks to be winning over publishers and printers.

Some fonts require purchase in order to use them; others come pre-installed in your word processing or page layout programs already licensed for you to use. Avoid free fonts available on the Internet (mostly TrueType). Some have serious technical issues that you will not want to discover after your book is printed.

Avoid any font that will not embed into a PDF (Portable Document Format—the file type most commonly requested by printers). If you do not have a license for your fonts, they will not save correctly into a PDF. If you are unsure, type a few words in each of your chosen fonts and convert that test file into a PDF. Most word processors will save files to PDFs using a simple "save as" command. If no error messages appear, the fonts are most probably all right.

There is no need to go wild with fonts. It is rare to use more than two to three fonts in a book's interior. Stick to the commonly used book fonts. You can be a little more creative with the font on the cover.

Type Size

For the main body of the book, make the font size big enough to read easily, and appropriate to the column width. Narrower columns can handle smaller fonts.

For adults, most fonts are readable between point sizes 10 and 12. Smaller font sizes are difficult to read. Smaller type is fine for captions or footnotes, down to 7 or 8 points, depending upon the font. Larger font sizes, 14 points or larger, should be reserved for large print books made for people with impaired vision. Larger font sizes are acceptable for headlines and subheads.

Leading

The term leading comes from a time when type was set by hand and thin strips of lead divided lines horizontally to create a space above and below each line.

Standard leading is two points greater than the type height for standard text and proportionally larger with larger sized text. Your body text may be 12 points tall with 14 point leading, whereas your cover font could be 48 points tall with 58 point leading—an amount proportional to the size of the large letters.

One way to decrease the density on the page (or lengthen a manuscript) is to increase the leading. Increasing the leading too much, however, will look like double spacing which is not attractive.

Emphasis

It is always better to make the reader feel emphasis with your words rather than using typesetting tricks. Italics is the most common way to show emphasis. Italics is also used to highlight foreign words, indicate book or movie titles, and the thoughts of a character—a rare occurrence in non-fiction.

Use bold, if you must, but only for short phrases. Paragraph after paragraph of bold text looks dense and uninviting.

Keep the exclamation points under control. If everything is important, nothing is—relatively. Avoid all capitals in running text unless you want the reader to feel that you are shouting your message.

There is no need to put everyday expressions in quotes, except to indicate irony. When air quotes became a popular hand gesture, they also proliferated in printed works. Try not to litter your book with unnecessary quotes. Save them for the places where you are actually quoting another author.

Avoid underlining, except as hyperlinks. Underlining had a place when typewriters offered little else, but underlining is not used for emphasis today.

Case

In English, when to use upper case and when to use lower case is fairly straight forward. Sentence case is used in paragraphs where capital letters begin sentences. Title case is used for headlines and subheads only. In title case, most words are capitalized except prepositions (by, to, from, of, on, with, at), articles (a, an, the), and coordinating conjunctions (and, but, or, for, and nor).

Capitals are used for proper nouns, such as the names of people (George Washington), businesses (General Motors), specific places (Savannah, America, the Mississippi Delta), nationalities (German), languages (French) and religions (Methodist).

Job or honorary titles are capitalized, but only when it refers to a specific person and precedes their name. So, there are presidents elected in the United States, but President Lincoln gets a capital in his title.

Capitals, like commas, can run amok. In book publishing, fewer capitals are preferred. If in doubt, use the lowercase letter.

Letter Spacing and Kerning

Letter spacing and kerning affect the distance between letters. Letter spacing (tracking) affects the spacing between all letters. Adjusting the letter spacing can open up the look of a page and make some fonts easier to read. In most cases, however, your software will correctly determine letter spacing. On occasion, altering letter spacing can help avoid orphans (more on this shortly).

Kerning adjusts the spacing between two, side-by-side letters to make them look more natural sitting next to each other. The auto-kerning feature in most software is fine for most body text. Kerning individual pairs of letters may be important, however, to make the large letters on your cover look their best.

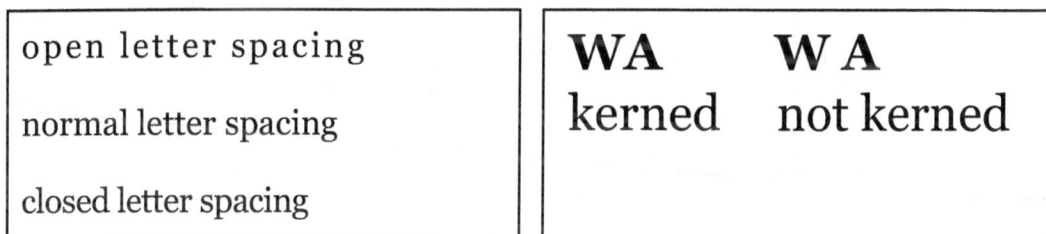

open letter spacing
normal letter spacing
closed letter spacing

WA   **W A**
kerned   not kerned

Letter spacing (left); Kerning (right).

Titles, Headlines, and Subheads

Titles, headlines and subheads are about hierarchy—clues to what is the most important. At the top of the hierarchy (and also in the largest font size and strength) are the chapter titles. Next are the headlines that should be bigger and bolder than subheads. If needed, create sub-subheads down to a second or third level.

The lowest level could be a run-in subhead where the subhead does not sit above the paragraph, but begins the paragraph and ends in a period (see below).

For most books, headlines and subheads should be aligned flush left. Centered or right-aligned headlines and subheads can work (albeit a challenge), but only over fully justified paragraphs. Whichever style you choose, be consistent.

Keep headlines and subheads short and sweet. Avoid having them run onto a second line, if possible. Headlines and subheads do not end in punctuation, except if you are using a run-in subhead, such as:

Tuesday. On the first sunny morning in a month, ...
Wednesday. We began to harvest ...

Aesthetically, headlines and subheads are never stacked one on top of another. There is always a paragraph in between them.

PUBLISH A PHOTO BOOK

Lorem ipsum dolor sit amet, consectetur adipisicing elit, sed do eiusmod tempor incididunt ut labore et dolore magna aliqua. Ut enim ad minim veniam, quis nostrud exercitation ullamco laboris nisi ut aliquip ex ea commodo consequat. Duis aute irure dolor in reprehenderit in voluptate velit esse cillum dolore eu fugiat nulla pariatur. Excepteur sint occaecat cupidatat non proident, sunt in culpa qui officia deserunt mollit anim id est laborum.

Headline Headline Headline

Lorem ipsum dolor sit amet, consectetur adipisicing elit, sed do eiusmod tempor incididunt ut labore et dolore magna aliqua. Ut enim ad minim veniam, quis nostrud exercitation ullamco laboris nisi ut aliquip ex ea commodo consequat. Duis aute irure dolor in reprehenderit in voluptate velit esse cillum dolore eu fugiat nulla pariatur. Excepteur sint occaecat cupidatat non proident, sunt in culpa qui officia deserunt mollit anim id est laborum.

Subhead Subhead Subhead Subhead

Lorem ipsum dolor sit amet, consectetur adipisicing elit, sed do eiusmod tempor incididunt ut labore et dolore magna aliqua. Ut enim ad minim veniam, quis nostrud exercitation ullamco laboris nisi ut aliquip ex ea commodo consequat. Duis aute irure dolor in reprehenderit in voluptate velit esse cillum dolore eu fugiat nulla pariatur. Excepteur sint occaecat cupidatat non proident, sunt in culpa qui officia deserunt mollit anim id est laborum.

Sub-Subhead Sub-Subhead Sub-Subhead Subhead

Lorem ipsum dolor sit amet, consectetur adipisicing elit, sed do eiusmod tempor incididunt ut labore et dolore magna aliqua. Ut enim ad minim veniam, quis nostrud exercitation ullamco laboris nisi ut aliquip ex ea commodo consequat. Duis aute irure dolor in

Headlines and subheads.

Lorem ipsum dolor sit amet, consectetur adipisicing elit, sed do eiusmod tempor incididunt ut labore et dolore magna aliqua. Ut enim ad minim veniam, quis nostrud exercitation ullamco laboris nisi ut aliquip ex ea commodo consequat. Duis aute irure dolor in voluptate velit esse cillum dolore eu fugiat nulla pariatur. Excepteur sint occaecat cupidatat non proident, sunt in culpa qui officia deserunt mollit anim id est laborum.

Lorem ipsum dolor sit amet, consectetur adipisicing elit, sed do eiusmod tempor incididunt ut labore et dolore magna aliqua. Ut enim ad minim veniam, quis nostrud exercitation ullamco laboris nisi ut aliquip ex ea commodo consequat. Duis aute irure dolor in reprehenderit in voluptate velit esse cillum dolore eu fugiat nulla pariatur. Ex-

cepteur sint occaecat cupidatat non proident, sunt in culpa qui officia deserunt mollit anim id est laborum.

Lorem ipsum dolor sit amet, consectetur adipisicing elit, sed do eiusmod tempor incididunt ut labore et dolore magna aliqua. Ut enim ad minim veniam, quis nostrud exercitation ullamco laboris nisi ut aliquip ex ea commodo consequat. Duis aute irure dolor in reprehenderit in voluptate velit esse cillum dolore eu fugiat nulla pariatur. Excepteur sint occaecat cupidatat non proident, sunt in culpa qui officia deserunt mollit anim id est laborum.

Lorem ipsum dolor sit amet, consectetur adipisicing elit, sed do eiusmod tempor incididunt ut labore et dolore magna aliqua. Ut enim ad minim ve-niam, quis nostrud exercitation

1. Lorem ipsum dolor sit amet, consectetur adipisicing elit, sed do eiusmod tempor incididunt ut labore et dolore magna aliqua. Ut enim ad minim veniam, quis nostrud exercitation ullamco laboris nisi ut aliquip ex ea commodo consequat. Duis aute irure dolor in reprehenderit in voluptate velit

2. Lorem ipsum dolor sit amet, consectetur adipisicing elit, sed do eiusmod tempor incididunt ut labore et dolore magna aliqua. Ut enim ad minim veniam, quis nostrud exercitation ullamco laboris nisi ut aliquip ex ea commodo consequat. Duis aute irure dolor in reprehenderit in voluptate velit

Correct paragraph spacing.

Paragraphs

Paragraphs are the basic building block of your book, so make paragraphs look their best.

The first paragraph in a chapter or after a headline or subhead should not have an indent—all other paragraphs should.

Indents should not be created by using a tab or by spacing over. Create a style with a first-line indent instead. If you turn your manuscript over to a typesetter full of extra spaces or tabs, he or she will have to remove them which will cost them time and you money.

Set your indent to one-quarter of an inch (.25") and not larger unless you are using big type for the visually impaired. Unfortunately, many word processing programs have the default set to an ungainly half inch (.5").

Never use a double return to create space between paragraphs. Most of the time, you will not need extra space between paragraphs, the indent will give the reader enough of a visual break. If you want more white space on the page, create a paragraph style with slightly more space above each paragraph.

Quotes

If you transcribe a document or quote another author directly, the entire paragraph(s) should be indented from both sides to form a narrower block of text. Create a bit more space above and below quoted paragraphs, as well. Quoted paragraphs should be fully justified (explanation below).

Justified Text

In books, paragraphs should be fully justified not justified ragged right. That is, they should look like a square block of text. In the era of typewriters, ragged right was unavoidable. The type along the right-hand edge of the page was uneven (ragged). Modern software creates much better looking fully justified text blocks.

Fully-justified text may be difficult in captions if there is only one or two lines in the caption. One potential problem with full justification whether in a caption or a paragraph is the text on the last line. If there are only a couple of words, full justification will spread the words out to the right-hand edge leaving unnaturally large spaces between the words. Most word processing programs give you a way to keep the last line of each fully justified paragraph together on the left.

Use centering and ragged right justification sparingly; in fact, almost never. Poetry with short lines can be centered, but a full paragraph that is centered is difficult to read.

Hyphenation

Most of the time, automatic hyphenation is fine because it avoids creating rivers of white down the page which disturbs the reader's ability to move smoothly

Justified Ragged Right

Lorem ipsum dolor sit amet, consectetur adipisicing elit, sed do eiusmod tempor incididunt ut labore et dolore magna aliqua. Ut enim ad minim veniam, quis nostrud exercitation ullamco laboris nisi ut aliquip ex ea commodo consequat. Duis aute irure dolor

Ragged right.

Justified Ragged Left

Lorem ipsum dolor sit amet, consectetur adipisicing elit, sed do eiusmod tempor incididunt ut labore et dolore magna aliqua. Ut enim ad minim veniam, quis nostrud exercitation ullamco laboris nisi ut aliquip ex ea commodo consequat. Duis

Ragged left.

Fully Justified Correctly

Lorem ipsum dolor sit amet, consectetur adipisicing elit, sed do eiusmod tempor incididunt ut labore et dolore magna aliqua. Ut enim ad minim veniam, quis nostrud exercitation ullamco laboris nisi ut aliquip ex ea commodo consequat.

Fully Justified Incorrectly

Lorem ipsum dolor sit amet, consectetur adipisicing elit, sed do eiusmod tempor incididunt ut labore et dolore magna aliqua. Ut enim ad minim veniam, quis nostrud exercitation ullamco laboris nisi ut aliquip ex ea commodo consequat.

Fully justified correctly (left); Fully justified incorrectly (forced outward spacing) (right).

from left to right, word to word. On occasion, automatic hyphenation will result in lines of hyphens stacked on top of each other (see above left). If this happens, you can artificially hyphenate a few words to make the paragraph look better.

Watch for odd hyphenation breaks. You would not want menswear to become men-swear, or therapist to become the-rapist.

Widows and Orphans

Widows and orphans are bits of text that do not fit neatly into the column grid.

Widows are created when: the last line of a paragraph appears on the following page or at the top of the next column; a headline or subhead is in one column (page) but the paragraph that follows it is in another column (page); or the last bullet in a list is in another column (page).

Page layout programs have much better tools to control widows and orphans than do word processors, including ways to control white space and hyphenation, commands to keep lines together, and the ability to alter the length of a column to force a line into the next column.

If you are using a word processor, one way to control widows is to add a hard return before a widowed headline to force it into the next column or onto the next page. If you have a widowed bullet or a widowed line, see if you can cut the text

Widows and orphans.

above without changing the meaning to allow enough space for the line or bullet to remain with the paragraph or list.

Orphans are created when: the first line of a paragraph appears in one column (page) but the rest of the paragraph appears in the next column (page); the last word of a paragraph is left on a line by itself.

One way to control orphans is to turn on or off automatic hyphenation for the paragraph. This may shift another word onto the last line of the paragraph. Another option is to alter the text without altering the meaning, so there are fewer words to fit in the paragraph.

Initials and Acronyms

How you handle initials and acronyms is a matter of preference as long as you are consistent throughout.

How you handle people known only by their initials is a matter of style. Typically, there are no spaces between initials, so D.S. Yates rather than D. S. Yates.

Acronyms typically do not have periods between the letters, so NASA rather than N.A.S.A.

Some acronyms, such as AM and PM, are typically set in small caps (AM and PM) rather than in full caps, although some style guides use a.m. and p.m. (or am and pm) instead. Small caps are a function of the font, although not all fonts have a small caps option.

Web and Email Addresses

Because we are in the Internet age, your book may include website URLs (website addresses), or email addresses. In electronic books (eBooks), these addresses can be made into hyperlinks so that the reader can click on the link to be taken to the website, or to launch an email program. In printed books, it is up to you whether or not you leave the color and underlining that word processing programs add when addresses are hyperlinked. Most word processors use a bright blue for hyperlinks, which may not be readable in print. Changing them to black will help. Increasing the letter spacing in website addresses also makes them easier to read.

Punctuation

Punctuation can make or break meaning. If you have not already read Lynne Truss's book, *Eats, Shoots & Leaves: A Zero Tolerance Approach to Punctuation*, you should. Single-handedly, she is conducting a rather hilarious war on the proliferation of commas.

Dashes and Hyphens

Hyphens are used to create compound adjectives, such as state-of-the-art computer. Hyphens are used for compound numbers (forty-four books), double last names (Sir Watkin Williams-Wynn), and spelled-out fractions (two-thirds). Hyphens once were used to distinguish all pre-fixes (pre-arranged), but less so today. If eliminating the hyphen would cause confusion with another word (recovered a lost wallet versus re-covered a sofa), then use the hyphen.

Dashes are not hyphens, nor double hyphens. Fortunately, most word processors will turn double hyphens into an em dash. Unfortunately, most word processors do not know the difference between the em dash and the en dash.

An en dash, a dash approximately the width of the letter n, is used to indicate duration, so October–December (October through December), or 10–12 (ten to twelve).

An em dash, a dash approximately the width of the letter m, is used when you want the reader to pause a bit longer than they would for a comma, but not as long as they would for a period. Em dashes are a matter of preference. Many authors will use parentheses to set off a change in thought, others prefer em dashes.

En and em dashes do not have spaces—before or after them.

Ellipses

Ellipses, a series of three periods (...) with a bit of extra space in between, are used to indicate a long pause in thought, or that material was left out of a quote.

Fortunately, if you put three periods in a row without adding a space in between, most word processors will display them correctly.

If you end a sentence with an ellipsis, you still need a period to end the sentence, so there will be four dots.

Ellipses require a full space before and a full space after.

Special Characters

Special characters include bullets, copyright symbols, and accent marks on foreign language words. These special characters are found in glyph or symbols menus. Fortunately, many word processors and page layout programs automatically insert correct accents on common words such as cliché.

Serial Commas

Although Lynne Truss is waging an admirable war on the proliferation of commas, sometimes the serial comma is needed when listing items. For example, you could eliminate the last comma from a list such as bananas, oranges, and apples. If however, you eliminated the last comma from, "To my siblings, Mom, and Grandma," you would be implying that your mother and grandmother were your siblings (i.e. "To my siblings, Mom and Grandma").

It is up to you how you handle serial commas, as long as meaning is clear.

Quotation Marks

Quotation marks are not apostrophes. Quotation marks are the curly-cue-looking marks that face one way at the beginning of a quote, and the other way at the end. Make this simple on yourself by turning on the "smart quotes," in your word processing or page layout program and avoid fonts that do not have true, left and right quotation marks.

Quotation marks should not be used for emphasis. Use italics if you want to get the reader's attention. Use quotation marks for direct quotations, to alert readers that a term is being used in a non-standard way such as for irony or sarcasm, or to replace the words "so-called."

Place commas and periods inside quotation marks. Colons and semi-colons belong outside quotation marks. Place question marks or exclamation points inside if they belong to quoted material, otherwise outside.

Semi-Colons

Semi-colons are used to link two independent clauses together. Most of the time, however, you can use a period and start a new sentence with the same effect.

You can also use a semi-colon to link items in a list together where a comma could cause confusion. For example, "some people choose to go places by motorized vehicles, cars, motorcycles or buses; but others, for different reasons, choose to walk, bicycle or roller skate."

Apostrophes

Apostrophes are used to indicate possession (e.g. John's book), to create contractions (e.g. don't) and to indicate the omission of letters, so Rock and Roll becomes Rock 'n' Roll because both the "a" and the "d" in "and" are replaced with an apostrophe.

A single, straight apostrophe indicates feet (e.g. 125'). A double, straight apostrophe indicates inches (e.g. 3").

In the 80s, means the temperature is in the 80s. In the '80s, means the decade of the 1980s (or 1880s). There is no apostrophe when referring to a decade (1850s) unless you are indicating possession (1850's clothing styles).

Lines, Rules, and Strokes

The terms lines, rules and strokes all mean a line. Most often lines are used in the header to separate the book title or chapter title from the body text.

If you use lines, choose a numbered point size for the thickness of your lines. Avoid the hairline setting, because "hairline" is interpreted differently by each printer's machinery, so the results may be unexpected.

Color

If a caption is placed on top of a dark photograph, using white type is a better option than choosing a lighter area of the photograph where the type would interfere with the image.

If the interior of a longer narrative is color throughout, you can use color for headlines and subheads to make them stand out. Black text is still the easiest to read, so if you use a color for headlines or subheads, choose one that is dark enough to be read easily, and use the same color throughout the book for consistency. Any dark color can work, although people with red-green color blindness will appreciate it if you avoid those two colors.

Cross-References

You may need to include cross-references to chapters, numbered sections, illustrations or pages. The only way to create cross-references without creating a lot of extra work for yourself, is to leave a visual indicator in the text (e.g. [XXXXX]), and wait until the final page proofs are available before adding the appropriate reference.

Most photo books do not need cross-references except in the index. You can accomplish much of the same with good explanations in foot- or endnotes.

Clean Up Your Manuscript Files

Before you begin typesetting, clean up your manuscript files. One common habit of people who learned to type on typewriters is to put two spaces before the beginning of a new sentence. Modern word processors use proportional spacing at the end of sentences so they do not need the extra space. Use the Find/Replace command to search for two spaces and replace them with a single space. Repeat this task until the software indicates that no more replacements have been made. This will eliminate the extra spaces created by the old typewriter trick of spacing over instead of using tabs, as well.

Remove extra tabs. Paragraphs should not be created by tabbing over. They should be given a style with a first-line indent instead (see Creating Styles below).

Eliminate double returns using Find/Replace. Double returns should not separate paragraphs. The first-line indent in the next paragraph will be enough to distinguish when one paragraph ends and the next begins.

Extra space is used to indicate the start of a new section or a change in topic where a new chapter or headline is not necessary. Double returns are not used to create this extra space. Instead, create a paragraph style to govern this situation, with even more space above the paragraph than that above a subhead, but less than a double return.

Look for odd line breaks, out of place page breaks, and missing punctuation.

Once your manuscript is clean, you can begin creating styles to govern how the text will look.

Create Styles

Most word processing and page layout programs allow you to create styles for different types of text (paragraphs, headlines and so on), and then apply the style when appropriate.

The easiest way to start formatting an entire chapter is to create a style for the majority of the body copy and apply it to the entire chapter. Then you can create new styles for first paragraphs that do not have indents, headlines that could be in bigger or bolder text than the body, and image captions that should be somewhat smaller than the body text.

In most software, each time you encounter a need for a new style, you can manually format the text, and then select that text to create a new style—the software will copy each of the attributes of the new text into the new style. After you create the new style, simply highlight text and apply the new style when needed.

❧

If you do not believe you can typeset the book yourself, you could hire a book packager to help you. Most photo books will not need professional services to look their best. If, however, you have a great deal of text or documented research that accompanies the photographs, a book packager can help you get from manuscript to beautifully published book.

Working with a Book Packager

Book packagers (designers) offer layout and design services, including book design, typesetting, image preparation, cover design and in some cases indexing. Most book packagers will offer these services together or individually, depending upon your needs.

Interior Design

Provide your manuscript along with a few examples of layouts you like to the book packager so they can understand the type of book you have written, as well as your style preferences. Acquiring good examples may necessitate a trip to a library or bookstore with a good collection of photo books.

Photo books, in particular, tend to be highly content specific, so choosing a nice-looking computer manual may not do you much good either. Using a beautiful photo book as your guide is probably best. A book designer who has worked with full-color books before may have suggestions for you.

Most book designers will offer two to three designs plus two rounds of revisions before you pay more than the initial quote. The better you can explain or demonstrate what you want at the outset, the more likely the designer is to create what you are looking for in the first round of designs.

Typesetting

Most of the time, if you have a professional design your book, you will also have them typeset the book because you may not use the same software they use, so there would be no way to hand over the master layout to you. Before you submit your manuscript for typesetting, clean up any overlooked double spaces, tabs and section breaks. Then proofread carefully so you are not paying the typesetter to do that for you.

Print it out. A printout is a way to be sure that nothing is missing or misplaced in the manuscript files. Check it over carefully first. If you find errors and make corrections to the manuscript, print a clean copy for the typesetter.

Image Preparation

You cannot prepare your images for the correct display size at the correct resolution until you have a layout in order to know how big or small each image must be in order to fit into the grid. If you have scanned the images at sizes larger than what will be needed, much of the hard work should already be done. Your book packager can then help you to correctly size the image for the book's layout.

Indexing

Few photo books meant for personal enjoyment include an index. If you plan to sell the book, however, you may need to include one. Not all book designers offer indexing services, although some do. Using a book packager or a professional indexer can be costly because he or she must read the manuscript in order to determine what should or should not be indexed, and that takes time.

Often called a poor man's index, you can make the job of indexing easy for a book packager by printing a copy of the final layout, and highlighting the items to be indexed. The highlighted copy along with a style sheet of how you want names, places and subjects indexed should be enough for your book packager to take care of the indexing for you.

Another option is to mark the index entries for yourself in your word processor. Index tags from Word import into InDesign, for example, and most book designers accept Word documents. Before you spend the time to index this way, make certain that the book packager can import your index tags.

Cover Design

Every book should have a cover worthy of the work it took to write the book. Book packagers offer cover design services, or you may want to use a cover designer—a graphic artist who only designs covers. Either way, he or she will need to know whether the book will be available for sale. Commercial books have different requirements than books solely for your family's enjoyment. The elements of a book cover meant for commercial sale are described in Chapter 21: Designing the Cover.

The cover will be the last part of your project finalized because spine width is dependent upon the final page count and the paper used, which may be different from printer to printer. In most cases, you will receive a template from your printer after you have a final page count, so that the dimensions and spine width are correct in the template. The designer can assemble the elements ahead of time and make final adjustments to the file when the page count is known.

File Formats

Most book packagers can work with any type of file format generated by one of the common word processors (.doc, .docx, .wpd) as well as plain text files (.txt) or rich text files (.rtf). Most word processors will also convert their native file formats to something more common such as a Microsoft Word file, if that is what the designer prefers.

Ask before converting anything. Converting to a plain text file will eliminate all of your formatting. Converting to a PDF is not helpful either, since PDFs are not easily re-formatted.

Portfolio

Before you ask about cost, look at the designer's work. You want to make sure that he or she has experience preparing books for a printer. Many book packagers have an online portfolio or can send you examples.

Another option is to hire someone who is looking to create a portfolio piece and is willing to do whatever it takes to finish the job to your satisfaction—at a lower price. Students and people who are learning the craft are often willing to work for much less than established book designers.

Cost

Book packagers charge for some services by the piece (image preparation), other services by the page (typesetting), and a few services by the hour (indexing). If you would rather have the designer give you a bid for the whole project, they will need to know the approximate page count and number of illustrations. They will set limits on the number of designs and revisions they will give you on the interior and cover. If you reject the initial round of designs all together, you may have to pay an additional fee to see more designs.

Write a Formal Proposal or Contract

Once you have a cost estimate from the designer, write an additional proposal making your expectations clear about what work will be taken care of by the designer, and what you are responsible for providing to him or her. Include firm deadlines and a do-not-exceed price—the price beyond which you cannot go. Most designers will give you an estimate with a price range since it is difficult to know exactly what you will or will not like until the work is started. You may want to make more changes than what the original agreement calls for, which may necessitate a new estimate. The designer should take care of any errors that are their fault, but be prepared to pay extra if you edit once the typesetting is done.

❧❧

Typesetting is all about making your manuscript easy to read. Choosing appropriate fonts and type sizes, spacing between letters and lines, and justifying body text are the heart and soul of the typesetting rules. If you can also avoid common punctuation errors, and eliminate any widows and orphans, your book's interior will look like it was typeset by a professional.

Chapter 18

Typesetting the Front Matter

This chapter will take you through the front matter in the order each element appears in most books, from the first item (the endsheets) to the last item (the introduction). How many of these front matter pieces are appropriate for your book is project specific. A photo book solely for the enjoyment of family may not need much beyond the title page.

Almost every front matter element should begin on a right-hand (recto) page which means that there may be blank pages within your front matter. Beginning each new section on a right-hand page is a publishing convention—a tradition, but in the interest of saving space, many publishers today are running each successive part on the next available page.

There are not many examples in this chapter because you will find working examples in the front matter of this book.

Endsheets

In hardcover books, endsheets are used to reinforce the attachment from the cloth cover to the sewn-together pages of the interior, so you will find an endsheet in the front and the back of the book. If you are using an offset printer, you may be able to choose the photograph, illustration or design for your endsheets. Other printers have stock designs for you to choose from, although many use a common endsheet.

Endsheets are not necessary to hold the covers onto softbound (paperback) books, therefore, are not used. With some printers, it is possible to print a photograph or illustration on the inside cover of a paperback book, but it is almost always an extra charge. Most print-on-demand printers do not offer this option.

Frontispiece

A frontispiece is an illustration on the left-hand (verso) side facing the title page. These are common, mostly in high-end coffee table books.

Although an illustration could go on the reverse side of the endsheet, a frontispiece is usually a separate page using the same paper as the interior, rather than the heavier endsheet paper.

Endorsements or Blurbs

Endorsements are also called blurbs. It is common for publishers with commercially available books to solicit short blurbs from well-known authors or experts. The best blurbs belong on the cover or dust jacket flaps. Any others go on pages before the half-title page, and these pages are not numbered.

It is uncommon for family photo books to include blurbs, although it could be fun if you are taking new photographs to include in the book to capture quotes from family members to use as blurbs as you are taking the photographs. If you are going to solicit them, five or six will do. Keep them short and sweet. If you are soliciting a well-known author or expert, offer a blurb already written for his or her approval or to edit as he or she sees fit.

Blurbs are typically set in the main body font, in quotes. The name of the blurb's author follows on a separate line either centered or flush right, followed by a line containing any titles, awards or books he or she has written, also centered or flush right. Use italics for book titles.

Half-Title Page

A half-title page was used more than a century ago to identify an unsold book. In those days, books were printed, but not bound until sold, so that the new owner could choose the binding. Today, half title pages are not necessary but if you include one, the reverse side should be blank.

The half-title page should be typeset in whatever font you have chosen for your chapter headers, but big enough to make a statement, placed about one-third of the way down the page.

Ad Card

One option for the reverse side of the title page is to include an ad card—a list of other books you have written. Look at the ad card in this book. It begins with: "Other books by the author" and lists the titles. You could begin with: "Author of ..." or "Also by ..."

The ad card is typeset in the main body font, flush left, but justified ragged right. If you are only listing titles, full justification may stretch the words apart unnaturally.

Title Page

Typeset the title in the same font and size as the half-title page, and place it about one-third of the way down the page. The title should be followed by the subtitle in the same font but smaller. The author's name should be placed about two-thirds of the way down the page, followed by the publishing company, and the city where the book was published (the city of the publishing company not the printer) at the bottom. If you have a logo for your publishing company, it can go on this page, as well.

The reverse side of the title page is the copyrights page.

Copyrights Page

The copyrights page belongs on the back of the title page and should include:

- The title and subtitle
- The author's name
- The publisher's name and physical address
- A copyright notice (the symbol and year)
- The name of the copyright owner
- The expression "all rights reserved" to give you the maximum protection in case of copyright infringement
- A disclaimer, if needed. Most books today include one even if not needed.
- Publishing history (edition or print run if there has been more than one)
- Printed in the United States of America (or wherever the book was printed)

If you plan to sell your book commercially or to libraries, also consider:

Library of Congress (LOC) Cataloging-in-Publication Data [LCC CIP]. The CIP data is bibliographic data prepared by the Library of Congress to help libraries and book dealers correctly catalog the book.

Before the book is published, apply for the CIP Program online (www.loc.gov/publish/cip/).

You can also create your own CIP data, called the Publisher's CIP data, if you do not want to wait months for the Library of Congress to do this for you.

Library of Congress Catalog Number (LCCN or PCN—Preassigned Control Number). A Library of Congress catalog control number (or preassigned number) is a unique identification number given by the LOC, that is included in their national database available to libraries, book stores and other commercial suppliers. Before your book is published, apply for a Library of Congress PCN (www.loc.gov/publish/pcn/).

International Standard Book Number (ISBN). An ISBN is like the Social Security number for you book. It is a unique number assigned by the U.S. ISBN Agency run by the Bowker Company (www.isbn.org). From the website, you can purchase a single ISBN, a block of ten, a block of 100, and so on. A single ISBN costs $125.00. A block of ten costs $295.00.

If you are planning to publish through a print-on-demand printer, many offer ISBNs free of charge. The only drawback to using one of your printer's ISBNs is that the printer becomes the publisher of record, and not you or your publishing company. For many photo book authors, however, using the printer's free ISBN is the simplest way to go.

The copyrights page should be typeset in the main body font, but the majority of the text will be set at a point size small enough to fit all of the above information onto one page. Use the copyrights page of this book as a guide.

Dedication

Many authors use the dedication page to thank whoever has been the greatest influence while creating the book. Most dedications are short. Longer tributes belong in the acknowledgments section.

The dedication page should be typeset in the main body font, in Roman (plain) text or italics.

Dedication pages are optional. If used, they should occupy a right-hand page, and the back should be blank.

Acknowledgments

Acknowledgments are your opportunity to thank anyone who helped you find photographs, research or write the book. Acknowledgments are optional.

If used, be rigorous when checking the spelling of each person's name, and if they have a title, use the correct, most recently earned title.

Acknowledgments begin on a right-hand page, and can be placed after the dedication, after the preface, within the preface, or in the back matter. If your acknowledgments run an odd number of pages, the last page should be blank.

Acknowledgments should be typeset in the main body font, and if there are many paragraphs, should follow the rules for the rest of the book. If there is a single paragraph, it can be set in italics about one-third of the way down the page.

Epigraph

An epigraph is a pertinent quote that sets the tone for the book, and is optional. Epigraphs are sometimes used on the first page of each chapter.

If the epigraph is typeset on a right-hand page, the back of the page should be blank. Epigraphs can also go on the left-hand page facing the table of contents, if that page is blank.

Epigraphs should be in quotes, in the main body font, in Roman (plain) text or italics. The author's name (or anonymous, if not known) should be placed on a line beneath the quote, followed by the source of the quote on another line. If the source is a book title, it should be typeset in italics.

Table of Contents

The table of contents (TOC) begins on a right-hand page. If there is only one page, the reverse side should be left blank. If the contents run more than one page, they are called contents *only* and can be set *either* on a left-right, two-page spread (pages ii and iii, for example), or beginning on a right-hand page with the remainder on the next left-hand page (pages iii and iv, in this case).

The table of contents can be set in either the main body font or the font you have chosen for your headlines and subheads. The page numbers should be typeset with a right-aligned tab to keep the right-hand edges of the page numbers even down the page.

The table of contents should show the number of the first page of each part of the front matter, the parts (or sections), each chapter, the back matter and the index. How much else you include beyond the chapter number, is up to you.

You could include the chapter title (if there are chapter titles), and a running list of subtitles to give the reader an idea of what to expect in each chapter. The example (below) from Buzzy Jackson's book *Shaking the Family Tree* uses a running narrative to give readers an idea of what is included in each chapter.

Illustrations

The nature of a photo book is book full of images, so a list of illustrations may seem silly. If, however, your book has many non-photo illustrations such as charts, you could include a list of illustrations (also called a list of figures). If the illustrations correspond closely with the text, the list is probably not necessary because the information will be provided in the captions, descriptive text or footnotes.

A list of illustrations should include the name (or a description) of the illus-

CONTENTS

Ask Yourself Why You're Doing This; or, Genealogy for
Beginners   1
An introduction to the world of genealogy and how I got interested in it. Here I provide an outline of how to do genealogical research and, coincidentally, a map of the book's structure.

They See Dead People But I Stick to the Living; or, Join Your
Local Genealogical Society   18
Seeking help from experienced genealogists, I join my local genealogical society. I begin my family research by interviewing my parents and by asking myself how much I really know about my family tree. Answer: not much.

Interview Your Relatives and Go to Your High School Reunion;
or, Rust Never Sleeps   39
Having exhausted my parents' fund of knowledge (and my own), I travel to Michigan to conduct interviews with extended family, seek access (mostly denied) to family Bibles, and visit my grandparents' graves for the first time. A few weeks later I attend my twentieth high school reunion, which offers another type of family connection.

Table of Contents.

tration, plus the page number where it occurs. The page numbers should be typeset with a right-aligned tab to keep the right-hand edges of the page numbers even down the page. The back side of a list of illustrations should be blank.

Tables

Lists of tables are common in scientific literature and occasionally in military histories but are uncommon in photo books. If you need one, the back of the page should be left blank. A list of tables should be typeset in the same way as a list of illustrations.

Foreword

A foreword is statement about the book written by someone other than the author. Forewords are common in biographies of famous people, but not common in photo books.

If you include one, a foreword longer than two to three pages should have a title of its own with the author's name at the beginning, rather than at the end, which is typical for short forewords.

The foreword should be typeset in the main body text and follow the same rules as the body as far as paragraphs, headlines and subheads. If your foreword runs an odd number of pages, the next page should be left blank so that the next section will begin on a right-hand page.

Typeset the following using the same rules as the foreword:

Front Matter	Body	Back Matter
Preface	Epilogue	Postscript
Methods	Afterword	About the Author
Contributors		Glossary
Chronology		Colophon
Characters		
Permissions		
Prologue		

Preface

A preface is optional. It is a way for you, the author, to address the reader directly. A preface is one place to explain the reasons you undertook this project, or your research methods. Many authors include their acknowledgments in the preface. If you do, there is no need for another section of acknowledgments elsewhere.

Methods

A methods section (also called editorial method) is used in scholarly works where the author's analysis needs explanation. In a photo book, you may want to alert readers to certain information, if the explanation is important before they begin looking at the photographs or reading the text. Some of this could be included in footnotes or endnotes rather than in the front matter.

Contributors

A list of contributors is optional. If someone provided expertise that calls for more than a simple acknowledgment, a list of contributors is the place to give credit along with a short explanation describing how each person or group helped you with this project.

Chronology

A chronology can be helpful if the order of events is not clear, as may happen, for example, in a collection of letters, or in a diary with missing entries.

Use a chronology to provide a broader historical context. For example, a list of events preceding the events pictured in your photographs may help readers understand why the photographs were taken.

A chronology can also serve as a quick reference if your book covers multiple families or time lines.

A chronology should begin on a right-hand page, unless it would be simpler for the reader to use a left-right page spread.

Characters

Occasionally, in fiction you may find a list of characters. In a photo book, captions should serve this role. If there are people important to the family but who are not pictured, you could use a list of characters or genealogical charts to include them.

If you include a list of characters, alphabetize by last name followed by a comma and the first name as well as a short, descriptive paragraph about the character. Typeset the names in bold or italics either as subheads or run-in subheads.

Permissions

If you have only a few places where you need to acknowledge permissions given to use material for the book, they could be placed in a footnote, an endnote, an image credit or a sidebar. A list may be easier if you have many permissions to acknowledge.

A list of permissions can be placed in either the front or the back matter and should begin on a right-hand page. You can organize the list of permissions in order as the items occur, or alphabetically by repository to avoid repeating information if many items came from one repository. When describing sources, give the location in the book by chapter and (or) page, then use the same style as endnotes or footnotes, typically using either *Evidence Explained* or *The Chicago Manual of Style*.

Prologue

A prologue is used in fiction to set the scene for the story and is told in the voice of one of the characters rather than by the author. A prologue is an unusual feature in most photo books.

Second Half-Title Page

If the front matter is long, you can use a second half-title page to give readers a visual clue where the body of the book begins. The second half-title page should look exactly like the first half-title page. This is another unusual feature for a photo book.

Introduction

If your photo book also has narrative, use an introduction to explain your purpose or goals in writing the book.

The introduction, although technically a part of the front matter, is the beginning of the narrative. The introduction should follow the typesetting rules for the body, with one exception. Although the page numbers in the preceding front matter sections are set in lowercase Roman numerals, switch to Arabic numerals when you begin the introduction.

Some publishers will continue the page numbers from the front matter, so if the last page of the front matter was page viii, then the first page of the introduction would be page 9. Others will restart the numbering with page 1 on the first page of the introduction. The first style is more traditional, although the latter style is becoming more common.

❧ ❧

Much of what can be included in the front matter is optional. The sections that *are* necessary are the title page, the copyrights page (if the book will be distributed to anyone other than family), and a table of contents if there is also narrative, not just photographs. Beyond that, it is up to you as the publisher to decide what else to include.

Chapter 19

Typesetting the Body

Most of the typesetting for the body of the book with narrative longer than captions is about the paragraphs, headlines and subheads covered in the previous section. The remainder is how to create first pages different enough to give the reader a visual clue that a new section or chapter is beginning.

Parts or Sections—First Pages

If you have divided the manuscript into parts or sections, you will need an opening page for each. These pages should act as dividers and should be right-hand pages with the reverse side left blank unless you wish to use an epigraph or illustration there.

Typeset the part or section title in large letters about one-third of the way down the page using the same font as your title and subtitle. You can use the part or section title alone, or include a mini-table of contents for the section.

Neither the front nor the back of this page should have a running header or a page number, but these pages contribute to the page count. So even though they should not have page numbers on them, count the pages following a part or section divider as if they did.

Chapters—First Pages

The first page of each chapter should be easy to find while thumbing through a book. Traditionally, chapters begin on a new page on the right-hand side. If you end up with many blank pages because chapters have an uneven number of pages, you can ignore the convention to minimize the number of blank pages—with two exceptions: chapters *must* begin on a *new* page (whether left or right) and Chapter One *must* begin on a *right-hand* page.

Chapter titles are optional, but numbers are not. If you use titles, they should be consistent in tone from one chapter to the next. In other words, do not use a whimsical title for one, and a serious statement for the next.

Chapter numbers start at one and are consecutive no matter what section they are in, so that chapter numbers are never repeated.

The first page of a chapter should not have a page number or a running header. The chapter number and (or) title should begin at least two inches from the top of the page, but could be as low as one-third of the way down the page with the body text beginning about half-way down the page.

Footnotes or Endnotes

Whether you put your source citations in footnotes or endnotes is up to you. Opinions are divided about whether readers would rather refer to an endnotes page or read footnotes as they occur in the text.

If you use footnotes, leave enough room between the text and the footnote to make it obvious, or use a rule (line) in between. Most word processing and page layout programs create footnotes for you, so they are not technically footers because the amount of space they occupy will change from page to page depending upon how many notes there are on each page.

If you use endnotes, place them either at the end of the chapter, or together in the back matter.

Section II Mary James (1849–1902) and John Nathaniel Hammet (1844–1900)	**Section 2** Mary James (1849–1902) and John Nathaniel Hammet (1844–1900) Chapter 8: Luella Ann Hammet Chapter 9: James William Hammet Chapter 10: Corrinne Sophie Hammet Chapter 11: Mary Louisiana Hammet Chapter 13: Winston George Hammet Chapter 14: Nelson Grant Hammet

Section divider with number and title (left); Section divider with mini-table of contents (right).

Typical formatting for footnotes or endnotes is as follows:

1. Author (first then last), *Title in Italics* (City of publication: Publisher, date), p. number.

Epilogue

An epilogue is a final note from you, the author, or as a continuation of the main narrative to bring closure to the book.

Afterword

An afterword, is a way for you, the author, to give your final thoughts. Set the book into a larger context within the family, let readers know about additional research you are doing, tell a funny story that wraps up the book, or give the reader an enticing preview of your next book.

Conclusion

If you did not do so in the epilogue, use the conclusion to provide a brief summary of the main points.

Chapter 4

Lorem ipsum dolor sit amet, consectetur adipisicing elit, sed do eiusmod tempor incididunt ut labore et dolore magna aliqua. Ut enim ad minim veniam, quis nostrud exercitation ullamco laboris nisi ut aliquip ex ea commodo consequat. Duis aute irure dolor in reprehenderit in voluptate velit esse cillum dolore eu fugiat nulla pariatur. Excepteur sint occaecat cupidatat non proident, sunt in culpa qui officia deserunt mollit anim id est laborum.

Lorem ipsum dolor sit amet, consectetur adipisicing elit, sed do eiusmod tempor incididunt ut labore et dolore magna aliqua. Ut enim ad minim veniam, quis nostrud exercitation ullamco laboris nisi ut aliquip ex ea commodo consequat. Duis aute irure dolor in reprehenderit in voluptate velit esse cillum dolore eu fugiat nulla pariatur. Excepteur sint occaecat cupidatat non proident, sunt in culpa qui officia deserunt mollit anim id est laborum.

Lorem ipsum dolor sit amet, consectetur adipisicing elit, sed do eiusmod tempor incididunt ut labore et dolore magna aliqua. Ut enim ad minim veniam, quis nostrud exercitation

Chapter 4

Our Family Moves West

Lorem ipsum dolor sit amet, consectetur adipisicing elit, sed do eiusmod tempor incididunt ut labore et dolore magna aliqua. Ut enim ad minim veniam, quis nostrud exercitation ullamco laboris nisi ut aliquip ex ea commodo consequat. Duis aute irure dolor in reprehenderit in voluptate velit esse cillum dolore eu fugiat nulla pariatur. Excepteur sint occaecat cupidatat non proident, sunt in culpa qui officia deserunt mollit anim id est laborum.

Lorem ipsum dolor sit amet, consectetur adipisicing elit, sed do eiusmod tempor incididunt ut labore et dolore magna aliqua. Ut enim ad minim veniam, quis nostrud exercitation ullamco laboris nisi ut aliquip ex ea commodo consequat. Duis aute irure dolor in reprehenderit in voluptate velit esse cillum dolore eu fugiat nulla pariatur. Excepteur sint occaecat cupidatat non proident, sunt in culpa qui officia deserunt mollit anim id est laborum.

Lorem ipsum dolor sit amet, consectetur adipisicing elit, sed do eiusmod tempor incididunt ut labore et dolore magna aliqua. Ut enim ad minim veniam, quis nostrud exercitation ullamco laboris nisi ut aliquip ex ea commodo consequat. Duis aute irure dolor in reprehenderit in voluptate velit esse cillum dolore eu fugiat

Chapter with number (left); Chapter with number and title (right).

ڡڡ

Because most of the typesetting for the book concerns paragraphs, headlines, subheads and running headers, what is left is to create visual breaks for parts (sections) and the first page of each chapter, and to decide where to place the source citations—in footnotes or endnotes.

Chapter 20

Typesetting the Back Matter

The back matter begins when the narrative ceases and you have had your last word as the author—well, almost. Back matter typically includes appendices, endnotes, a bibliography and an index. Your back matter could also include a postscript, an about the author section, a glossary, errata, a colophon, an excerpt from another book, and an order form.

The following front matter can be placed in the back matter if you prefer: acknowledgments, lists of illustrations, tables, contributors, and permissions.

Postscript

A postscript is a place to add something you were unable to include in the book. If you came across additional research, for example, give a brief synopsis. Or, if you are planning an additional photo book tell readers about it in the postscript.

About the Author

An about the author section is optional. It is an opportunity to tell the reader who you are and why you wrote the book. It should include a brief biography and a photograph is customary. Often, a brief version is placed on the back cover, or a longer version on the dust jacket flap of a hardcover edition.

Appendices

Items in an appendix may explain, elaborate or clarify information that do not fit neatly into the narrative. Each appendix needs a title, a number or a letter. The first appendix should appear on a right-hand page. Each subsequent appendix could begin on the next available page, right or left, to avoid blank pages.

Addendum

An addendum is a section of new material that was unavailable when the book was written. Often, an addendum is added in a subsequent edition, updating information without a complete re-write.

Glossary

A glossary is optional, but appreciated if you use: foreign words; jargon or technical phrases (common if you are describing a process or a profession from a century or more ago); words used during an earlier era but not used today; or unfamiliar slang (e.g. military slang).

Alphabetize glossary terms followed by a brief explanation.

Endnotes

If you want to place endnotes in the back matter, they should begin on a right-hand page, be organized by chapter, and then by note number. Leave extra space before the start of each chapter's endnotes to create a visual break.

Bibliography

While a formal bibliography is optional in a photo book, readers may be interested in what books and articles you consulted in addition to any original source material you used.

You will find standard bibliographic style guides for published materials in *The Elements of Style* by William Strunk and E.B. White, or *A Manual for Writers of Term Papers, Theses, and Dissertations* by Kate L. Turabian.

Your bibliography could be organized by family, location, research facility or topic. If you organize in a way other than alphabetical by author's last name for the whole list, use a subhead to indicate the start of a new section, alphabetize within the section, and leave space before the subhead as a visual break.

Index

All non-fiction books that will be sold or used in libraries must have an index. The first place many family members will look is the index, to see if they are listed. Fortunately, most word processing and page layout software makes it possible to create index tags electronically within the body text, which are compiled into an index once the final layout is finished. It is important to compile the index last, however, to make certain text has not shifted from one page to the next during any final editing or touch ups to the layout.

Unfortunately, there is not one, single set of rules for creating an index. Most publishing houses have their own criteria, as do professional indexers. As the publisher, you have a great deal of latitude in what you will include.

Indexing takes time and adds pages to the book, but, first and foremost, it should be a useful tool. Be careful not to let the task of indexing determine the contents. It is not uncommon to find books where material in the beginning is over-indexed, and material at the end is under-indexed because the indexer tired of the process.

There are three types of index listings to consider: names, places and subjects.

Every person mentioned should be included in the index. A full-name index has become the standard for genealogical works thanks to the persistence of genealogists such as Birdie Holsclaw. Your index should adhere to this standard. Besides, it is the first place your family members will look, to see where they are mentioned.

Indexing places is helpful to other people researching the area.

Indexing subjects is a little trickier because it is hard to know what subjects are the most important to include. If you have spent time talking about battles, or the details of a profession, or have discussed the manufacturer of your grandmother's bone china, those are the kinds of subjects worth including.

An index is not merely a list of names and places, it is a way for people to retrieve information quickly, so any subject you think would help the reader find what they are looking for will be appreciated.

Index the whole book—everything from the dedication to the appendices—with a couple of exceptions. There is no need to index the colophon or copyrights page, nor the bibliography because it is already alphabetical by author's name and therefore easy to search. Endnotes or footnotes may be a different matter, if you have included other explanatory material in the note. If there are relevant entries in the explanatory material, then index it.

Basic Index Formatting

The index should begin on a right-hand page and be typeset in the body font, one or two points smaller. Each page should have a running header and page numbers, the same as the rest of the book. Use hanging indents to keep the alphabetical first letter flush left, but the remainder of the listing along with the page numbers, indented about one-quarter of an inch. Use a slightly larger space between listings than the line leading for wrapped text to create a visual break or to add a bit of white space to the page.

When you begin a new letter in your alphabetical list, use a subhead in bold that is slightly larger than the index body text.

Some publishers use bold page numbers to indicate illustrations, and bold italicized page numbers to indicate boxed text or tables. If you have created a list of illustrations or tables in the front matter, there is no need for this type of formatting in your index.

Page numbers are formatted according to long-standing tradition. Information that occurs on sequential pages is formatted with an en dash in between the numbers, but only if the discussion of the subject is continuous across those pages. For example, a person may be mentioned on page 140 and again on page 141, but there is *not* a continuous discussion of this person, so the formatting would be 140, 141. If there had been a continuous discussion of that person, the formatting would be 140–141. This is a subtle difference and not crucial.

Most software-generated indexes will create a list of numbers separated by commas. You can save space in the index by combining a long list of consecutive page numbers (140, 141, 142, 143, 144), into a shorter run of 140–144. Whether you follow the long-standing convention of using the en dash only to indicate a continuous discussion of the subject, is up to you, although using the en dashes correctly is more accurate.

In a photo book, there may be chapters where the same individual is mentioned on every page. Another way to cut down on the number of pages where an individual is indexed, is to give the reader the first page plus a symbol (e.g. * or # or +) on which a major player is mentioned in a chapter, but no subsequent page numbers. If you shorten the number of listings this way, explain it at the beginning of the index—true of any deviation from convention—so that the reader knows what to expect.

There is no need to indicate how many times an individual, place or subject is listed on a single page. An index points the reader to the page, it does not absolve the user of reading what is there.

Formatting Subjects

Main subjects should be flush left, then broken down into minor subjects. The minor subjects should be indented one-quarter of an inch using a hanging indent so that any wrapping page numbers fall at half an inch. Main subjects are capitalized; minor subjects are not unless they begin with a proper noun. If you include a cross-reference, the word "see" should be in italics before the cross-reference subject. The following is an example:

Wagon
 Conestoga 33, 70, 104
 repair, *see* wainwright
 trains 21-24, 47

Formatting Place Names

Formatting place names can be tricky if the place is known by more than one name during different time periods. The New Netherlands is a good example. If your ancestors lived in the Manhattan area during Dutch rule, they would have lived in New Netherlands, not New York. If you are unsure whether your readers will be acquainted well enough with the location to know that New Netherlands became New York, you may want to include a cross-reference.

New Netherlands, *see also* New York.

Another way to deal with place names where the location is the same but the name is not, is to include an explanation, such as:

Denver, Denver County (then Arapahoe County), Colorado
Denver, Arapahoe County (now Denver County), Colorado

Index geographic names the way a reader would look for them, so:

The Dalles, Oregon.
> The Dalles, Oregon, not Dalles, The, Oregon because "The Dalles" is recognized as the place name.

Elms, The.
> However, if you have a property name such as The Elms, it would be indexed as Elms, The and not The Elms. (Indexing can be tricky.)

Florence, Italy.
> Florence not Firenze (for an English-speaking audience)

Pear Cottage.
> Pear Cottage, not Cottage, Pear

If you use abbreviations in your place names, do so consistently, such as:
> St. Louis or Saint Louis, but not a mixture of the two
> Ste. Genevieve County for Sainte Genevieve County

Or:
> Ste. Genevieve Co. (if you also consistently abbreviate county using Co.)

Formatting People's Names

Surnames are not universal, and they can be inconsistent over time. That makes them tricky to index if you have included people whose families are the same, but whose surnames are different. In general, whatever rule you followed for the text, repeat in the index, except where alphabetizing by your software becomes a problem. Not all software alphabetizes the same way. Microsoft Word, for example, will treat De la Rosa differently than de la Rosa, giving priority to the capitalized version. The index will show both versions, but the capitalized version will come first.

Most software will treat names with spaces in them differently than names without, so these words would be alphabetized as:

> De la Rosa
> Deify
> Delarosa

Detrimental
Di Larosa

If the number of listings between the two versions of De la Rosa is substantial, use a cross-reference (e.g. *see* Di Larosa or *see* Du Larosa) so that the reader knows to look for another spelling. A different way to deal with this is to explain at the start of the index that you have made all versions of Vandergard (Vander Gard, Van Der Gard, van der Gard) the same for the purposes of indexing only.

If there are people with the same name, do something to distinguish them in the index, for example:

Josiah Smith (1830–1899)   33, 89, 90
Josiah Smith (1864–1919)   60, 71, 90
Josiah Smith (1880–1956)   78, 91, 106

Or:

Josiah Smith (the elder)   33, 89, 90
Josiah Smith (the baker)   60, 71, 90
Josiah Smith (the son)   78, 91, 106

If you have many people listed with the same surname, so you will list the surname once, flush left, then alphabetize the first names indented one-quarter of an inch (.25") with the hanging indent leaving any wrapping page numbers indented one-half inch (.5"). For example:

Foster
    Allen 71, 77
    Bruce 50
    Carter 44

If you have a long list of people under the same surname, when you reach the next column or page, repeat the surname followed by (cont.).

Foster (cont.)
    Wesley
    William, Jr.
    William, Sr.

Women's names can be problematic because in order to create the most useful index, you need to refer to women by both their maiden and married names, if appropriate, and on occasion, by multiple married names. The following are examples of how to handle this.

If a woman's name was Mary Jane Jones Rankin Scarborough, meaning she was born as Mary Jane Jones, married a Rankin and subsequently married a Scarborough, she should be listed as:

Jones, Mary Jane (*see* Rankin, Mary Jane, *see* Scarborough, Mary Jane)
Rankin, Mary Jane (Jones)
Scarborough, Mary Jane (Jones) (Rankin)

People with hyphenated surnames should be listed under both names as well. For example:

Gowan-Saroyan, Jane (*see* Saroyan, Jane Gowan)

If there are women who are referred to by *only* their married names, they should be listed as:

Brice, William (Mrs.)—not, Brice, Mrs. William.

If there were many women named Mrs. Brice, for example, they would all alphabetize under Brice, M (for Mrs.) and not under the letter of their husband's first name where they should.

Incorrect:
Brice, Keith
Brice, Mrs. Adam
Brice, Mrs. William
Brice, Nathan

Correct:
Brice, Adam (Mrs.)
Brice, Keith
Brice, Nathan
Brice, William (Mrs.)

The use of titles such as Miss and Dr. is a matter of preference in the index, unless Miss Shaw or Dr. Reynolds is the only name you have for those individuals. If you have only a last name and a title, then the titles belong in the index.

In a transcription, using a name as you find it is proper; in an index, not necessarily. For example, if you find the name Daniel, Dan'l and Dan in the body text, in the index, you may not wish to have three listings for the same person under each of these iterations. If it is clear that you are referring to the same person, use the best, most complete name—Daniel.

If there are people who are referred to by only one name, or by none at all, include whatever you need to, to reference that individual:

Horace (the watchmaker)
Negro girl (b. ca 1850)
Susannah (the neighbor)

The same goes if you have a surname but no first name, for example:

Halford (cotton buyer)
Rosenkranz, Miss (housekeeper)
Surry, Miss (teacher)

If you have people who used a nickname that does not suggest their formal name, and then use a cross-reference, such as: Rogers, Buzz (*see* Rogers, Alden).

Formatting Institutional Names

Formal names should be indexed as they are presented:

All Saints Cathedral
Miss Porter's School
Van Pelt Cemetery

These places could also be indexed under subject headings:

Cemeteries
Van Pelt Cemetery

Churches
All Saints Cathedral

Schools
Miss Porter's School

Institutions with the same name should include a way to differentiate one place from the next:

Old Burying Ground (Boston, MA)
Old Burying Ground (Waverly, NH)

Institutions using people's names can be tricky, as well. For the most part they should be indexed as written, so either:

Harrison Trimble High School
Or:
Trimble, Harrison. *See also* Harrison Trimble High School
But not:
Trimble, Harrison (High School)

In the 19th century, it was common for people to name their businesses after themselves. The best way to list them is both as they appear *and* by the founder's last name, for example:

C. Madison & Co.
Madison, Charles. *See also* C. Madison and Co.
Madison (C. Madison & Co.)

Index legal cases the same way as business names above. First by the full name of the case, usually plaintiff versus defendant, and then by the surname of the defendant followed by the full case name, so:

Delaney vs. Richards
Richards (Delaney vs. Richards)

Index consistently so that readers can find information quickly and easily.

Errata

An errata section is used to alert the reader to any errors that were discovered during production that are uncorrected in the narrative. For publishers who run thousands of books in a single press run, these sections are necessary because the publisher will not issue a corrected edition until the print run is sold out. Fortunately, if you use one of the print-on-demand printers that does not charge to upload a new version, you can correct errors as you find them by uploading a new interior file. There would be no need for an errata section.

An errata section is organized in order of the errors with the chapter number and page number, followed by what is listed and the correction. For example:

Chapter 2, page 26: 21 May 1767 should read 21 May 1867
Chapter 2, page 33: Richard S. Burton should read Richard L. Burton

Remember: Each time you make changes that move words from one page to another, you must re-create the index.

Colophon

A colophon is the design and production credits for the book: who created the cover and interior, the fonts and paper used, and the name of the printer. This information can also go on the copyright page above the copyright notice and cataloging data.

Excerpt

If you have written other books, or are writing or planning to write additional books, include an excerpt from another book at the end of this one, especially in an electronic version. In an electronic version you can also include a live link to your website, a blog where you will update readers on the progress of a new book, or to a place where the other book(s) is sold. Include the full links in your print edition as well so interested readers can find you online.

Include something exciting or useful in the excerpt. Then, tell the reader why they may be interested in other books you have written. Ask readers to check out the link. This is referred to as a "call to action" in marketing. You could also include a line such as, "If you enjoyed this book and would like to purchase a copy for a family member ... "

Format the excerpt the same way as the body text. If you have many other books, list them at the end of the excerpt so that interested readers can browse your list of titles. Include links for each of those titles as well.

Order Form

Including an order form is one way to make sure an interested person who has found your book in a library has a way to contact you to buy their own copy. Not everyone uses the Internet to place orders, even today.

An order form should occur on the last page, and should include:

- Your name or your company name
- Your address (where they should send the order)
- Your website address
- A call to action ("If you enjoyed this book and would like to buy a copy for a family member ...")
- All titles available (cross-sell your other books)
- The price of each item
- Shipping and handling charges for each item
- A discount for ordering more than one book (free shipping perhaps)
- Any additional merchandise you have to offer (photographic reprints or family tree charts, for example)
- A place to total the order
- A place to fill out their name, address, email address (make this area big enough for the person ordering to write legibly)
- An explanation of the payment methods you will accept (check, money order, PayPal or credit card)

Creating order forms can be tricky. Find a good catalog order form and use it as your guide.

❧❧

In the back matter, you have an opportunity to include whatever did not fit easily into the body of the book, or to clarify terms used or mistakes discovered after the typesetting was finished.

The most important item in the back matter is the index. Every non-fiction book that will be sold in a store or used in a library must have one, including a photo book.

As the publisher, everything else in the back matter is up to you.

❧

Working with an Indexer

Most photo books do not need the services of a professional indexer. You know your material as well as any indexer could. Professional indexing is often necessary for complex non-fiction or scientific works, but you should be able to either create the index yourself as you typeset, or be able to work with your book packager to do so. If you choose to hire an indexer, consider the following:

Portfolio

A professional indexer should be able to give you the titles of books he or she has indexed, and an electronic copy of an index or two.

What to Include

Your index should include every name mentioned in the book, along with the names of groups or institutions. Include place names that are significant. The indexer may be able to suggest subject headings to you, since subjects are more commonly what professional indexers categorize, rather than names.

Fees

Professional indexers charge either by the page, or by the hour. If your indexer does not have much experience, pay by the page. Pay by the hour, only when hiring an accomplished indexer. Using a professional indexer can often run as much as book packaging or editing costs. If you have to choose, put the money into editing first, and then into the layout and design. Leave the indexing for last.

Final Layout

A professional indexer must work from your final layout—with all of the typesetting in place and pages established—in order to create an accurate index. Before you give the final layout to the indexer, make certain all revisions or corrections have been made. Then, print a final copy.

After the indexing is complete, if you make revisions to the text that alters on which page the indexed words appear, you will pay dearly to have the indexer make corrections.

Write a Formal Proposal or Contract

Use a formal proposal to indicate how the index is to be returned to you or your book packager—as a Word document, or an unformatted plain text document, for example. Make your expectations for the index and deadlines clear. If you have agreed to pay by the hour, include a do-not-exceed price to keep the indexer from running wild with your budget.

❧❧

It may seem as if there are a lot of rules to follow for typesetting, but it is the attention to detail in the typesetting that will make your book look like it has been professionally published.

Chapter 21

Designing the Cover

It would be nice to think that readers do not judge books by their covers, but in reality, they do. Not only do they judge whether they want to buy the book, but often a book with a poor cover will go unread, simply because it looks uninviting. In a photo book, choosing a cover image is one of your most important decisions because that image carries with it the promise of what the reader will see in the throughout the book.

Oftentimes, the title on photo books are left as an afterthought because the images take such priority. If your book is solely for the enjoyment of family you may not need a title. Your cover image could speak for the contents of the book.

If your photo book will be sold (or given) to libraries or bookstores, it must have a title. If you have not given much thought to your book's title while you were writing, once you start designing the cover, you must. In fact, choosing the right title and making it look good on the cover may be the most difficult element of cover design. Fortunately, there is a fairly simple formula for the other elements expected on the front and back covers as well as on the spine.

Choosing a Good Title

The title will affect the perception readers have of the book and as such, the title should be the most prominent item on the cover. While it is tempting to use a title that is also a clever play on words (e.g. Deep Roots and Long Branches), if you want potential *buyers* to know what they can expect in the book, it is best to be specific in the title or subtitle.

You could use "Descendants of ... " or "Ancestors of ... " or "The Unusual Lineage of ... " plus the names of the main characters, a time period or a region to distinguish your family from others with the same surname.

Most online bookstores will list both your title and subtitle in the short listings, so, if you prefer, you can use a shorter title followed by a more lengthy, explanatory subtitle.

The following are examples of good titles:

Up the Mississippi: The Laidlaw Family of England, New Orleans and Illinois

Descendants of Abial Washburn (1841–1899) and Susannah Cooke Washburn (1850–1919): From Georgia to Tennessee and Back

Handcarts Across the Plains: The Hubert Miller Family from Illinois (1830) to Oregon (1850)

These titles are not as good:

Our Family
The Third Generation
The Browns of Ohio

On the cover, typeset the title in a font large enough to be readable in a small thumbnail online. Online bookstores and eReaders will display your cover this way and often the small image is all a potential buyer has to evaluate the book.

Cover Layout Basics

How your cover is designed depends upon how it will be bound—hardbound, hardbound with a dustcover, or softbound (paperback).

A paperback cover is printed on a single sheet that wraps from the front around the spine to the back. It will be printed at a size larger than the book's pages, and then attached to the book with glue and trimmed so that the page and cover edges are smooth and even.

Hardbound covers can be made from either cloth or paper. They are glued to stiff boards to form a solid cover. A paper cover for a hardbound book will look like modern textbooks—full color with a glossy coating. Paper covers for hardbound books are designed even larger than those for softbound books because they must wrap around the edges of the boards and glued down to form part of the inside cover. An endsheet will be glued over the edges of the cover.

Cloth covers are made of anything from linen to leather, depending upon the printer's equipment and how much you are willing to pay. Cloth covers, typically, do not have much more than the title and the author's name. Many cloth-covered books also have a full-color, paper dust jacket that wraps around the cloth cover. The dust jacket uses flaps inside the front and back covers to keep it secure.

Whether you are designing a paper cover or a dust jacket, your printer should have a template for you to follow. Many printers have template generators that

			Bleed Edge
			Trim Edge
			Safe Area Edge

CATEGORY/SUBCATEGORY   LOGO

SALES MESSAGE

OTHER BOOKS

BOOK
COVER
IMAGE

TITLE:
SUBTITLE

TITLE:
SUBTITLE

ISBN PRICE

"BLURBS"

BY
AUTHOR'S NAME

ABOUT THE AUTHOR

BAR CODE

WEBSITE ADDRESS   AUTHOR

IMAGE

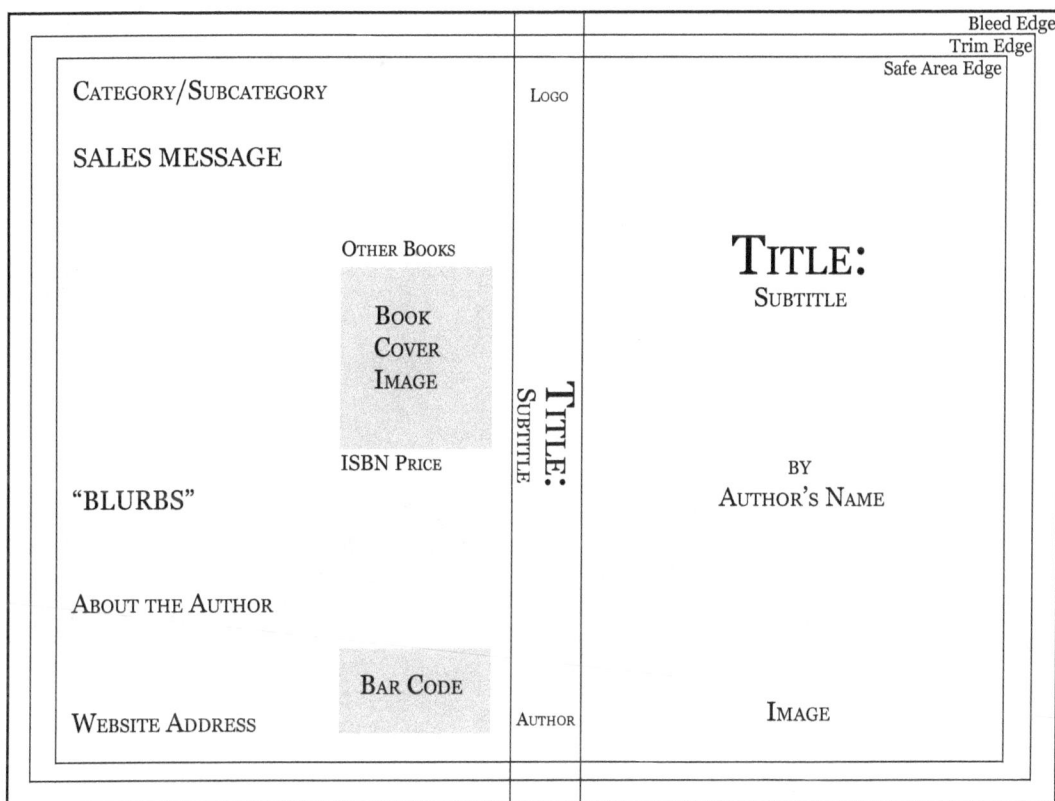

Cover elements.

will give you an exact size based upon the number of pages in the book, which will determine spine width. You can assemble the elements at any time, however, and create the final cover once you have a page count.

Cover templates will have three areas defined by the edge of the element: the bleed edge, the trim edge and the safe area.

The *safe area* is the innermost area that allows for any slippage when the printed cover is attached to the book's interior. Most templates will give you three safe areas, one each for the front cover, the back cover and the spine. The safe areas are away from the edges of the spine and the front and back covers. Keep all text, as well as the barcode, and any logo images within the safe areas.

The *trim edge* is where the book will be trimmed once the cover is applied to the interior pages so that the finished book will have clean, smooth edges.

The *bleed edge* is the area where photographs or solid background color should reach, so that when the book is trimmed, there is no danger of leaving a white line around an edge because nothing was printed in that area.

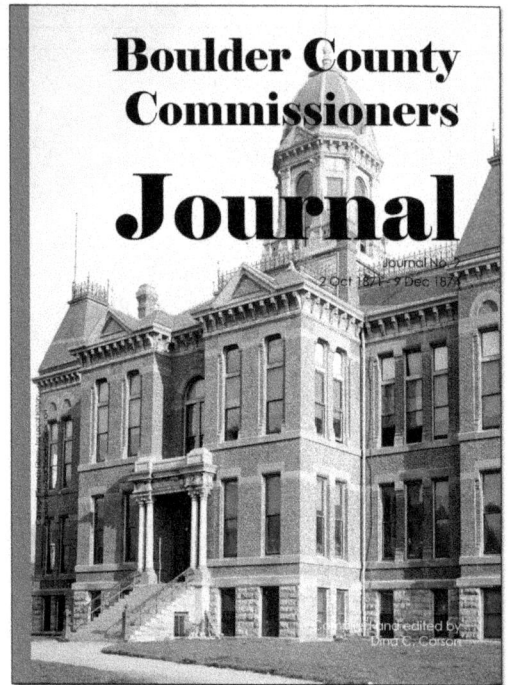

Cover photograph properly placed (left); Cover photograph making the title difficult to read (right).

Cover Elements

Covers have three elements: the front, the spine, and the back. Most covers are designed in a single piece, and when laid flat, the front cover will be on the right-hand side, the spine in the middle and the back cover on the left.

If you use a print-on-demand printer that has an online cover generator—not a template but a design tool—you may be able to design the cover in three separate parts. Using one of these cover generators, however, will give you fewer options than designing the cover yourself.

If you design your own cover, create it as a single piece. You can use a word processor (although not ideal), an image editing program, a page layout program or a vector graphics editor such as Adobe Illustrator. One of the benefits of using a page layout program or a vector graphics editor is that they are built for creating cover files—to combine images with crisp, sharp type.

For ideas, take a look at Book Cover Archive (www.bookcoverarchive.com). This website offers a gallery of book covers created by professionals.

Front Cover

The front cover should get the reader's attention. The title should be the most prominent element on the cover, set in a font that is easy to read. The following are popular cover fonts: Baskerville, Franchise, League Gothic, and Trajan.

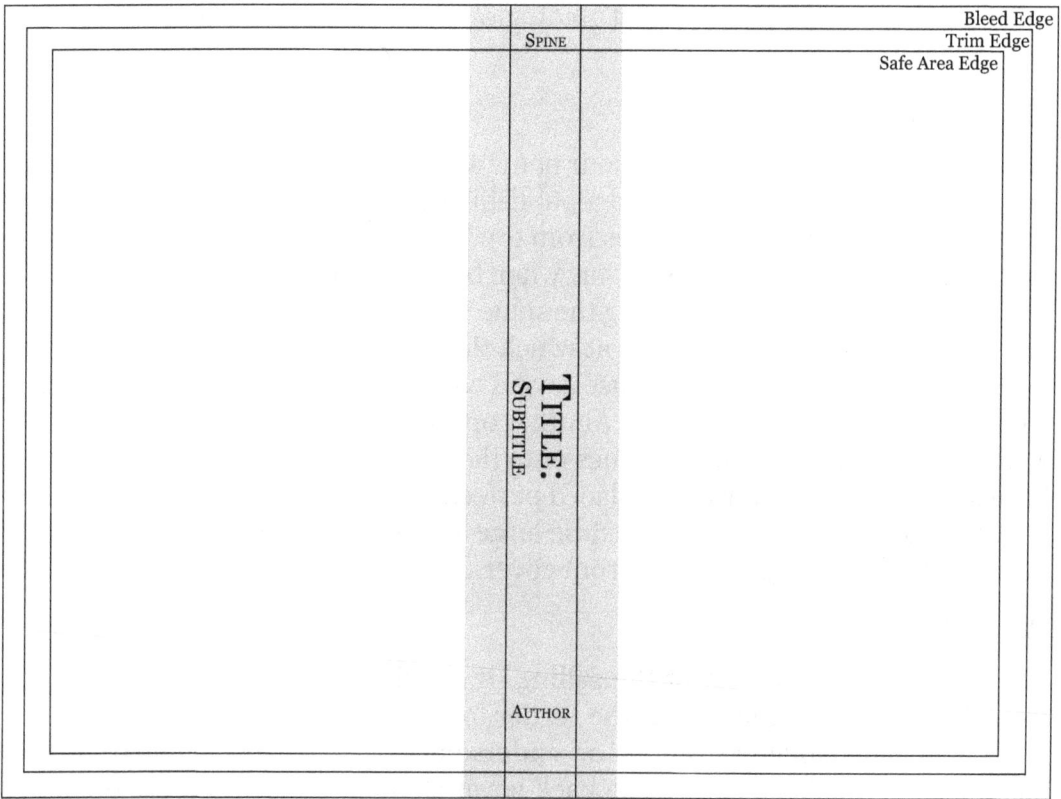

Spine wrap.

For the background, use a photograph, a color, or a texture as long as the area where the title and subtitle are placed is plain (subtle) enough that the reader has no trouble reading the text at a glance. Avoid background elements that are too busy and those that do not create enough color contrast with the title text.

If you use an image, choose one that says something about the contents. The illustration shows two covers with the same title, but uses the background photograph in a different way. The key to making a book cover image look great is finding one that leaves a large, nearly solid area where you can place the title in a contrasting color. The cover on the left has enough plain sky to read the title and subtitle clearly. The closeup cover image does not.

If you do not have an appropriate photograph in your own collection, you may be able to find a historic photograph that you could license, or you could purchase an image from one of the online rights-managed image companies for a few dollars.

Size and resolution matter and your cover image is likely to be the largest image you use for this project. The resolution should be 300 ppi at a size big enough to cover the bleed area. A cover with a 2.5" spine, for example, would measure 19.5" x 17.5" which is 5850 pixels by 5250 pixels.

If you cannot find the perfect photograph for the cover, blocks of color or subtle patterns also work.

The Spine

The spine will contain your title, your name as the author (full name, initials plus last name, or last name only), and a publishing company logo, if you have one.

The lettering on the spine goes from top to bottom—never the other way—so that all of the titles read the same way when books are spine out on the bookshelf.

The tricky part about designing the spine is making the elements (background image) stop at precisely the point at which the cover bends, either to the front or back. One way to avoid this is to use a solid color, a texture, or a photograph that continues across the entire cover. Another option is to create a spine wrap, where a graphic element or color continues onto the front and back covers to disguise a little slippage if the cover is not placed perfectly during production.

The typeface on the spine must be large and legible, and typically, the same one you used for the title on the front cover.

Back Cover

The back cover does most of the selling. It should explain why the reader will want your book and gently asks the reader to buy a copy.

If you have solicited blurbs or endorsements, your best endorsement(s) should go on the back cover. The back cover should include a bit about you as the author, or why you have written the book. If there are other books you have written, there may be room to mention those books, or to show their covers, page count, ISBNs and price.

If you have a website where the book is sold, the URL should appear prominently on the back cover.

If you plan to sell your book commercially through a print-on-demand printer (such as Lulu or Amazon), you must place an ISBN barcode at the bottom right corner about one-quarter inch from the spine. The barcode can also include the price, although price is optional.

Some printers will include the barcode for you in their template. If you are using one of the ISBNs belonging to your print-on-demand printer, the barcode will be placed on the cover as you create it. If you are printing through an offset printer and must purchase an ISBN barcode, you can do so online. There are many companies offering barcodes for as little as $10. You will receive an EPS (.eps) image by email to use in your design. If you are purchasing your own ISBNs from the Bowker Company, they also offer barcodes for sale.

The other element you will need if you plan to sell your book to libraries or bookstores is a subject heading in the top left corner of the back cover. This is to give the librarians or bookstore employees an idea where to categorize the book.

Book Industry Standards Advisory Committee (BISAC) codes are the standard across the industry for subject headings. If you search online for BISAC codes, you will find a complete list. For a photo book that is also a family history, the code will be Reference/Genealogy. For other photo books, use the closest BISAC code to the contents of the book. If you are using a print-on-demand printer, this question will come up as you are creating a listing for your book. Some printers make it easy to search for the BISAC code, others do not. Some printers allow you to list two or more categories, others do not. Search online for the complete list, then use the best subject heading on the back cover.

Advanced Cover Design

The following are additional tips for designing effective covers:

First, go to Amazon.com and take a look at Todd A. Stone's book, *Novelist's Boot Camp*. This is a simple cover, in two colors, black and olive, but it says something about what is in the book, and does so simply.

Now take a look at *Virginia Historical Genealogies* by John Bennett Boddie. This is a black-and-white cover that is about as simple as is possible, but it does not re-produce well as a thumbnail on screen. Arguably, this is a well-written book, but does the cover give you that impression? This book has been around for more than fifty years, so it is hard to be critical of a cover that was designed before major printing technology changes. However, the contents are deserving of a better cover.

Using Color

To make areas of solid black (such as your title text) look its best, use the formula for rich black, which is: 40% cyan, 40% magenta, 40% yellow, 100% black. You will notice that these are in CMYK colors. CMYK is the color palette most printers prefer. If you are designing your cover in your word processor or image editing program, you may not be able to choose the CMYK color palette, so the colors you are seeing on screen in the RGB palette may look slightly different when printed. Page layout and vector graphics programs are designed for working in CMYK.

Limit the cover's color palette to two or three colors and their various tints. That should be a sufficient variation unless you are using a photograph. If you are, choose colors from the photograph for other elements such as the subhead "About the Author" on the back cover. As with interior text, black text is still best for most elements on the cover.

If you need help choosing colors that look good together, use a good color picker. There are apps and online color wheels available, or buy one of Jim Krause's books, *Color Index*, or *Color Index 2*. If you want to go all out, buy one of the Pantone Color Guides (www.pantone.com).

Selecting great color combinations is not easy. If your spouse will not let you choose your own shirts, ask for help choosing colors for your book cover.

Other Cover Considerations

Once you have a cover design in mind, scale it down to a small thumbnail of one inch by one and a half inches (1" x 1.5"). This is how your cover will appear to people shopping at an online bookstore. A thumbnail image is how you will present the cover on your blog, website, Facebook, on a bookmark, or business card to give away to interested family members or other buyers. If the title is not easy to read at the thumbnail size, then revise the cover for those uses with bigger, bolder text.

Save your cover in different sizes. You may need an eBook version (600 pixels x 800 pixels), an online bookstore version (Amazon's requirement is 1880 pixels x 2500 pixels), one for your blog or social media (400 pixels x 600 pixels), and a small thumbnail 90 pixels x 108 pixels (the standard cover size in Amazon's email promotions).

If you have plans for writing more than one book, consider using a branded look, that is, the same layout with different colors or photographs so that the books look like they belong together.

❧❧

If you cannot design a cover yourself, the following are tips for working with a cover designer.

Working with a Cover Designer

Before you hire a cover designer, ask about the designer's experience. Cover design is a specialty, and most graphic designers have never designed a book cover. Most book packagers, however, either have cover designers on staff, or use freelancers who are familiar with book cover design.

Take a look at Book Cover Archive (www.bookcoverarchive.com). This website offers a gallery of book cover designs. Show the prospective designer four or five styles that you like, but be open to suggestions.

In addition to cover ideas, bring along a two or three paragraph synopsis, to help the designer understand the content of your book. The cover design should complement the content.

Portfolio

Ask to see the designer's book cover portfolio. Evaluate the full covers, front, spine and back, to make sure the designer is familiar with the elements needed for a commercially available book.

Estimate

Ask for an estimate. Most cover designers will offer two or three designs, plus two rounds of revisions before you start paying more than the initial estimate. You may even find that the cover designer has a few standard layouts that you can choose from to save money. Include a do-not-exceed price in the agreement, so the designer cannot go wild with changes before you have a chance to revise the estimate.

Deadlines

Make your expectations clear and set firm deadlines. Let the designer know when you will have a final page count, and when you expect the final cover finished once the page count is given. The designer should have the cover essentially ready, needing only a few minor adjustments once the page count is final.

File Type and Resolution

Let the designer know what type of file and resolution you need (usually a PDF) and any special instructions provided by your book printer. In addition, ask for web-ready book cover images in the different sizes you may need—an eBook version (600 pixels x 800 pixels), online bookstores (Amazon's requirement is a cover of 1880 pixels x 2500 pixels), and a small thumbnail 90 pixels x 108 pixels (the standard cover size in Amazon's email promotions). Make sure the final cover looks good and that the title is readable, even at the smallest thumbnail size.

Write a Formal Proposal or Contract

Use a formal proposal to indicate how and when the cover should be delivered to you—on a thumb drive, an external hard drive, an archival DVD, or through a file sharing service. Make sure deadlines for payment and a finished cover are clear. Include all prices and payment terms.

✥

Your cover is the ambassador for your book. Some family members will want a copy even if it comes as loose leaf sheets wrapped in newspaper. Most readers, however, will form an impression of the book's contents by looking at the cover. When designing your cover, you should be able to find many suitable possibilities from the hundreds of thousands of non-fiction books already published. Use one as your guide. Bottom line: all of your hard work writing the book deserves to be covered in something beautiful, and representative of the quality of the contents.

Chapter 22

Preparing the Final Files

Most photo books are printed. However, some of your readers may prefer an electronic version, or, if you are not interested in selling the book, an online version may be a good choice to distribute it as widely as possible. You may choose to do all three or some combination of the three.

While this book focuses mainly on print publishing, there are ways that you can use what you have produced for print to also publish electronically or online. What follows are brief descriptions of the differences in setup between print and electronic or online versions. For complete instructions, please consult *Set Yourself Up to Self-Publish: A Genealogist's Guide.*

Final Files for Print

How you prepare your final files depends upon your printer. Most printers want PDF files because they are the least problematic. If you send a file in a word processing format such as Word, and you have used a font that the printer does not have, the text may re-format in a way you do not intend. By creating a PDF, there are rarely any font issues because the process of creating the PDF embeds the fonts into the document. Creating a PDF is, in some ways, like taking a snapshot of your manuscript. It will create a file that looks exactly like your manuscript file whether you created it in a word processing program or a page layout program. Most word processing and page layout software will save documents as PDFs.

Create Final PDFs

If you are using one of Adobe's software products to create your PDF (Acrobat or InDesign, for example), there are different PDF settings, including press quality or high quality print (what we want for a printed book), smallest file size (appropriate for emailing the book), and several other settings in between. The best settings for printed material are: Press Quality, High Quality Printing or PDF/X 1a:2001. Most page layout programs will give you a choice in PDF settings, your word processor may not. In most cases, the printed book will still look fine.

If you use a digital or offset printer, ask for their preferred PDF settings before saving your files. Most print-on-demand printers, on the other hand, will accept whatever file you upload, so the responsibility for creating a file that will look its best when printed is up to you.

After creating the PDF, print it out and check it over carefully by comparing the printed version to your original to make sure nothing shifted or was lost in the conversion. This is the process of typescript editing (mentioned in Chapter 15: Editing Your Manuscript). This is the time to catch widows and orphans, captions that do not match images, and other errors. Take a ruler and scan each line one at a time for errors. You may be surprised at what crept in as elements were typeset. The following are common post-typesetting errors:

- Widows and orphans
- Missed or incorrect formatting styles
- Hard returns mid-sentence
- Missing punctuation
- Incorrect quote marks (the symbol for inches)
- Spacing around images
- Spacing between different types of text blocks
- Images that fade into the page (missing outlines)
- Images that do not fit the grid
- Placeholder images not final images (at resolutions too low for print production)
- Pages that are mis-numbered

Uploading Files for Print

If you have created your final layout in chapters so that they are easier to work with, it is safer to send the printer a single file so there is no chance the files could be printed out of order. Programs such as InDesign will take your individual files and combine them into a single book-length PDF. The full version of Adobe Acrobat will also combine individual PDF files into a larger book-length file.

If you must upload your manuscript files individually, the best way to make sure they are printed in the correct order is to begin each file name with a number so that the computer arranges them in the correct order. If you followed the advice in Chapter 14: Creating the First Draft, you should be ready to go.

If you need to number your files now, the following is another way to make sure the computer arranges them in the correct order.

Unfortunately, if you number your files starting with a one (1), and you also have an eleven (11), the computer may order the files this way: 1, 11, 2.

The only way to avoid this is to count the total number of files, and use a sufficient number of zeros preceding the file number to force the computer to put the files in the correct order.

If there are fewer than ten files, there should be no issues, as the computer will number those files from one (1) to nine (9) in order. If there are ten or more files but fewer than one hundred, create two digit numbers from 01 to 09, so that subsequent numbers will be in the correct order. If there are more than one hundred files, file names require two zeros in front of the numbers from one (001) to nine (009), and a single zero before each and every number from ten (010) to ninety-nine (099). Numbers greater than one hundred will fall in order correctly.

Once you upload the files, the best way to see whether or not the files were placed in their proper order is to order a proof copy. Many print-on-demand printers offer a digital PDF proof for you to download. This should not cost you anything, but proofing on screen and proofing in print are different. You will catch different errors. It is worth the money to print a proof copy as well.

Examine the digital and print proofs carefully page by page. You may be surprised what you find. Missing punctuation and incorrectly applied styles are common errors. Watch for places where widows or orphans were created by text shift. It happens. Make sure your illustrations remain in place along with any captions or credits.

Other Information About Your Book

Once you start the process of uploading files to a print-on-demand printer, requesting ISBNs or creating marketing materials for your book, you will need the following information. Keep it gathered in a convenient place so that you can cut and paste whatever is required by vendors or websites.

If you have purchased your own ISBNs, much of this information will inform the book-buying community about your book. If you use a print-on-demand printer, they will ask for much of this information when you upload your files. Each printer has slightly different requirements. What follows is the information asked for most often.

Title

Title. Keep the title and subtitle separate.

Subtitle. Keep the title and subtitle separate.

Author and Publisher

Primary Author. List your name as the primary author. If you have co-authors or other contributors, you should have a chance to add their names.

Author Biography. Write a few paragraphs about yourself as the author and why you wrote the book.

Publisher. If you are acting as your own publisher, you have a choice whether to create a publishing company, or not. For tax and legal reasons you may wish to do so. One sign that you are a self-publisher, however, is naming the publishing company after yourself.

Language and Printing Location

Language. The primary language of the book.

Country. The country in which the book was published, not printed.

Important Dates

Copyright Year. The year in which the book was finished. Although your copyright existed from the time you put pen to paper, most publishers use the most current year as the copyright date, so that readers know that the information is current.

Publication Date. This is a fictional date used by the publishing industry to schedule book reviews ahead of the book's official launch. Use the date when your book is available for sale.

Audience

Target Audience. Unless you are writing a children's book, the audience will always be "Trade."

Metadata

Together, the title, license, description, category and keywords make up the metadata—cataloging information about your book that is key to book sales. Any mis-matches in the metadata will make it difficult for the big databases (online book catalogs) to place your book in front of the right potential buyers.

License. Indicate that you own the copyright to your work, that you are not re-packaging a work already in the public domain.

Description. This is your sales language, your chance to interest potential readers. Some sites use descriptions as short as 200 characters, others as long as 4000. Have several descriptions ready with the most important information wrapped up in the shortest description, and additional detail in the longer descriptions. If you want to sell your book, the description may be one of your most important marketing tools. Lulu describes "providing too little detail in the description" as the greatest mistake of new authors.

Category. Many printers will use the BISAC codes, others have a search option, still others make it as confusing as humanly possible. When in doubt, if

Genealogy is not a main category, look for Reference/Genealogy & Heraldry. A secondary category could be History (U.S. History, European History, etc.) plus the local area where the book takes place (U.S. History/Midwest).

Keywords. Most sites allow five or more keyword phrases separated by commas. Choose the five most important and put those first. For most photo books that are also family histories, the keywords should be about the surname and the location(s) where the family lived. For example, Campbell Family History, Campbell Genealogy, Abraham Campbell Family, or Campbell Family Kentucky. If the book covers broader subjects, use keywords for those subjects. If you are able to add more keyword phrases, do. More keywords will help potential readers find the book. Think of the phrases another researcher interested in the family would use to find the book. There are keyword search programs online that can help with this, such as Google Adwords Keyword Planner (adwords.google.com). This tool is free, but you must create an account to use it.

ISBN and Price

ISBN. If you have your own ISBN, use it. If you do not, leave this blank and the printer will assign one of theirs to you.

Price. Choose a price higher than the wholesale price if you want to make money. Another reason you may wish to choose a price higher than the wholesale price is to give the distributor (printer) the opportunity to price the book at a discount. Book buyers love bargains, but if you price the book at the wholesale cost, the distributor cannot sell the book for less than what it costs to manufacture it.

The following are a few items particular to Amazon (CreateSpace), Lulu and Bowker (the ISBN Agency).

Amazon (CreateSpace)

Distribution. Amazon offers the following outlets for distribution: Amazon. com, Amazon Europe, Create Space eStore, Bookstores and Online Retailers, and CreateSpace Direct. If you are using one of their ISBNs your book is also eligible for distribution to libraries and academic institutions—a plus for Reference/Genealogy books.

Prices. If you have chosen distribution outside of the United States, choose US Dollars, Euros, and British Pounds. Google's online currency calculator can help convert U.S. dollars to English pounds or euros. Round the prices up to the nearest .99 or .95, as prices ending that way have become customary.

Option to Publish on Kindle. If you use CreateSpace to publish your print book they will give you the option to create a Kindle version.

Lulu

Private Access. One of my favorite features of Lulu is that you can publish a book and keep it completely private, meaning that only you can order copies. This is appropriate for books that you may wish to distribute to family members that have information about living people you would not want distributed outside the family.

Direct Access. Direct Access gives you a private URL to direct family members to buy the book for themselves. This option gives you less control over distribution than private access, but it is a good option if you have family spread out all over the country, and you want them to be able to buy their own copies and have the books delivered directly to them.

General Access. Any book you assign as general access will become available through Lulu's catalog as well as other online booksellers' catalogs.

Bowker Company (ISBN Agency)

ISBN 10. Older ISBNs had only 10 digits. If you have a newer ISBN it will have 13 digits. There is a calculator on the site to convert it to the older 10 digit version. This site asks for both, and checks one against the other for accuracy.

ISBN 13. The ISBN for your book.

LCCC. A Library of Congress Catalog Number.

Medium. Medium is the format of the book, usually print or eBook, unless you have chosen to distribute it as an audiobook, or on CD or DVD instead.

Format. In most cases the format will be paperback or hardbound.

Title Status. If you want the book industry to know that your book is available for sale, use Active. You can use the term Forthcoming, if you are months away from publishing. Be sure, however, to come back and change the status. The big databases that the book sellers use will show the book as unavailable until you change the status to Active.

Price Type. Choose Retail Price.

Keep a file with this information gathered in one place. When you are ready to let others know that you have a book available, having these details handy will save time.

SECTION 5

For most family photo books, marketing is not as much about making sales as it is about contacting the people who would be interested in seeing your book or adding it to a library collection, and providing information about where they can obtain a copy. Marketing—spreading the word—is about using methods that get results at a cost you can afford, in both money and time.

Baby Steps

If your intent for writing your book is solely to provide a beautiful legacy to family members, then once they have copies, you can stop marketing.

Next Steps

If, however, you would like your book to remain available well past the current generation, contribute it to the major genealogical collections around the country. I know that some family photographs are personal, but contributing your photo book to a genealogical collection is one way to preserve those photographs into the future. Assuming your photographs are the family's legacy, and not deeply personal, another way to keep those images alive is to establish a sales channel that will last awhile. Creating a website for the book or selling the book through an online bookseller such as Amazon are two ways to keep the book out in the marketplace long after you have turned your attention to other projects.

Giant Leaps

If your book is full of images that would be of interest to the general public, then by all means, market the book wherever you can. Your book may help another genealogical researcher answer questions about a collateral line or the era in which your family lived. Your photographs may be a collection so unique that you should share them. There may be many people who are interested in your book that you will remain unaware of unless you spread the word far and wide.

Note: In this section, the expression "pitch" means to make an appeal or to make your case about your book.

Chapter 23

Creating a Marketing Plan

Quite often, when I speak to groups about marketing anything related to genealogy, I get moans and groans about not wanting to "sell" something. Not all selling is the equivalent of selling used cars. Some of you will generously give your books away to family members. If you have the means to do so, hooray.

Many of you will sell your book, if for no other reason than it is more practical for your family members to order a copy online and have the printer ship the book to them directly, than for you to buy hundreds of copies, store them (and dust them), and have to run to the post office every time someone orders one.

In this section, marketing (and its side-kick, selling) is more about getting the word out that you have a book available, than becoming a tycoon selling books to unsuspecting cousins.

Marketing 101

Marketing has five elements: identifying the target market, determining a method to reach out to the target market effectively, giving interested people a reason to buy, showing them where they can buy, and asking them to do so.

Identify the Target Market

Most of you will have more than one target market. For this discussion, a target market is a group of people with similar interests. The reason you want to narrow down a wide group of potential buyers into narrow target markets is to be able to reach them effectively. People who have similar interests tend to gather in the same places, belong to the same (or similar) groups, read the same books or magazines, and use the same websites. Once you identify where you can reach the target market, you can let them know the book is available.

Reach Out to the Target Market

Let us use your immediate family as an example. Most people have multiple ways to reach parents, grandparents, siblings and children. You have phone numbers, email, and home addresses. That gives you many ways to reach this audience. You could call each person and discuss the book. You could create an email list and send a group email, or you could write a letter or create a sales sheet and send it to each family member's home. You could make an announcement on the social media your family follows. You could talk about the book at the next family gathering. Contacting your family should be easy. Unfortunately, you may not have as many easy options with other target markets.

Every target market has a way to contact the group and its members. You may have to decide, however, whether the effort or expense of reaching out to each target market is worth the cost.

Give the Target Market a Reason to Buy

In most cases, it is not enough to simply tell someone you have a book available. While your Mom will buy a copy without hesitation, other buyers will want to know what they will get out of reading your book. The most important part of your marketing plan is putting together a list of benefits.

Benefits are the reasons why a person will want to read your book. Distinguishing benefits from features can be confusing. The following are common book *features*:

- The book is 396 pages long.
- The book covers four generations.
- The earliest photograph is from 1865.
- The book covers the family's move west from the Ohio River Valley to the coast of Oregon.

By contrast, this is an example of a benefit-rich statement: "With cinematic power and beauty, bestselling author David Laskin brings to life the upheavals of the twentieth century through the story of one family, three continents, two world wars, and the rise and fall of nations." That description, taken from the dust jacket flap of David Laskin's *The Family*, sounds much more like an enticement to read the book than a list of facts, does it not?

Remember back in Chapter 22: Preparing the Final Files in the discussion about your book's description and how vital the description can be to sales? It is worth your time to write a compelling enticement to read the book. In fact, it is worth writing, and re-writing, if necessary. Once you have a vivid, enticing description, you can use it in all of your marketing materials.

Show the Target Market Where They Can Buy

Let potential book buyers know where they can buy a copy, whether by contacting you directly, by buying from your website or at an online bookstore such as Amazon. If you have multiple options for sales, give the buyer a choice. Not everyone is comfortable purchasing items online. And, if you want to offer autographed copies, state where those copies are available, as well. For some people, autographed copies are an additional inducement to buy.

Include a Call to Action

One of the biggest mistakes in marketing is forgetting to ask for the sale. You do not have to include an obnoxious, flashing "Buy Now!!!" button. A simple, "purchase your copy today" will do. Or offer free shipping if the buyer purchases a book by a certain date. Enticements to act sooner rather than later often work.

Setting the Price

Before you can sell your book, you have to determine its price. If you do not plan to make any money on the book, you can set the price a few cents over your wholesale cost.

In the publishing industry, the standard price is set at eight times (8x) the wholesale cost to account for the cost of marketing and fulfillment. That cost is based upon long print runs, however, that keep the wholesale cost of each book very low.

Realistically, your wholesale costs will be a bit higher and depending upon which type of printer you have chosen, the cost may be substantially higher. You will have to decide which is more important to you, making the book widely available—meaning keeping the retail price low—maximizing the amount you make on the sale of each book, or something in between. The higher you set the price, however, the fewer you will sell.

If you plan to offer an eBook version, understand that eBook readers do not expect to pay the same price for their electronic version as they would for a printed book. Amazon has recognized this fact and has structured their royalty payments to reflect what readers want. Amazon pays a royalty of 70 percent to any eBook priced under $9.99, but only a 30 percent royalty for books priced at $10 or higher. Amazon has analyzed a lot of buyer data to discover that $9.99 price point. Consider pricing your electronic version under $9.99.

For most photo books, making the book more widely available at a lower cost is the best way to get your hard work out there to the people who are interested in the photographs.

The Offer

Use the following formula to build your marketing pieces: attention-catching headlines and sub-headlines, text that supports the headlines while giving readers details, and a call to action. I have added bullets and keywords to the formula to make your offer easy to scan, and easy for the search engines to find if you post the offer online.

Headline

The headline should get the reader's attention and interest them enough to read more. For most photo books, this would include the people or the most important images in the book (e.g. Henderson Family Album With Photographs from 1860 Massachusetts, or New Book Shows the Only Known Photograph of George Custer on the Day of Little Big Horn).

Sub-Headlines

Sub-headlines break up the rest of the text into small, easy-to-read sections. Sub-heads also make it easy to scan the piece from beginning to end. Subheads are an opportunity for you to catch and keep the reader's attention (e.g. Three Rare Photographs of the Little Big Horn Battlefield).

Supporting Text

After each headline and sub-head, give the readers details from the book. Tell a quick story, allude to the contents, give something to pique the reader's interest.

Bullet Points

Give the reader a bulleted list of the book's main features:

- People covered
- The most important places or events covered
- Number of pages
- Number of photographs or illustrations (you could name any that are especially enticing [e.g. The only known photograph of great-grandfather Roger E. Mills])
- Price (include shipping and handling charges)
- ISBN (if you have one)

Keywords

If you will place your marketing piece online, include a few important keywords within the text to help the search engines find it. Using the example above, keywords could include: George Custer Rare Photograph, Little Big Horn Battlefield, and so on.

Call to Action

A call to action is a marketing term for asking the reader to buy (e.g. "Buy by November 1st and receive free shipping").

Pre-Publication Offers

One method publishers use to jump-start their sales is to send a pre-publication offer letting potential readers know that the book will be available soon, while offering a discount of some type as an enticement to buy before the book's release.

Before print-on-demand, the proceeds from a pre-publication offer was a way to pay for the first print run. It was also a way to fill the time between when the book went to the printer, and when the books were delivered. With print-on-demand, there is no longer much of a delay or the need to pay for an initial print run. Today, a pre-publication offer is more a thank-you to the people who purchase right away.

Ongoing Offers

Continue to market your book for as long as you want readers to buy it. Family photo books do not go out of style, so you could repeat your offer every now and again for years to come. Even after your family members have copies, there will be new members of the family who may enjoy reading the book as well. As the kids start having kids of their own, they may become more interested in their roots. In addition, there will always be a new generation of genealogical researchers who were unaware of their interest in your book when it was released.

Check Out the Competition

If you are ever at a loss for how to get the word out about your book, look for ways in which other authors are marketing their books. Check out book-related websites. Read the About the Author pages. Sign up for book-related emails. Check YouTube for book trailers. Spend some time on Amazon and other online booksellers' sites and read the description of similar books. Read the blurbs about the authors.

Learn from the best. Use the search engines to find all the marketing and publicity about a family-related book. David Laskin's, *The Family* would be a good model since it is a relatively new book, although not a photo book. David Laskin, however, is a Harvard-educated writer with some major-league writing credentials, so you may not be able to replicate precisely the kind of attention for your book that he has garnered for his. You should, however, be able to get some ideas for increasing sales of your book.

Create a Marketing Plan

For many authors, once a book is complete and that huge project is off the desk, it may be difficult to jump right back in to create awareness for the book. If you will create a plan with just one marketing technique per week over the first six months after your book is finished, you will be surprised at how many people you will reach. Like many things, you are more likely to accomplish your marketing goals if you write them down and schedule them on the calendar.

❦

The most important thing about marketing is being able to identify your target market, finding a way to contact these potential buyers, and describing your book in such a way that they simply cannot resist placing an order.

Chapter 24

Reaching Your Audience

If your photo book is meant for family members only, the first section of this chapter will help you contact them. If your book contains photographs that would be of interest to a broader audience, read on. With most books, it is best to identify the people who are the *most* likely to buy in order to save marketing money and time rather than trying to contact the biggest possible audience. The natural markets for your book are a starting point. There may be other, unanticipated buyers, however, who surface through your marketing efforts.

Family Members

The obvious target market for a family photo book is your family. The following are marketing techniques you can use with family members.

Email Campaign

Send an email announcing the book. Add a signature to your regular email so that each time you correspond, a message will go out showing you as the author, the title, a link back to your website or a place where the book is sold and any social media you are participating in that concerns the book. If you include "http://" before any website address, the link will become click-able within the email.

Ask family members to forward your book announcement email to anyone else who may be interested in the book. This is a good way to have family members help spread the word, especially if you do not have email addresses for each of the distant cousins.

Family Gatherings

Bring a few books with you to each and every family gathering in case there are people who have been waiting to buy directly from you.

Autographed Copies

Autographed copies are a nice touch when you know the buyer personally. They also make some books more valuable. In order to offer autographed copies, you must purchase enough books to keep a few on hand to fulfill the orders, or ask family members to bring their copies with them to reunions, or other family gatherings for you to sign.

Make an Announcement

Make an announcement on any social media sites where your family participates. Google+ has a new service called Google Hangouts (LIVE) that enables you to hold a town meeting of sorts with family using the Internet.

Send a Card

Some of your family members may not use email. There are services such as Send Out Cards (www.sendoutcards.com) that enable you to create a personalized card that the company will print and send through the postal service. Use your cover image and images from the book to create your personalized card. Have the description and buying information for the book ready to copy and paste into the card. Write a quick personal note, as well. Personal notes take only a few seconds to compose but mean a lot to the recipients.

Genealogical Researchers

Other genealogical researchers who are working on your family—whether as a direct line or a collateral line—may be interested in the book. The key to finding the people in any target market is to evaluate where they gather and make an announcement where they are likely to see it. In the announcement, do not try to sell directly. Let the group know that there is a new book out and where interested members can go for more information.

Family Trees with Links to Your Family

If you did not do so during your research, check the major genealogical research sites (Ancestry, FamilySearch, MyHeritage and FindMyPast) for member trees that link to your family and contact the owners of those trees.

Genealogical Forums

Many of the major genealogical research sites have forums by surname and location. You can leave a message for members in the forum. Use an informative headline (e.g. New Book Follows Four Generations of the Walter Richmond Family, 1844–1900). Within the post, use your description of the book. And, if you are posting in a locations forum, make ties to the location clear (e.g. New Book about Walter Richmond Family, 1844–1900, of Bainbridge, Indiana).

Some of the older forums have stopped accepting new posts, but their older posts remain online and contain contact information. Although you can no longer post a message, you could contact anyone who is researching your family.

Blogs

Finding a surname based blog will be relatively easy because so many people are blogging, but finding a surname-based blog that is also researching family history is not. My best suggestion is that you use both "family" and "genealogy" in your keywords when you search.

Surname Groups

Look at Cyndi's List (www.cyndislist.com) for surname groups and reunions. The categories list alone will keep you busy. Some links will take you to personal websites, and others to surname societies or newsletter websites.

Conferences

If your family stayed in one area of the country for a substantial amount of time, ascertain whether there is a regional genealogical conference where you could post an announcement for attendees. There may be descendants who are still in the area. Most conferences sell inexpensive advertising space in their giveaway bags or programs that you could use to make your book announcement.

Contact as many like-minded researchers as you can find. They may have a greater interest in your book than some of your distant family members.

Local Historians

How much you can interest local historians or history buffs in your family photo book depends upon how many local historical photographs you included. If you do, contact local historians and make your pitch, mentioning the photographs that may appeal to them.

Historical Societies and Their Museums

If the images in your book will appeal to local historians, the local historical society may appreciate being able to offer a special deal to their members. Offer to give society members a discounted price in exchange for mentioning the book in their member newsletter and on the society's website. Set up a special landing page on your website where society members can go to place a discounted order.

The most likely opportunity for in-store sales may be at a local historical museum bookshop. There you will find like-minded local history buffs who buy local history books. Approach a museum shop buyer by making the book's ties to the community obvious in your pitch.

Offer a small discount if the museum shop buys only one book, and a larger discounted price if they buy three or more books. Most museum shops will not stock an abundance of any one book until they see how well the book will sell.

Not every historical museum is connected to a historical society. The independent museums in the area may be willing to sell your book, as well.

Living History Societies and Re-Enactors Groups

Re-enactors are individuals who are so fascinated with how people lived during an era that they spend time and money re-enacting what life was like then. If your family photo book includes images about an era, a profession, war-time, or military groups, there may be a society of like-minded historians who may be interested.

One of the most interesting re-enactors I have found is a Victorian Photographer who demonstrates historically accurate wet-plate photography to interested photographers, and who takes photographs of re-enactors in Victorian dress. Check out Alex Burnham's website (historic-photographer.co.uk).

Collectors Groups

Although collectors will rarely refer to themselves as re-enactors, many of them have an interest in the historical era from which their collections came. As an example, consider the Winchester Arms Collectors Association (winchestercollector.org). They feature historical articles and host events for collectors. Collectors groups may be willing to feature an article about your book if there is a significant tie from the book to their members' interests.

The Press

The key to working with the press is making it easy for them to help you while meeting their deadlines. One way to get the attention of busy reporters is to join the website, Help a Reporter Out (www.helpareporter.com). Every day, reporters seek information from experts. To use the site effectively, do not overstate your expertise and respond to the digest of queries in a timely manner. The free account will send queries in your field of expertise three times a day. There is a paid option as well, if you want to become known to a wide range of journalists as an expert in a particular field. Help a Reporter Out is not the only press leads website available, but it offers a free option where many others do not.

Complete Strangers

"Complete strangers" is a difficult target market to define, but there are a few ways in which to reach interested individuals without knowing who they are.

Bloggers

For those of you who are unfamiliar with blogs, blogs are web-logs—a type of website. Blogging software makes blogs easy to update. The most recent post (information) remains at the top of the page until the next post comes along and moves the older information down or into an archive.

Blogs are popular because they are easy and inexpensive to set up. If you can use email, you can post (add information) to a blog. That said, for a blog to become popular, it must be fed and followed. In other words, you must add useful, helpful, interesting information to the blog regularly enough to satisfy the audience—the blog's followers. (You will find detailed instructions for creating a blog in *Set Yourself Up to Self-Publish: A Genealogist's Guide*.)

There are two primary ways to encourage bloggers to help get the word out about your book: to provide content for the blog, or to become a guest host providing interesting information to or answering questions by the blog's audience.

First, however, you must locate blogs that are appropriate to a conversation about your book. Any aspect of your book may be interesting to a blogger's audience. If, for example, you studied recipes that your 19th century ancestors would have used, then you may have information of interest to a historical cooking blog, or a blog that features unusual recipes.

Website

Host your own website with enough information about the book that someone who is doing similar research, either on the family, the time period or the place, could find the site using a search engine. Use appropriate keywords in the copy and the metatags to help the search engines correctly categorize the site. Look back at the cheat sheet of "Other Information About Your Book" you should have standing by and pump up the keywords to include the same type of information that other genealogical researchers, history buffs or collectors would use to find the website. (More about hosting your own website in Chapter 25: Selling Online.)

Email Signup

One way to make contact with complete strangers is to ask them for an email address when they visit your website. Many companies use this technique to send product or service offers. If you are not planning a regular newsletter, indicate that you will only be contacting them with news of the book, either when it is finished or when a second edition is offered so that they will not be fearful of dozens of emails a day clogging their email box.

Book Trailer on YouTube

Create a quick book trailer on YouTube showing some of the photographs from the book. You can create a book trailer quite easily using movie or slideshow software such as Windows Movie Maker or iMovie for the Mac. Watch a few episodes of Ken Burns's *Civil War* to see how the master uses still photographs and voice-overs to tell a compelling story. Search for book trailers on YouTube to see other examples.

Social Media Page or Group

Create a specialty page (fan page) or group for the book or a part of the contents that would appeal to other researchers, local historians or collectors. The expectation with a fan page or group, however, is that you will contribute to it regularly enough to keep members interested. If you do not have the time to commit to updating it at least once every couple of weeks, you may want to skip this step. I would give you the same advice about establishing a blog for the book. The expectation of people who read social media or blogs is that you will provide updated content often.

Make Yourself Available to Answer Questions

If you are able to help another person creating a family photo book, and are willing to answer questions about your research or how you worked with the images, say so on your website, a public blog, or a post to your social media account. The same goes for letting genealogical and historical societies know that you are willing to help their members, and give them a way to contact you. Being helpful can translate into book sales.

Libraries

Most libraries have limited budgets, and the books they want to buy are ones that patrons will check out over and over. In other words, libraries will buy the latest bestsellers but may not be interested in buying a family photo book unless they have a genealogical collection.

If your family has a local connection, it would be a grand gesture to send the library a free copy, along with a note about how your family is connected to the area. To go the extra mile, help the library's indexer by sending a list of the main characters with their birth and death years, along with a synopsis indicating how the family is connected to the area.

If you are planning to sell to the library market, however, the following are a few things to consider:

Obvious local ties. Libraries are more likely to buy if there are strong ties to the area, or if you have unique photographs showing the local area included in the book.

General appeal. If your family's story has broader, general appeal, make sure your description of the book includes that information.

Price. If you are able, offer the library a discount on the book or sell it to them at cost plus shipping. Librarians must look after their budgets.

Bookstores

In general, bookstores are lousy places to sell books. Bookstores play by a different set of rules than other retail outlets. Bookstores expect to put your books on their shelves, wait ninety days to see if the books sell, and if they do not, to return them to you for full credit. You pay the shipping to get the books to them; they return the books, and oftentimes, you get back books in no condition to re-sell.

Bookstores can be a good place to sell books if you can be there to give a talk about your book to an eager audience. Book signings are a long-standing tradition in publishing, but the only people who make money by signing books, are celebrities. If you are well known, you can sit and sign books for a couple of hours and make some money. If you are not well known, you must create a reason for people to come into the store, usually by offering a free, informative talk.

In either case, a bookstore hosting a book signing or a talk will expect to buy the books from you at a discount of about fifty percent. You will be expected to bring enough books to the store to satisfy the expected crowd, and the bookstore will sell the books at full price to the audience. Afterward, the bookstore will pay you the negotiated price for each book sold.

Non-Book Stores

The list of non-book stores is nearly endless. Any retail outlet that you can establish a tie with could sell your book for you. Books are sold at restaurants, tire stores, copy shops, outdoor stores, indoor stores, bait and tackle shops—nearly everywhere there is a cash register.

The best news regarding selling to non-book stores is that they do not expect to return the books. They will expect the same deep discount as bookstores and will likely take only a few copies to see how sales go. They also may expect a counter-top display. Fortunately, you can pick up an easy-to-assemble cardboard display form online or at most office supply stores.

Complimentary Copies

For the sake of posterity, other genealogical researchers, and the possibility that some major catastrophe will happen somewhere at some time, please send a complimentary copy of your book to the following major genealogical collections:

The Library of Congress
    101 Independence Ave, SE, Washington, DC 20540

The Family History Library
    35 North West Temple St, Salt Lake City, UT 84150

The DAR Library
   1776 D Street, NW, Washington, DC 20006

The Denver Public Library
   10 W 14th Ave Pkwy, Denver, CO 80204

The Allen County Public Library
   900 Library Plaza, Fort Wayne, IN 46802

The Wisconsin State Historical Society
   816 State St, Madison, WI 53706

The Midwest Genealogy Center
   3440 S Lee's Summit, Independence, MO 64055

The New York Public Library
   31-11 Thomson Ave, Long Island City, NY 11101

If you are able, add to your list the local libraries in the places depicted in the photographs. I have often been surprised by the amazing collections of local history in even the tiniest of local libraries.

❧

Reach out to people who may want to buy a copy of your book. As a rule, family photo books do not create enough in the way of interest or sales beyond the family or other genealogical researchers to create a full-blown marketing campaign. Occasionally, a photo book with general audience appeal will warrant such a campaign. If you are interested in a more extensive marketing campaign where you will expand your reach and your audience, generate publicity, or promote yourself as an author, consult *Publish Your Family History: A Step-by-Step Guide to Writing the Stories of Your Ancestors.*

Chapter 25

Selling Online

Selling your book online is a convenience for many readers, but also the most practical way to sell books. Bookstores are only interested in books that sell quickly, and convincing a bookstore to carry a family photo book can be difficult unless you have photographs that would be of interest to the public. Not to mention, that once the book is in the store, you must inspire interested readers to go there to purchase the book.

Fortunately, there are a multitude of ways to offer your book for sale on the Internet.

Create a Website

If you want to sell your book online at your own website, you will need a domain name, a web host with server space to hold your website files, a way to build the website, a method of sending files to the server, and a way to allow customers to pay for the book.

Domain Name

A domain name (also called a URL—Uniform Resource Locator) is the address where web browsers will locate your website in order to display it. Google's domain name, for example, is www.google.com. If you know a website's domain name, you can type it directly into the search bar.

You can obtain a URL through one of the many registrars online, such as:

• Register.com (www.register.com)
• Domain.com (www.domain.com)

Registering a domain name will cost anywhere from a few dollars per year to about twenty-five dollars per year. If you stop paying the annual fee, you will lose the domain, and Internet users will no longer be able to find your website.

Web Hosting

The files that make up your website must sit on a server (computer) that is connected to the Internet all the time.

You can obtain free server space for a website. The most popular free website hosts are:

- Weebly (www.weebly.com)
- Wix (www.wix.com)

The following are sites where you can obtain free space for a blog. The sites marked with an asterisk also have paid options. You can use a blog to sell your book online instead of a website, if you prefer.

- Blogger (www.blogger.com)
- WordPress (www.wordpress.com)*
- Squarespace (www.squarespace.com)*
- Tumblr (www.tumblr.com)

There are hundreds of others. Free websites or blogs include a domain name, although, it may be a subdomain of the company, such as, www.yourname.web-hostingcompany.com. If you have your own domain name, you could employ domain forwarding to point your domain name to the site. For example, your domain could be something simple such as www.WilsonFamilyPhotos.com. That is the URL you would print on your business cards or use in your email signature because it will re-direct anyone who types that address into their web browser to the site which may be located at a more complicated address such as www. wilsonfamilyphotos.domainhostingcompany.com.

Note: Domain mapping is a bit more detailed than simply forwarding. Once you establish the domain map, all of the interior files that the site creates will use only the shorter, easier domain name, rather than the complete URL. For example: www.wilsonfamilyphotos.domainhostingcompany.com/10-Best-Pictures-from-our-Reunion.html will become *www.wilsonfamilyphotos.com/10-Best-Pictures-from-our-Reunion.html* using domain mapping.

Many free website hosts offer simple HTML editing tools to help you create a website. How much control you will have over the look and the organization depends upon the type of tools offered. Blogs work a little differently than HTML sites. Blogs are built primarily upon templates that hold the code for the blog posts so that the latest post goes to the top until it is replaced with something newer. Most blogging software also allows you to create static pages, and to add widgets (code) to a sidebar so that readers can click a button to go to your payment system or shopping cart.

Free sites often place advertising on your web pages. Some free sites limit the number of pages you can create. Others limit server space (often impacting the number of images you can use on the website) or traffic (the number of people visiting the site at a time and in a single month). Free is fantastic, as long as the hosting company stays in business.

Another option is to purchase hosting for your website from an Internet Service Provider (ISP). Three of the biggest ISPs are:

- HostGator (www.hostgator.com)
- NetworkSolutions (www.networksolutions.com)
- GoDaddy (www.godaddy.com)

There are thousands of local and regional ISPs offering different levels of services at all price ranges.

Some ISPs offer web-building tools, many of which are drag and drop which means you do not need to know much about creating websites in order to use them. Most ISPs charge for a certain amount of server space before you have to buy more. If you have many large files, such as videos, you may need more space. Some ISPs also charge for traffic, so if you have a popular website, you may pay more for the number of people visiting the site. Thankfully, most ISPs allow a generous amount of space and traffic in their basic (least expensive) packages.

HTML Editor

If you do not have the option of using your ISP's website building tools, or want to have more control over the look and contents of your website, you will need a way to build it. The most common way to build a site is in the computer coding language HTML, using an HTML editor. HTML editors come in all levels of sophistication and price from free downloads found on the Internet to Adobe Dreamweaver (www.adobe.com). For the most part, you do not need the most sophisticated program available to sell your book online.

Note: If you choose a blog-based site, you will not need an HTML editor. The blog software contains all of the editing tools you will need.

Uploading Files

If you build a website using an HTML editor, you must upload your files to the server space reserved for your site by your Internet Service Provider (ISP). Some ISPs have file transfer protocol (FTP) tools available from your account dashboard. Others will give you an FTP address and you must use an FTP program to upload your files from your computer to the ISP's server. The following are some of the most popular FTP programs. Those with an asterisk are free.

- WS_FTP Pro (www.ipswitchft.com)
- SmartFTP (www.smartftp.com)*
- CuteFTP Pro (www.cuteftp.com)
- WiseFTP (www.wise-ftp.com)
- FileZilla (www.filezilla-project.org)*

Uploading files to or downloading files from the Internet is simple. To send new files to the Internet, you choose files from the panel showing your computer, and hit the arrow key pointing to the side showing the server's files. If you want to download files from the server to your computer, you choose files from the server side, and hit the arrow key pointing to the files on your computer.

Payment Method

If you want to sell your books online, you must provide a way to receive payment. You can use a simple form that readers can print and send to you in the mail with a check, but most people who shop online expect to pay online. The simplest way to accomplish this is to set up a business PayPal account. These accounts are one step up from personal accounts in that they allow you to pay for items, but also receive payment. And, the site will create the code for a unique "buy now" button for each product you wish to sell, that you can copy and paste into your website or blog allowing readers to make a purchase online.

Organizing Your Website

Organizing the website well is key. At a glance, readers should be able to look at the home page and understand what to do next.

Banner Images. Most websites use a banner across the top to identify the website, display a logo, and tell viewers what the website is about. Use the banner to show your book cover and give the title, subtitle and your name as the author.

Navigation. Every page of the website should have essential navigation (links or buttons), so that readers can go from place to place within the website without losing track of where they are, and without having to use the back button on their web browser repeatedly to access other sections of the website.

Place the essential navigation in a vertical column down the left-hand side of the website or across the top beneath the banner. These are the two most common areas for navigation, and where the reader will expect to find links.

Website Real Estate. Most websites are wider than they are tall to keep viewers from having to scroll. If you can, keep whatever information you wish to impart on each page short enough to keep scrolling to a minimum.

What to Include in Your Website

Once you have the essentials—the domain name, hosting space, a way to build the site, and a payment method—there are other elements that will help potential readers find your site, and obtain enough information to purchase the book.

Home Page. Your home page should let readers know enough about the book to make them want one. Include a book cover image (even if you have one in the banner area), along with a "buy now" button, and the same type of information you used in your press releases—headline with a hook, follow up paragraphs with who, what when where and why, as well as a call to action (asking the reader to purchase the book).

Autographed Copies. If you plan to offer autographed copies, let readers know how to request one. This should be a different process than your "buy now" button so that you can tell which books must come from your stock and be autographed, and which ones you can ship directly from your book printer to the buyer. If you are using PayPal to create your "buy now" buttons, simply set up a different button to indicate a request for an autographed copy.

Author. Use this page to promote yourself as the author, or to explain why you wrote the book and how you went about the research. Show your event schedule or give a list of lectures you have prepared about the book, and give interested readers a way to contact you to book a lecture.

Excerpts. Include an excerpt or two so that readers get a feel for the contents.

Reviews. If you have good reviews, put a few on your website or blog.

Social Media Links. If you are using social media to promote the book, use an icon for each of the social media sites where you are active (Facebook, Twitter, YouTube or others) to link to your page on those sites. If you have a video book trailer, you can use the YouTube icon to link to your YouTube channel (where viewers can see all of your videos), but the site also produces the code to embed a small video window into your website or blog.

Ask for an Email Address. If you are planning any ongoing communication with readers, ask them to give you an email address. You could also capture email addresses by adding some viral marketing pieces to the site. Viral marketing pieces are simple PDFs that people can pass on to others who may be interested.

Media Kit. If you are doing any publicity for the book, put your media kit online.

Contact Information. Give readers, people who may want to book you as a speaker, or members of the media a way to contact you.

Bookstore. Give readers information about other books you found helpful in writing your book. You can make a few dollars with your bookstore by becoming an affiliate of other online bookstores (see Affiliate Programs below).

Search Engine Optimization (SEO). In order for the search engines to correctly categorize your site so that users can find them you need the following:

Good Content. Search engines will look for matches between the content (the words on the page) and the keywords (metatags in the background). The closer the match, the more "relevant" the page is to the search term. In other words, if a person is searching for "Woodrow Wilson Family Photographs" and you include that phrase in the content and the keywords, your site will show up higher in the search engine's list than a site using "Woodrow Wilson History" in the text.

Clean Design. Clean design means error-free code. If you use blogging software or your ISPs website building tools, you should not have to worry about the code. If you use an HTML editor, as long as you follow the software's basic design process, you should have clean code. If you edit the code on your own—all bets are off. If you edit the code yourself, be sure to check each page for missing images or bad links.

Keywords that Make Sense. Most website-building software allows you to add keywords (metatags) to the code of the website that will remain unseen by the user. Keywords are used by the search engines to help determine relevance. By choosing your keywords or phrases wisely, you will help boost your website's rankings in the search engines. Keywords are separated by commas, and can include more than one word (e.g. Woodrow Wilson Rare Photographs, Woodrow Wilson Rare Photographs, Woodrow Wilson Presidential Photographs, etc.). Do not stuff the keywords with anything that is irrelevant to your book or the search engines will push your page rank down. Also, use the best eight to ten keywords or phrases. Any more than that, the search engines will ignore them.

Description Tags. Keywords are one metatag; the description is another. The description tag is what appears in search engine results underneath the headline link. It should give the viewer an idea of what the site is about in one sentence. Look at the first sentence of the description you wrote for your book. That sentence should hook the reader or pique his or her curiosity about the book, and is probably the best description for your website as well.

Title Tags. Each page in your website should contain a title tag. The title tag is what appears in the top left-hand portion of the web browser when visitors are on the site, but also is used as the click-able headline in the search engine results. A good title tag for the home page should be short and sweet (e.g. New book. Woodrow Wilson at Home: Family Photographs of the President.).

Image Tags. Image tags are used by the search engines to determine relevance. Image tags can boost your ranking by adding more keywords to the page. Image tags are also used by the "Images" tab on the major search engines, so if you tag an image with the names of each person in the image, anyone searching for those names may find your image which will lead them back to your website.

Image Basics Online

The goal when preparing images to use on the Internet is to keep the file sizes small enough that web pages load quickly. One way to accomplish this is to use thumbnail images with links to full-sized images so that readers have the option of looking at a photograph or a document at full size or downloading the larger image for themselves. Full-sized images can be used to order prints, as well, which is a nice way to share photographs with your family without having to print them yourself and send them.

If you place a full-sized image online, however, expect that people will save the image for themselves. If you do not want your images saved or used in ways you cannot control, there are ways to disable right clicks and copy/paste, or use thumbnail-sized images only, and give interested people a way to contact you for a full-sized image.

If your thumbnails are linked to larger images, explain that somewhere on the home page. Not everyone will understand that the thumbnails are click-able links unless you explain. Also post a warning about large file sizes so that readers are prepared for how long a full-sized image may take to download. Oftentimes, large images will take a minute or two to appear in a web browser making the viewer believe that nothing is happening and close the window prematurely.

Book Cover Image

Use your book cover image in the banner or in the right-hand column of the page. To keep pages loading quickly, convert your book cover image as you would any other image for the website. If you use a small thumbnail which can make the title hard to read, you can link it to a larger image or add your title, subtitle and author's name in the banner area in a larger font.

File Formats

Save full-sized images as smaller thumbnails using the "for the web" setting in your image editor, or at 72 ppi because the monitor cannot display an image at any higher resolution anyway. While web browsers will recognize and display TIFF, BMP, JPG, GIF, and PNG files, you will achieve the best quality with the fewest compatibility issues if you stick to JPG or PNG. Use PNG if you want to maintain a transparent background if the image is an icon or a logo, for example, with sharp lines and distinct areas of color. Use JPG for photographs, maps or illustrations. Play with the image format for your documents to see what gives you the best results. Typically, documents that are fairly clean, with easy-to-read handwriting will look fine as a JPG.

Animation

While you can include animated graphics, such as animated GIFs or flash animations on your website, please do so sparingly. Flashing or rotating graphics have fallen out of fashion and tend to annoy viewers.

If you have many images to share, create an animated slide show. The most common website building software have simple plugins that create slideshows, or you can use stand-alone software such as Adobe Flash (www.adobe.com) to create a file that plays like a video. Microsoft Movie Maker comes pre-installed on most Windows machines or is free to download. Macs have iMovie that is similar. Both iMovie and Movie Maker create web-ready video slideshows.

Another option is to find (or purchase) a flash gallery where the slideshow is already built, you just add the images. Search for "free photo gallery download" on the Internet and you will find hundreds of sites with flash galleries to download. One you have a flash gallery filled with images, upload it to the server and create a link to it in the navigation of the website.

Video

If you have video, you may want to use a thumbnail or link to take readers to a full-screen version of the video. If you create a "channel" on YouTube, you can store your video files there (saving server space that you may have to pay for), and YouTube will give you the code to bring a small video window into your website. You will copy and paste the code into the page on your website. Viewers will then click on the video window to play the video from your website.

Audio

Audio files also can be large. While audio alone can generate memories, you could use your audio as the soundtrack behind a slideshow, and load it on YouTube.

Websites can be a dynamic way to showcase what is in the book, add extras, share photographs and documents, and provide an easy way to sell books online.

Online Ads

Typically, I do not recommend that you purchase ads to sell your book because there are an infinite number of ways that you can plug your book without having to purchase advertising. However, there are a few ways that you can do so without busting your budget.

Adwords

Adwords is a Google company that sells advertising which appears in the Google search engine results (usually the top three listings on the page, plus the top ten items in the right-hand sidebar), and on selected websites that have allowed an advertisement window to be placed on the site. To purchase an ad, you will set up an account, choose the keywords you would like to bid on and set a budget for how much you are willing to pay per day to let the ad run. The best thing about Adwords is that you only pay if a viewer clicks on the ad and goes to your website. Because the best keywords for a photo book are not often searched, you may not pay a great deal to get interested people to your website to buy the book.

Note: Adsense is also Google company that pays for advertising if you allow an advertisement window to be placed within your website. It is a way to make a few dollars, but unless you have an often-visited website, do not expect much more than dinner or movie money.

Facebook Ads

Facebook advertisements show up in the news feeds on individual's facebook pages based upon what they have "liked" on other pages. In other words, if you choose "genealogy" in the likes and interests field, your ad will be shown to other people interested in genealogy. A recent search showed that choosing "genealogy" as an interest returned more than two million interested people. A search for "genealogy family history" returned only eighteen thousand, and "genealogy research" only sixteen thousand. Unfortunately, there is no way to know more specifically if any of these interested people are researching your family. Select the option to only pay for clicks to your website, which will narrow the number of people down considerably. The fewer clicks through, the lower the cost of the ad.

Trade an Ad

Make an offer to a local historical or genealogical society to trade ads. You host an ad for the society on your website, while they host an ad for your book on theirs. Agree to a length of time you will keep each other's ads up.

Book-Related Sites that Sell Ads

There are several book-related sites that sell advertising. The following are two of the most popular:

Ereader News Today. Ereader News Today (ereadernewstoday.com). This site sends emails to its subscribers daily that offer readers free and bargain books for their Kindles. This site also spreads the word through their Facebook page. If you want to price your book at $2.99 or less in order to reach their enormous audience, buying an ad on this site will help you do so. They also offer a Bargain

Books ad that takes 25 percent of whatever you sell through the ad, measured by their affiliate code through Amazon.

BookBub. BookBub (www.bookbub.com). This site offers bargain eBooks to their subscribers across many eReader platforms. You coordinate the sales price with each of your retail outlets (Amazon, Barnes&Noble, BooksaMillion, etc.) or through your eBook aggregator, if you used one. You purchase an ad based upon the genre and the sales price. Their primary focus is on fiction and, unfortunately; there is not a category listed for family histories. There are categories for Biographies and Memoirs as well as Advice and How-To, which may fit your book.

Online Bookstores

There are many bookstores besides Amazon that sell books online. If you are using one of the big print-on-demand printers, chances are good that your book will be included in the catalogs of:

- Amazon (www.amazon.com)
- Barnes&Noble (www.bn.com)
- Books-a-Million (www.booksamillion.com)
- Powell's Books (www.powells.com)
- Alibris (www.alibris.com)
- Abe Books (www.abebooks.com)
- Biblio (www.biblio.com)
- The Tattered Cover (www.tatteredcover.com)

If your book is not included in these catalogs automatically, look for the "publisher" information on their websites to see what you must do to have your book added. Amazon, however, remains the largest online book seller. As long as your book is listed there, you may not want to go to a lot of trouble to have your book listed in other online stores.

Wherever your book is listed online, use every tool available to enhance your listing. Make sure each site has a cover image. Enable all features that allow readers to get a feel for what the book entails. Add a description, an author biography or an excerpt. Everything you can do to help buyers find your book will increase book sales.

Amazon

The three most important sales tools on Amazon are the "Look Inside the Book" function, reviews that come from readers, and Author Central, where you can showcase yourself along with the book. These features have been discussed, but here is one more. On your book's listing, below the cover is a link to "share your own customer images." If you have other photographs related to the book that would entice readers to buy, by all means, add the photographs.

Affiliate Programs

One way to earn a little bit more for selling your own book is to join an affiliate program. Affiliate programs give you credit (and a percentage of the sale) every time someone goes to your website or opens your email, clicks through to the online bookstore, and makes a purchase. Amazon has one of the most comprehensive affiliate programs online.

One way to be helpful to your readers is to suggest other books (or products, if appropriate) to enhance the reader's experience. For example, if you have a travel guide, you could recommend travel gear or a translation guide that would be helpful while visiting the area your travel guide describes. For a family history, you could recommend other books about the area or era. Amazon does this expertly with their "customers who bought this item also bought" feature.

Amazon also has a "recommended for you" feature based upon your prior purchases. You could set up a "recommended reading" list with links to any books (or movies) you used in your research.

If you think viewers would appreciate buying from their favorite online bookstore, or in different eReader versions (Kindle, Android, etc.), set up multiple affiliate links giving readers a choice.

Each affiliate program will give you a coded link to the products on their website so that when viewers on your website make a purchase using the affiliate link, you get credit for the sale.

Online Non-Book Stores

Bookstores are not the only places books are sold online. There are online sales outlets such as eBay (www.ebay.com) where you can set up an account and sell items directly to eBay's buyers. There are also museum shops and historical or genealogical organizations that sell books.

Conduct a quick search of the area where the photographs were taken for a Chamber of Commerce, independent bookstores, a college or university, a local library, and what tourist attractions exist. You may be able to sell books through a local hotel or bed & breakfast.

You can negotiate with any place that has a website where products are already being sold to list your book on their website. They will collect the full retail price, send you payment for the wholesale price through PayPal or a wholesale page on your website, and you will ship the book to the reader.

❧❧

Selling online is one way to expand your audience because potential readers can find your book using a search engine. You will make the most per book if you sell directly to the reader, but there is something to be said for gaining access to the customer base of an existing group or online store. You may make more money by selling books at a discount through an association, for example, because of the larger volume of sales, than selling one book at a time through your website.

Conclusion

Whether you took only the baby steps or jumped headlong into the giant leaps, I am sure you have photographs that deserve to be preserved, shared and published for interested family members or researchers to appreciate.

I am confident that if you can do the research and follow the steps outlined in this guide, you can publish. Although most family photo books are published in print, if you choose to publish electronically, let me encourage you, once again, to publish at least a few copies in print to contribute to the major genealogical collections around the country. Your unique images deserve to be preserved and available to other interested researchers for generations to come.

If you are just beginning, I trust you are inspired enough to pick a project to publish. In fact, I hope to have inspired half a dozen projects you cannot wait to begin, and caused many more ideas to tumble around in your imagination.

If gathering the images is underway but the organizing and layout is not yet complete, I anticipate that you will reach out to family members and others who can be of assistance to gather images you do not have.

If you have inherited a box of documents or photographs, my aim was to motivate you to begin scanning and organizing, sharing with family, and preparing the images for when you are ready to create a stunning family heirloom.

If the images are sitting in your computer yearning to bust out of the bytes and into the hands of family members, I trust this guide has made you believe that you *can* publish and share the photographs only you have with other researchers or the next generation as a beautiful book.

About the Author

Dina C. Carson has been involved in publishing and genealogy for more than two decades. She brings her experience with all phases of book publishing to help first-time self-publishers create quality family or local histories that are both believable and achievable.

She is the coordinator of the Boulder Pioneers Project, a comprehensive look at the original source documents for Boulder County during the territorial period (1858–1876) and is the author of more than a dozen annotated indexes of Boulder County source materials.

She lectures frequently to genealogical, historical and philanthropic societies, gives workshops on publishing, pioneers and other topics, and is working with the Colorado State Archives on state-wide records indexing projects.

Although her formal education is in international law and economics, she owns Iron Gate Publishing, a publishing company that focuses on genealogy, local history and reunion planning. She is also a partner in Imagination Technology, a graphic design and marketing firm working with local businesses.

When she's not at a computer working on a publishing project, you can find her photographing the pioneer cemeteries of Colorado.

Bibliography

RESEARCH

Blumenson, John J-G. *Identifying American Architecture: A Pictoral Guide to Styles and Terms, 1600-1945*. New York, NY: W W Norton, 1981.

Butchart, Ronald E. *Local Schools: Exploring Their History*. Nashville, TN: American Association for State and Local History, 1986.

Carpenter, Will. *The Life and Times Of ...: Researching and Writing American Local History*. Cookeville, TN: HistoryWorks, 2009.

Carson, Dina. *Directory of Genealogical and Historical Societies, Libraries and Museums in the U.S. and Canada, 2014*. Niwot, CO: Iron Gate Publishing, 2014.

Danzer, Gerald A. *Public Places: Exploring Their History*. Nashville, TN: American Association for State and Local History, 1995.

Davidson, James West and Mark Hamilton Lyle. *After the Fact: The Art of Historical Detection*. Boston: McGraw Hill, 2000.

DeBlasio, Donna M. *Catching Stories: A Practical Guide to Oral History*. Athens, OH: Swallow Press, 2009.

Dudley, Roger L. *In Their Time: A Timeline Journal for Placing Family Events into Historical Context, 1000-2076*. Denver, CO: Warfield Press, 2013.

Evans, Tonya Marie and Susan Borden Evans. *Literary Law Guide for Authors: Copyright, Trademark and Contracts in Plain Language*. Philadelphia: Literary Entrepreneur Series, 2003.

Field, Marion. *The Writer's Guide to Research: An Invaluable Guide to Gathering Material for Features, Novels and Non-Fiction Books*. Oxford, England: How to Books, 2000.

Filby, William. *A Bibliography of American County Histories*. Baltimore, MD: Genealogical Publishing Company, 2000.

Foster, Gerald. *American Houses: A Field Guide to the Architecture of the Home*. Boston, MA: Houghton Mifflin, 2004.

Hart, Cynthia and Lisa Samson. *The Oral History Workshop: Collect and Celebrate the Life Stories of Your Family and Friends*. New York: Workman Publishing Company, 2009.

Henderson, Nancy. *The Genealogist's U.S. History Pocket Reference: Quick Facts & Timelines of American History to Help Understand Your Ancestors*. San Diego, CA: Family Tree Books, 2013.

Howe, J. and Delores A. Fleming, Emory L. Kemp, Ruth Ann Overbeck. *Houses and Homes: Exploring Their History*. Walnut Creek, CA: Alta Mira Press, 1997.

Hunt, R. Douglas. *American Farms: Exploring Their History*. Malabar, FL: Krieger Publishing Co., 1996.

Jacobson, Judy. *History for Genealogists: Using Chronological Time Lines to Find and Understand Your Ancestors*. Baltimore, MD: Clearfield Publishing Co., 2009.

Jones, Thomas W. *Mastering Genealogical Proof*. Arlington, VA: National Genealogical Society, 2013.

Kammen, Carol. *On Doing Local History: Reflections on What Local Historians Do, Why and What it Means*. Nashville, TN: The American Association for State and Local History, 1986.

Kammen, Carol. *The Pursuit of Local History: Readings in Theory and Practice*. Walnut Creek, CA: Alta Mira Press, 1996.

Kerr, K. Austin and Amos J Loveday, Mansel G Blackford. *Local Businesses: Exploring Their History*. Nashville, TN: American Association for State and Local History, 1990.

Kyvig, David E. and Myron A. Marty. *Nearby History: Exploring the Past Around You, 2nd Edition*. NY: Alta Myra Press, 2000.

Lynch, Daniel. *Google Your Family Tree*. Baltimore, MD: FamilyLink, 2008.

McAlester, Virginia and A. Lee McAlester. *A Field Guide to American Houses*. New York, NY: Knopf. 1984.

Mills, Elizabeth Shown. *Evidence Explained: Citing History Sources from Artifacts to Cyberspace*. Baltimore, MD: Genealogical Publishing Co, 2007.

Ritchie, Donald A. *Doing Oral History*. New York: Oxford University Press, 2003.

Szucs, Loretto Dennis and Sandra Hargreaves Luebking. *The Source: A Guidebook to American Genealogy, 3rd Edition*. Provo, UT: Generations Network, 2006.

Urend, James P. *Places of Worship: Exploring Their History*. Nashville, TN: American Association for State and Local History, 1990.

Yow, Valerie Raleigh. *Recording Oral History: A Guide for the Humanities and Social Sciences, 2nd Edition*. Walnut Creek, CA: AltaMira Press, 2005.

WRITING

Ackerman, Angela and Becca Puglisi. *The Emotion Thesaurus: A Writer's Guide to Character Expression*. Jupiter, FL: JADD Publishing, 2012.

Ackerman, Angela and Becca Puglisi. *The Negative Trait Thesaurus: A Writer's Guide to Character Flaws*. Jupiter, FL: JADD Publishing, 2013.

Ackerman, Angela and Becca Puglisi. *The Positive Trait Thesaurus: A Writer's Guide to Character Attributes*. Jupiter, FL: JADD Publishing, 2013.

Amato, Joseph A. *Rethinking Home: A Case for Writing Local History*. Berkeley, CA: University of California Press, 2002.

Barany, Beth. *The Writer's Adventure Guide: 12 Stages to Writing Your Book (for Novelists and Creative Nonfiction Writers)*. Oakland, CA: Barany Pub, 2009.

Beckett, John. *Writing Local History*. Manchester, England: Manchester University Press, 2007.

Bickham, Jack M. *The 38 Most Common Fiction Writing Mistakes (And How to Avoid Them)*. Cincinnati, OH: Writer's Digest Books, 1997.

Blake, Gary and Robert W. Bly. *The Elements of Technical Writing: The Essential Guide to Writing Clear, Concise Proposals, Reports, Manuals, Letters, Memos, and Other Documents in Every Technical Field*. NY: Simon & Schuster Macmillan Company, 1993.

Block, Lawrence. *Spider, Spin Me a Web: A Handbook for Fiction Writers*. NY: William Morrow Paperbacks, 1996.

Block, Lawrence. *Telling Lies for Fun and Profit: A Manual for Fiction Writers*. NY: William Morrow Paperbacks, 1994.

Block, Lawrence. *Writing the Novel from Plot to Print*. Cincinnati, OH: Writers Digest Books, 1985.

Borg, Mary. *Writing Your Life: An Easy-to-Follow Guide to Writing an Autobiography*. Fort Collins, CO: Cottonwood Press, 1990.

Bowerman, Peter. *The Well-Fed Self-Publisher: How to Turn One Book into a Full Time Living*. Atlanta, GA: Fanove Publ, 2007.

Boyer, Carl III. *How to Publish and Market Your Family History, 4th Edition*. Santa Clarita, CA: Carl Boyer, 1993.

Brohaugh, William. *Write Tight: How to Keep Your Prose Sharp, Focused and Concise*. Cincinnati, OH: Writer's Digest Books, 1993.

Browne, Renni. *Self-Editing for Fiction Writers: How to Edit Yourself Into Print*. New York, NY: Harper Paperbacks, 2004.

Carpenter, Will. *The Life and Times Of ...: Researching and Writing American Local History*. Cookeville, TN: HistoryWorks, 2009.

Casagrande, June. *It was the Best of Sentences, It was the Worst of Sentences: A Writer's Guide to Crafting Killer Sentences*. New York: Ten Speed Press, 2010.

Cheney, Theodore A. Rees. *Writing Creative Nonfiction: How to Use Fiction Techniques to Make Your Nonfiction More Interesting, Dramatic and Vivid*. Berkeley, CA: Ten Speed Press, 1991.

Chicago Manual of Style, 16th Edition. Chicago: University of Chicago Press, 2010.

Clark, Roy Peter. *Writing Tools: 50 Essential Strategies for Every Writer*. New York, NY: Little, Brown and Company, 2008.

Clausen, John. *Too Lazy to Work, Too Nervous to Steal: How to Have a Great Life as a Freelance Writer*. Cincinnati, OH: Writer's Digest Books, 2001.

Cleaver, Jerry. *Immediate Fiction: A Complete Writing Course*. NY: St Martin's Griffin, 2005.

Collier, Oscar and Frances Spatz Leighton. *How to Write & Sell Your First Nonfiction Book*. NY: St. Martin's Press, 1994.

Collins, Brandilyn. *Getting Into Character: Seven Secrets a Novelist Can Learn from Actors*. NY: John Wiley & Sons, 2002.

Dalton, Judy. *The 29 Most Common Writing Mistakes and How to Avoid Them.* Cincinnati, OH: Writer's Digest Books, 1985.

Dibell, Ansen. *Plot: How to Build Short Stories and Novels that Don't Sag, Fizzle, or Trail Off in Scraps of Frustrated Revision—and How to Rescue Stories That Do.* Cincinnati, OH: Writer's Digest Books, 1988.

Dickson, Paul. *War Slang: American Fighting Words and Phrases since the Civil War.* Washington, D.C.: Brassey's, 2004.

Edgerton, Les. *Hooked: Write Fiction That Grabs Readers at Page One and Never Lets Them Go.* Cincinnati, OH: Writer's Digest Books, 2007.

Einsohn, Amy. *The Copyeditor's Handbook, 3rd Edition: A Guide for Book Publishing and Corporate Communication.* (Berkeley, CA: University of California Press, 2011).

Ellis, Sherry. *Now Write! Nonfiction: Memoir, Journalism and Creative Nonfiction Exercises from Today's Best Writers.* New York, NY: Tarcher, 2009.

Embree, Mary. *The Author's Toolkit: A Step-by-Step Guide to Writing and Publishing Your Book (Revised Edition).* New York: Allworth Press, 2003.

Finley, Carmen J. *Creating a Winning Family History.* Arlington, VA: National Genealogical Society, 2010.

Franklin, Jon. *Writing for Story: Craft Secrets of Dramatic Nonfiction.* New York, NY: Plume, 1994.

Friedlander, Joel. *A Self-Publisher's Companion: Expert Advice for Authors Who Want to Publish.* San Rafael, CA: Martin Bookworks, 2011.

Fruehling, Rosemary T. and N. B. Oldham. *Write to the Point! Letters, Memos, & Reports that Get Results.* New York, NY: McGraw-Hill Book Co, 1988.

Garrison, Webb. *The Encyclopedia of Civil War Usage: Everyday Language of Soldiers and Civilians.* Nashville, TN: Cumberland House, 2001.

Gaughran, David. *Let's Get Digital: How to Self-Publish, and Why You Should.* US: Arriba Arriba Books, 2011.

Genealogy Publishing Service. *How to Write & Publish Your Family Book.* Franklin, NC: Genealogy Publishing Service, 1992.

Gerard, Philip. *Creative Nonfiction: Researching and Crafting Stories of Real Life.* Cincinnati, OH: Waveland Pr Inc, 2004.

Goldfarb, Ronald L. and Gail E. Ross. *The Writer's Lawyer: Essential Legal Advice for Writers and Editors in All Media.* NY: Times Books, 1989.

Gouldrup, Lawrence P. *Writing the Family Narrative.* Salt Lake City: Ancestry Publishing, 1987.

Gutkind, Lee. *In Fact: The Best of Creative Nonfiction.* New York, NY: W. W. Norton & Company, 2004.

Gutkind, Lee. *Keep it Real: Everything You Need to Know About Researching and Writing Creative Nonfiction.* New York, NY: W. W. Norton & Company, 2009.

Gutkind, Lee. *The Art of Creative Nonfiction.* New York, NY: Wiley, 1997.

Hale, Constance. *Sin and Syntax: How to Craft Wickedly Effective Prose*. New York, NY: Broadway, 2001.

Hart, Jack. *Storycraft: The Complete Guide to Writing Narrative Nonfiction*. Chicago: University of Chicago Press, 2011.

Hatcher, Patricia Law. *Producing a Quality Family History*. Salt Lake City: Ancestry, Inc., 1996.

Howard, V. A. and J. H. Barton. *Thinking on Paper: Refine, Express, and Actually Generate Ideas by Understanding the Processes of the Mind*. New York, W Morrow, 1986.

Kawasaki, Guy and Shawn Welch. *APE: Author, Publisher, Entrepreneur—How to Publish a Book*. US: Nononina Press, 2013

Kempthorne, Charley. *For All Time: A Complete Guide to Writing Your Family History*. Heinemann, NH: Boynton/Cook Publishers, 1996.

Kidder, Tracy and Richard Todd. *Good Prose: The Art of Nonfiction*. New York: Random House, 2013.

Kitchel, Dwain L. *Writing and Marketing a Family History in the 1990s*. Knoxville, TN: Tennessee Valley Publicatiions, 1990.

Kramer, Mark. *Telling True Stories: A Nonfiction Writer's Guide from the Nieman Foundation at Harvard University*. New York, NY: Plume, 2007.

Krull, Kathleen. *12 Keys to Writing Books that Sell*. Cincinnati, OH: F&W Publications, Inc. 1989.

Lashier, Kathleen. *Grandma [Grandpa], Tell Me Your Stories*. Waverly, IA: Cq Products, 1992.

Lashier, Kathleen. *Mom [Dad], Share Your Life With Me*. Waverly, IA: Cq Products, 1992.

Lashier, Kathleen. *To the Best of My Recollection*. Waverly, IA: G&R Publishing, 1996.

Leland, Christopher T. *The Creative Writer's Style Guide*. Cincinnati, OH: Writer's Digest Books, 2002.

Levin, Donna. *Get that Novel Started and Keep it Going until You Finish*. Cincinnati, OH: Writer's Digest Books, 1992.

Lopate, Phillip. *To Show and to Tell: The Craft of Literary Nonfiction*. New York: Free Press, 2013.

Lukeman, Noah. *The First Five Pages: A Writer's Guide to Staying Out of the Rejection Pile*. New York, NY: Fireside, 2005.

Lukeman, Noah. *The Plot Thickens: 8 Ways to Bring Fiction to Life*. New York: St. Martin's Griffin, 2003.

Marshall, Carl and David Marshall. *The Book of Myself: A Do-it-Yourself Autobiography in 201 Questions*. New York, NY: Hyperion, 2007.

Marshall, Evan. *The Marshall Plan for Novel Writing: A 16-Step Program Guaranteed to Take You from Idea to Completed Manuscript*. Cincinnati, OH: Writer's Digest Books, 1998.

McCutcheon, Marc. *Building Believable Characters*. Cincinnati, OH: Writer's Digest Books, 1996.

Merriam-Webster's English Usage Dictionary. New York: Merriam-Webster, 2010.

Morris, William. *Morris Dictionary of Word and Phrase Origins, 2nd Edition*. New York, Collins Reference, 1988.

Noble, William. *The 28 Biggest Writing Blunders (And How to Avoid Them)*. Cincinnati, OH: Writer's Digest Books, 1992.

Noble, William. *Noble's Book of Writing Blunders (And How to Avoid Them)*. Cincinnati, OH: Writers Digest Books, 2006.

Noble, William. *Writing Dramatic Non-Fiction*. Forest Dale, VT: Paul S Eriksson, 2000.

Nuwer, Hank. *How to Write Like an Expert About Anything: Bring Factual Accuracy and the Voice of Authority to Your Writing*. Cincinnati, OH: Writer's Digest Books, 1995.

Obstfeld, Raymond. *Fiction First Aid: Instant Remedies for Novels, Stories and Scripts*. Cincinnati, OH: Writer's Digest Books, 2002.

Orion, Dean. *Live To Write Another Day, A Survival Guide for Screenwriters and Creative Storytellers*. US: Sky Father Media, 2013.

Perl, Sondra. *Writing True: The Art and Craft of Creative Nonfiction*. Boston, MA: Wadsworth Publishing, 2006.

Plotnik, Arthur. *Spunk & Bite: A Writer's Guide to Bold, Contemporary Style*. New York, NY: Random House Reference, 2007.

Polking, Kirk. *Writing Family Histories and Memoirs*. Cincinnati, OH: Betterway Books, 1995.

Poynter, Dan. *Writing Nonfiction: Turning Thoughts into Books*. Santa Barbara, CA: Para Publishing, 2007.

Pyne, Stephen J. *Voice & Vision: A Guide to Writing History and Other Serious Nonfiction*. Cambridge, MA: Harvard University Press, 2011.

Q&A a Day: 5-Year Journal. New York, NY: Potter Style, 2010.

Rampolla, Mary Lynn. *A Pocket Guide to Writing History*. Boston, MA: Bedford-St Martin's, 2007.

Raymond, Stuart A. *Genealogical Jargon for Family Historians*. Bury: Federation for Family History Societies, 2005.

Reminiscing: 21st Century Master Edition. Itasca, IL: TDC Games, n.d.

Rodale, J.I. *Synonym Finder, Completely Revised*. New York: Grand Central Publishing, 1988.

Roerden, Chris. *Don't Murder Your Mystery: 24 Fiction-Writing Techniques to Save Your Manuscript from Turning up D. O. A.* Rock Hill, SC: Bella Rosa Books, 2006.

Rubie, Peter. *The Elements of Storytelling: How to Write Compelling Fiction*. NY: John Wiley & Sons, 1995.

Rubie, Peter and Gary Provost. *How to Tell a Story: The Secrets of Writing Captivating Tales*. Cincinnati, OH: Writer's Digest Books, 1998.

Schmidt, Victoria Lynn. *Story Structure Architect: A Writer's Guide to Building Dramatic Situations and Compelling Characters*. Cincinnati, OH: F&W Publications, 2005.

Sellers, Heather. *Page After Page: Discover the Confidence and Passion You Need to Start Writing and Keep Writing (No Matter What!)*. Cincinnati, OH: Writer's Digest Books, 2005.

Silverman, Sue William. *Fearless Confessions: A Writer's Guide to Memoir*. Athens, GA: University of Georgia Press, 2009.

Smith, Michael C. and Suzanne Greenberg. *Everyday Creative Writing: Panning for Gold in the Kitchen Sink, 2nd Edition*. Lincolnwood, IL: NTC Publishing Group, 2000.

Stewart, James B. *Follow the Story: How to Write Successful Nonfiction*. NY: Touchstone, 1998.

Strong, William S. *The Copyright Book: A Practical Guide, 4th Edition*. Cambridge, MA: MIT Press, 1993.

St. Maur, Suzan. *How to Write Winning Non-Fiction: The Complete Writing and Publishing Handbook for Non-Fiction Authors*. London, England: Publishing Academy, 2010.

Stone, Todd A. *Novelists' Boot Camp: 101 Ways to Take Your Book from Boring to Bestseller*. Cincinnati, OH: Writer's Digest Books, 2006.

Strunk, William and William Strunk, Jr. *The Elements of Style (Updated 2011 Edition)*. New York: The Style Manual Press, 2011.

Szucs, Loretto Dennis. *Family History Made Easy*. Salt Lake City: Ancestry Publishing, 1998.

Truss, Lynne. *Eats, Shoots & Leaves: A Zero Tolerance Approach to Punctuation*. New York, New York: Gotham, 2004.

Tuchman, Barbara W. *Practicing History: Selected Essays*. New York: Ballantine Books, 1935.

Turabian, Kate L. *A Manual for Writers of Research Papers, Theses, and Dissertations, 8th Edition*. Chicago, IL: University of Chicago Press, 2013.

Walsh, Bill. *Lapsing into a Comma: A Curmudgeon's Guide to the Many Things that Can Go Wrong in Print—And How to Avoid Them*. New York: McGraw-Hill, 2000.

Walsh, Bill. *The Elephants of Style: A Trunkload of Tips on the Big Issues and Gray Areas of Contemporary American English*. New York: McGraw-Hill, 2004.

Walsh, Bill. *Yes, I Could Care Less: How to Be a Language Snob Without Being a Jerk*. New York: St Martin's Griffin, 2013.

Wilson, Lee. *Make it Legal*. NY: Allworth Press, 1990.

Zinsser, William. *Inventing the Truth: The Art and Craft of Memoir*. NY: Mariner Books, 1998.

Zinsser, William. *On Writing Well*. New York, NY: Harper Paperbacks, 2006.

Zinsser, William. *Writing About Your Life: A Journey into the Past*. New York, NY: Da Capo Press, 2005.

Zuckerman, Albert. *Writing the Block Buster Novel*. Cincinnati, OH: Writer's Digest Books, 1994.

PRODUCTION

Ashford, Janet and John Odam. *Start with a Scan: A Guide to Transforming Scanned Photos and Objects into High-Quality Art, 2nd Edition*. Berkeley, CA: Peachpit Press, 2000.

Blatner, David and Glenn Fleishman, Steve Roth. *Real World Scanning and Halftones: The Definitive Guide to Scanning and Halftones from the Desktop*. Berkeley, CA: Peachpit Press, 1998.

Bonura, Larry S. *The Art of Indexing*. New York, NY: John Wiley & Sons, 1994.

Bringhurst, Robert. *The Elements of Typographic Style*. Point Roberts, WA: Hartley & Marks, 2008.

Carter, David, ed. *Big Book of Design Ideas*. New York, NY: Harper Collins, 2000.

Cohen, Sandee and Robin Williams. *The Non-Designer's Scan and Print Book: All You Need to Know About Production and Prepress to Get Great-Looking Pages*. Berkeley, CA: Peachpit Press, 1999.

Ctein. *Digital Restoration from Start to Finish*. London: Elsevier, 2010.

de Bartolo, Carolina. *Explorations in Typography: Mastering the Art of Fine Typesetting*. 101 Editions, 2011.

Evans, Poppy. *Designer's Survival Manual: The Insider's Guide to Working with Illustrators, Photographers, Printers, Web Engineers, and More ...* . Cincinnati, OH: How Design Books, 2001.

Felici, James and Frank Romano. *The Complete Manual of Typography: A Guide to Setting Perfect Type*. San Francisco: Peachpit Press, 2002.

Hendel, Richard. *On Book Design*. New Haven: Yale University Press, 1998.

Hoff, Henry B. *Genealogical Writing in the 21st Century: A Guide to Register Style and More*. Boston: New England Historical and Genealogical Society, 2002.

Krause, Jim. *Color Index—Revised Edition*. Cincinnati, OH: HOW Books, 2010.

Krause, Jim. *Color Index 2*. Cincinnati, OH, HOW Books, 2007.

Lee, Marshall. *Bookmaking, 3rd Edition: Editing, Design, Production*. New York: Norton & Co., 2004.

Lupton, Ellen. *Thinking with Type: A Critical Guide for Designers, Writers, Editors and Students, 2nd Revised and Expanded Edition*. NY: Princeton Architectural Press, 2010.

Masterson, Pete. *Book Design & Production: A Guide for Authors and Publishers*. El Sobrante, CA: AEonix Publishing Group, 2007.

McClure, Rhonda R. *Digitizing Your Family History: Easy Methods for Preserving Your Heirloom Documents, Photos, Home Movies and More in a Digital Format*. Cincinnati, OH: Family Tree Books, 2004.

Pantone Graphics. *Formula Guide: Solid Coated & Solid Uncoated*. Carlstadt, NJ: Pantone Graphics, 2014.

Smith, Brian R. *Dollarhide Numbering for Genealogists—An Authorized Guide for the Serious User*. Orting, WA: Family Roots Publishing, 2011.

Spaltro, Kathleen. *Genealogy and Indexing*. Wheat Ridge, CO: American Society of Indexers, 2003.

Sperry, Kip. *Abbreviations & Acronyms: A Guide for Family Historians*. Orem, UT: Ancestry, 2000.

Steinhoff, Sascha. *Scanning Negatives and Slides: Digitizing Your Photographic Archive*. Santa Barbara, CA: Rocky Nook, 2009.

Tally, Taz. *Avoiding the Scanning Blues: A Desktop Scanning Primer*. Upper Saddle River, NJ: Prentice Hall, 2001.

Wellisch, Hans H. *Indexing from A to Z*. Bronx, NY: The H. W. Wilson Company, 1991.

Wheildon, Colin. *Type & Layout: How Typography and Design can Get Your Message Across—Or Get in the Way*. NY: Strathmoor Press, 1995.

White, Jan V. *Great Pages: A Common-Sense Approach to Effective Desktop Design*. London: Serif Publishing, 1990.

Williams, Robin. *The Mac is not a Typewriter, 2nd Edition*. San Francisco, CA: Peachpit Press, 2003.

Williams, Robin. *The Non-Designer's Design Book, 3rd Edition*. San Francisco, CA: Peachpit Press, 2008.

Williams, Robin. *The Non-Designer's Type Book*. San Francisco, CA: Peachpit Press, 1998.

MARKETING

Amir, Nina. *Authorpreneur: How to Build a Business around Your Book*. Los Gatos, CA: Pure Spirit Creations, 2014.

Daffron, Susan C. *Publishize: How to Quickly and Affordably Self-Publish a Book That Promotes Your Expertise*. Logical Expressions, 2011.

Eager, Rob. *Sell Your Books like Wildfire: The Writer's Guide to Marketing and Publicity*. Cincinnati, OH: Writer's Digest Books, 2012.

Gaughran, David. *Let's Get Visible: How To Get Noticed And Sell More Books*. US: Arriba Arriba Books, 2013.

Kremer, John. *1001 Ways to Market Your Books: For Authors and Publishers*. Taos, NM: Open Horizons, 2006.

Levinson, Jay Conrad. *Guerrilla Marketing, 4th edition: Easy and Inexpensive Strategies for Making Big Profits from Your Small Business*. Wilmington, MA: Mariner Books, 2007.

Miller, J Steve. *Sell More Books! Book Marketing and Publishing for Low Profile and Debut Authors: Rethinking Book Publicity after the Digital Revolutions*. Acworth, GA: Wisdom Creek Press, 2011.

Schriever, Norm. *The Book Marketing Bible: 99 Essential Marketing Strategies for Self-Published and First-Time Authors, or any Writer Looking to Skyrocket Sales.* Seattle: Amazon Digital Services, n.d.

Scott, David Meerman. *The New Rules of Marketing & PR: How to Use Social Media, Online Video, Mobile Applications, Blogs, News Releases, and Viral Marketing to Reach Buyers Directly.* Seattle: Amazon Digital Services, 2013.

Scott, Steve. *61 Ways to Sell More Nonfiction Kindle Books.* US: Amazon Digital Services, n.d.

Weber, Steve. *Plug Your Book.* Falls Church, VA: Weber Books, 2007.

Index

Order Form

If you borrowed this copy from a library or would like to order a copy for a frien
or family member, please send a check or money order to: Iron Gate Publishing,
P.O. Box 999, Niwot, CO 80544. Our books are available online to institutions
through Lightning Source, to individuals at Amazon.com and on our website:

www.irongate.com

Set Yourself Up to Self-Publish: A Genealogist's Guide
     ISBN 978-1-879579-99-6 $19.95 + $5.00 S&H

Publish Your Genealogy: A Step-by-Step Guide for Preserving Your Research
for the Next Generation
     ISBN 978-1-879579-62-0 $24.95 + $5.00 S&H

Publish Your Family History: A Step-by-Step Guide to Writing the Stories of
Your Ancestors
     ISBN 978-1-879579-63-7 $24.95 + $5.00 S&H

Publish a Local History: A Step-by-Step Guide from Finding the Right Project
to Finished Book
     ISBN 978-1-879579-64-4 $24.95 + $5.00 S&H

Publish a Memoir: A Step-by-Step Guide to Saving Your Memories for Future
Generations
     ISBN 978-1-879579-65-1 $24.95 + $5.00 S&H

Publish a Biography: A Step-by-Step Guide to Capturing the Life and Times of
an Ancestor or a Generation
     ISBN 978-1-879579-66-8 $24.95 + $5.00 S&H

Publish a Photo Book: A Step-by-Step Guide for Transforming Your
Genealogical Research into a Stunning Family Heirloom
     ISBN 978-1-879579-67-5 $24.95 + $5.00 S&H

Publish a Source Index: A Step-by-Step Guide to Creating a Genealogically
Useful Index, Abstract or Transcription
     ISBN 978-1-879579-68-2 $24.95 + $5.00 S&H

Publish Your Specialty: A Step-by-Step Guide for Imparting Your Research
Expertise to Others
     ISBN 978-1-879579-76-7 $24.95 + $5.00 S&H